Law of Attraction & Manifestation

This Edition Includes: Law of Attraction for Amazing Relationships, Money, Abundance, Self-Love, Motivation + Manifestation Exercises

by Elena G.Rivers

Copyright @ 2017-2020 by Elena G.Rivers

All rights reserved. No part of this publication may be reproduced, stored in a retrieval system, or transmitted, in any form or by any means, electronic, mechanical, photocopying, recording, or otherwise, without the prior written permission of the author and the publishers.

The scanning, uploading, and distribution of this book via the Internet or via any other means without the permission of the author is illegal and punishable by law. Please purchase only authorized electronic editions and do not participate in or encourage electronic piracy of copyrighted materials.

ISBN: 978-1-80095-060-3

Legal Notice:

This book is copyright protected. It for personal use only.

Disclaimer Notice:

Please note the information contained in this book is for inspirational and entertainment purposes only. Every attempt has been made to provide accurate, up to date, and completely reliable information. No warranties of any kind are expressed or implied. Readers acknowledge that the author is not engaging in the rendering of legal, financial, health, medical, or professional advice. By reading this book, the reader agrees that under no circumstances are we responsible for any losses, direct or indirect, which are incurred as a result of the use of the information contained within this book, including, but not limited to, errors, omissions, or inaccuracies.

The information provided in this book is for entertainment purposes only. If you are struggling with serious problems, including chronic illness, mental instability, or legal issues, please consult with your local registered health care or legal professional as soon as possible. This book is not a substitute for professional or legal advice

Contents

About This Book 7

Part 1 – Book 1 *Law of Attraction - Manifestation Exercises* 9

    Introduction 11

    Chapter 1: The Truth about Manifesting 13

    Chapter 2: Lower-Level Teachings 15

    Chapter 3: Upper-Level Teachings 34

    Chapter 4: Making Sense of it All 44

    Chapter 5: 30-Day Challenge 49

Part 2 - Book 2 *Self-Love Handbook* 51

    Introduction- Why Self-Love is the Only Way to Create the Life You Love and That Loves You Back 53

    Chapter 1 Step #1Emotional Peeling 65

    Chapter 2 Step #2Making Friends with Your Emotions on a Deeper Level 75

    Chapter 3 Step #3Control Your Precious Mind As If Your Life Depends on It Because It Does 80

    Chapter 4 Step #4The Number One Self-Love Trick to Eliminate Limiting Beliefs and Self-Doubt 87

    Chapter 5 Step #5Expressing Kindness 95

    Chapter 6 Step #6Creative Self Expression 98

    Chapter 7 Step #7Positive Reminders and Your Own Magic Pendulum 101

    Chapter 8 Step#8Magnifying LOA Combine Action with Attraction 103

Part 3 – Book 3 *Law of Attraction to Make More Money* 107

    Introduction 109

    Mindset Shift #1 Is Your Desire Good for You? 116

    Mindset Shift #2 Grow Your "No" Muscle 122

    Mindset Shift #3 The Biggest Mistake Behind Finding Your *Why* 125

    Mindset Shift #4 The LOA KISS Method 132

    Mindset Shift #5 The Most Powerful Word for a Bad Day (aka Your Manifestation Bridge) 133

    Mindset Shift #6 Own Yourself 140

Mindset Shift #7 The Resourceful Method 144

Mindset Shift #8 Your LOA Stamina to Keep Believing & Achieving 146

Mindset Shift #9 Abundant Mindset Mastery 147

Mindset Shift #10 Be on the Other Side 149

Mindset Shift #11 The Invisible Force That Makes You Fail or Succeed (and how to use it to manifest what you want) 150

Mindset Shift #12 Your Net Worth Starts with Self-Worth 151

Part 4 – Book 4 *Law of Attraction for Motivation* 155

Introduction 157

Chapter 1 Reconnecting with Your Inner Guidance 164

Chapter 2 Vision for Life and Vision Boards 171

The Mistakes to Avoid 171

Chapter 3 The # 1 Motivation Killer and How to Mindfully Release It to Live Your Best Life 180

Chapter 4 The Mental and Emotional Peeling to Welcome the New and Get Rid of the Old 190

Releasing Pressure and Judgment to Feel Free and Naturally Motivated 192

Chapter 5 How to Deal with Adversity and Keep Taking Inspired Action 194

Chapter 6 How to Deal with Self-Sabotage 197

Chapter 7 The Best LOA Tools to Stay Motivated 199

Mindful Exercises to Raise Your Vibration First Thing in the Morning 199

Conclusion 204

Part 5 - Book 5 *Law of Attraction for Amazing Relationships* 207

Introduction 209

Chapter 1: Thoughts, Beliefs, and Reality 211

Chapter 2: The Link between Thoughts and Emotions 216

Chapter 3: Who Are You? 217

Chapter 4: The Law of Attraction Works through You! 219

Chapter 5: The Vibrational Level of Your Life 223

Chapter 6: About your Vibe 226

Chapter 7: Love: The Evolution of Consciousness 232

Chapter 8: When the Lines of Communication is Crossed 234
Chapter 9: The Face of God...237
Chapter 10: The Mirror of Relationships 239
Chapter 11: Using the Law of Attraction in Relationships 242
Chapter 12: Conscious Relationships.. 244
Chapter 13: Law of Attraction Exercises for Relationships 247

Part 6- Book 6 *Law of Attraction for Abundance* 261

Introduction..263
Chapter 1: The Secret Behind the Secret..265
Chapter 2: From Nothing to Something 266
Chapter 3: The Illusion of Separation 269
Chapter 4: Meditation 273
Chapter 5: The Vibrational Universe 274
Chapter 6: Meditation on the Self... 286
Chapter 7: The Law of Attraction and Money................................... 289
Chapter 8: Law of Attraction Mindset 295
Chapter 9: How to Remove Resistance 296
Chapter 10: The Pathway to Reconnection 299
Chapter 11: What Do You Really Want? 301
Chapter 12: Intentions and Life Purpose 302
Chapter 13: Your Ultimate Desire... 309
Chapter 14: Making Sense of it All 311
Conclusion 313

Personal Message from Elena... 315

Free LOA Newsletter + Bonus Gift.. 317

More Books by Elena G. Rivers... 320

About This Book

Dear Reader, Thank You so much for taking an interest in this publication. It really means a lot to me. My intention was to compile the best of my earlier works to create a truly transformative, all in one, special book edition to assist you in mastering the Law of Attraction.

With this special volume, you will gain the manifestation tools and a deep understanding of how to use the Law of Attraction to mindfully create a life you desire.

Here's exactly what you will discover:

Part 1 – Book 1 – *Law of Attraction - Manifestation Exercises* - Understand the Law of Attraction and manifestation basics and start applying what you learn even before you're done reading this book (you can thank me later!)

Part 2 – Book 2 – *Self-Love Handbook Magnified with the Law of Attraction* – Discover how self-love can help you raise your vibration and manifest faster. At the same time, find the courage to let go of your fears, doubts, and negative energies that hold you back from living your full potential.

Part 3 – Book 3 – *Law of Attraction to Make More Money* – Many people ask me how to use LOA specifically to manifest more money. Some of them use different LOA techniques yet are still not attracting what they want. The problem? To use LOA successfully, you also need to work on your mindset. And this is precisely what you will discover with the *Law of Attraction to Make More Money*!

Part 4 – Book 4 – *Law of Attraction for Motivation* – To manifest what you really want, you need to know who you really are. You can't manifest successfully if you're stuck in your old mindset, motivation, and energies. In other words, you need to know what makes you tick! Suppose you feel stuck or can't achieve your goals. In that case, you can learn how to use the Universal Laws to uncover your authentic motivations and start manifesting your dream reality almost on autopilot!

Part 5 – Book 5- *Law of Attraction for Amazing Relationships* – This book contains all you need to know to master your personal and professional relationships so that you can become a magnet for kind, loving, and authentic people who appreciate you for who you really are. Spoiler – it all starts with the relationship you have with yourself!

Part 6 – Book 6 – *Law of Attraction for Abundance* – True abundance means that you can transform negative into positive. So that you can start attracting beautiful things, events, and circumstances into your life while feeling confident you have the power to be the director of your life.

Part 1 – Book 1

Law of Attraction-

Manifestation Exercises:

Transform All Areas of Your Life with Tested LOA & Quantum Physics Secrets

You create your own universe as you go along.
– Winston Churchill

Introduction

The Law of Attraction has been highly publicized and has become the topic of books, CDs, and seminars. *The Secret*, a 2006 best seller, brought the Law of Attraction to the forefront for millions of people. Many have tried to put the Law of Attraction into practice only to end up with mixed results or disappointment. The most fundamental reason for this is that most discussions about the Law of Attraction approach it from a perspective that is limited by our belief system. When I think of my childhood, I remember an old poster that I had on the wall of my room. The poster showed a seagull gracefully soaring against a vast blue sky with the words, "They can because they think they can." For every person who has not been able to manifest as they hoped, these words echo the reason why.

As long as we try to manifest from the mindset of the average person, we will not be able to experience our potential for manifesting. The reason is that conscious manifesting requires shifting from the common mindset to one that is conducive to manifesting. The problem is not that manifesting is difficult. The problem is that most of us lack control of our manifesting abilities. Unless we learn to take charge of the manifesting process, we will be like a person who gets behind the wheel of a car who has never learned to drive.

I need to clarify a statement that I just made. Learning to manifest consciously is less about taking "charge" as it is learning to allow and accept our current experience of life. Perhaps a more accurate way to describe manifesting is to compare it to trying to remember someone's name. We try to remember the person's name without success. When we stop trying to remember the name, the name comes to us. Manifesting works the same way. The universe, or consciousness, does not make an effort to manifest. Manifesting occurs effortlessly. At every moment of our lives, new manifestations are appearing before us, manifestations that we attracted. We just have to contemplate our bodies to recognize this. At every moment, new cells are replacing old cells, and complex physiological processes are occurring. Each of these new cells or physiological processes is the result of a new potential manifesting itself.

To become conscious manifesters, we need to do the same thing that we would do anytime we want to learn a new skill, which is to look for someone who is already doing it and model them. By learning to model the qualities of the universe, we can become conscious manifesters. This book explores the characteristics of consciousness (I use *universe* and *consciousness* interchangeably throughout this book) and how to adopt these characteristics in our lives. Adopting the characteristics for manifesting is the secondary reason behind why this book was written. My ultimate hope is that by embracing these qualities, you will discover <u>the truth of who you are</u>, which is more profound than anything you could ever manifest.

Part 1 - Law of Attraction – Manifestation Exercises

I attract to my life whatever I give my attention, energy, and focus to, whether positive or negative.
– Michael Losier

Chapter 1: The Truth about Manifesting

The truth about manifesting is that we have been doing it every moment of our lives; we are just unaware of it. It is the lack of this awareness that leads us to believe that manifesting does not work for us, or that it works with limited results.

Anytime that we dream at night, we experience ourselves as a projection of our sleeping self. The projected self, the dream self, experiences and engages with its dream world. Just as in our waking life where we believe we are a separate entities inhabiting the "real world," our dream self believes that it's separate in its dream world.

It is only when awaken that we realize that which we experienced during the night was just a dream. What we often do not take time to contemplate is that our sleeping self-manifested both our dream self and its dream world. Unlike our waking experience, our sleeping self-manifested our dream experience without any effort.

Both our dream experience and our "real world" experience are projections of consciousness. We can think of the manifestation process like an old movie or a slide projector. Unlike the modern day projectors that are digitized, older movie projectors worked by projecting a beam of light through a film strip or slide, as in the slide projector. The image from the film strip or slide is then projected on to a screen. Similarly, we project consciousness, or awareness, on thought. Thought is like an individual frame of a film strip or slide. It is projected by the light of consciousness onto to the screen of our minds, resulting in what we refer to as "experience." In this case, the screen is also consciousness. In fact, the thought, projection of thought, resulting experience, and the screen itself are all aspects of consciousness.

Going back to the movie projector metaphor, the image that appears on the screen and the screen itself are inseparable, just as the image and the projected light are inseparable from each other. The challenge that we have in manifesting is that we believe that we are separate from that which we want to manifest. Just as the light beam is inseparable from the image, we are inseparable from that which we want to manifest. It is this sense of separateness that creates our sense of difficulty in manifesting.

If you can entertain the parallel between the manifestation process and the dream world, here is a metaphor for the truth of who you are, and that metaphor is deep sleep. Deep sleep is like a slide projector without a slide. The beam of light travels into empty space without any slide to project.

Deep sleep is like the movie projector without a film strip. The only thing that is being projected is the light itself.

During deep sleep, you have no sense of separation since there is nothing to experience, and you lose all sense of yourself. For this reason, deep sleep is a metaphor for pure consciousness.
All manifestation arises from consciousness. Without consciousness, no manifestation could exist. You are the projection of pure consciousness. Your experience of yourself, and your world, are the projected images of your mind. The more that we can adopt the characteristics of pure consciousness, the more we can successfully manifest.

Because everyone is at a different level of self-awareness, the next chapter will focus on techniques that most people can identify with. In Chapter 3, we will discuss advanced techniques for challenging your beliefs and perceptions of being a separate self and provide you the opportunity to explore deeper levels of awareness. Ultimately, it's the realization of who you are at the most fundamental level that will allow you to take your manifestation ability to a whole new level.

Part 1 - Law of Attraction – Manifestation Exercises

The entire universe is a great theatre of mirrors.
– Alice Bailey

Chapter 2: Lower-Level Teachings

The lower the level of our resistance, the higher the frequency of our life condition will be for manifesting. This understanding dates back to the origin of religion. There are fundamental tenets that have been exposed by most, if not all religious traditions that can guide us in lowering our resistance. These tenets were proposed by the original teachers of the religions that we know today, such as Jesus and the Buddha. The reason why these teachers exposed these tenets is because they understood that all of our sufferings could be relieved by lowering our resistance and raising the frequency of our life condition.

The tenets that I speak of are not a mystery. Most of us have been taught of their importance since we were children. They include forgiveness, appreciation, humbleness, gratitude, intention, and service to others. In addition to these tenets, I have added the unity or oneness of life. Though this tenet may be less known, it is implicit to all the other tenets. The following is what the Bible says of these tenets:

- **Forgiveness:** *But I tell you, love your enemies and pray for those who persecute you.* Matthew 5:43
- **Appreciation or Gratitude:** *Make a joyful noise unto the LORD, all ye lands.* Psalm 100
- **Humbleness:** *Be completely humble and gentle; be patient, bearing with one another in love.* Ephesians 4:2
- **Intention**: *Turn from evil and do good; seek peace and pursue it.* Psalm 34:14
- **Service to others:** *Feed the hungry, and help those in trouble. Then your light will shine out from the darkness, and the darkness around you will be as bright as noon.* Isaiah 58:10
- **Oneness:** *On that day you will know that I am in My Father, and you are in Me, and I am in you.* John 14:20

The fact that these tenets are universal points to the mutual understanding by the founders of the world's religions. These founders understood the manifestation process. However, their true intent was often misconstrued when their teachings were transcribed into writings. What was intended to be a parable was taken literally. The wisdom that was attributed to Jesus or the Buddha exists within the depth of the lives of each one of us. Learning to manifest is about getting in touch with the part of ourselves which is universal.

Part 1 - Law of Attraction – Manifestation Exercises

Manifesting is the natural outcome of a vibrational universe where all of existence has a vibrational quality to it. Imagine the strings of a guitar, violin, or any other stringed instrument. Each string vibrates at a specific frequency, which is why each string creates a unique sound. The tighter the string is, the higher the frequency of the sound that it creates. Conversely, the looser the string is, the lower the frequency of its sound. Just as with the guitar string, everything in this universe has its own frequency, which is a result of the how energetic its vibration is.

Another example of the universe's vibrational nature is that of electromagnetic waves, waves that affect every aspect of our lives. Electromagnetic waves form a spectrum of various energy levels, and each energy level has its own quality. When electromagnetic waves vibrate at a very high frequency, they create gamma rays, x-rays, and ultraviolet light. In the middle of the spectrum, we find visible light, and at the lower end of the spectrum, we find microwaves and radio waves. Gamma rays can be used to treat cancer. X-rays make it possible for doctors to identify bone fractures. Ultraviolet light, while invisible, is the light that comes from the sun. We use it to disinfect, stimulate the production of Vitamin D, and get tanned. Microwaves make it possible to cook foods using a microwave oven while radio waves make it possible for us to listen to the radio. The only difference between all of these electromagnetic waves is their frequency.

Just as we cannot get a tan by exposing ourselves to gamma rays, or listen to the radio using visible light, we cannot attract what we want if our lives are not at the right vibrational level. It's the vibrational nature of the universe that makes the Law of Attraction operate.

We attract into our lives that which is a vibrational match to our own lives. What determines our vibrational level is our level of resistance toward life and ourselves, and our resistance is created by our minds, meaning the ego.

At the beginning of this chapter, we discussed the tenets of forgiveness, appreciation, humbleness, gratitude, intention, service to others, and oneness of existence. These tenets work toward lowering our resistance while raising our vibrational level.

We will discuss the significance of each of these tenets in the manifestation process, which will be followed by practical ways to apply them in your daily life. But before we go on to discuss these tenets, we need to backtrack to my earlier statement that we are always manifesting. By understanding this statement, you will grasp what it means to be a "conscious manifester."

With every intention we have, we manifest something into our life. Because most of us are not aware of this, we may believe that we have difficulty manifesting. In truth, we cannot avoid manifesting. We are manifesting without being aware of it! Rather than questioning our ability to manifest, a better question would be how we can take greater control of the manifestation process so that we attract what we desire, rather than that which was unintended. The following discussion of the tenets will explain how they serve us in taking control of our manifestations.

Part 1 - Law of Attraction – Manifestation Exercises

It is the combination of thought and love which forms the irresistible force of the law of attraction.
– Charles Hammel

Forgiveness

One of the key aspects of using the Law of Attraction is learning to lower our resistance. Resistance refers to when we do not accept a thought, feeling, emotion, other people, situation, or event.

Whenever we resist anything in life, we are giving it our attention. When we do not forgive others for their actions, we give our attention to those thoughts, emotions, and feelings that we have for the situation. The emotions of anger or resentment that we hold onto receive ongoing nourishment from the attention that we provide them. With time, these emotions will manifest themselves as disorders within the body, disorders of the mind, and they will become the overriding force that cancels our conscious attempts to manifest that which we desire.

Our intentions to attract that which we desire are based on our conscious level of thinking. However, the depth of those emotions that we hold onto, due to not forgiving, may become subconscious. At the subconscious level, our inability to forgive will turn on us. If we hang on to the emotions of anger or resentment, they will infiltrate our sense of self. At this stage, manifestations of physical and mental disorders start taking root. That said, this does not mean that you should forgive when you are not ready to, as that can be a source of problems as well.

If we feel pressured to forgive when we do not feel like it, then we are also creating resistance. Not only are we creating resistance, we are dishonoring our own feelings, which will also hamper our ability to consciously manifest and cause us to lose alignment within ourselves.

We lower our resistance when we learn to forgive, as the adage states: Forgiveness is more for the sake of the forgiver than it is for the forgiven. In short, not forgiving others, and attempting to forgive when we are not ready, will create major problems manifesting, especially the manifestations of happiness, self-trust, and well-being.

So how do we walk this tightrope of forgiveness? We honor ourselves by learning to listen to our feelings. If you are not ready to forgive, do not try to change how you feel. However, when you feel ready to move on, here are some suggestions on how to release your resistance:

Exercises

Journal Writing

1. Start keeping a journal and write in it daily. You can use this journal for all of the exercises that we will be discussing. Starting with the tenet of forgiveness, journal about the things that have angered or hurt you. When you write, write from the heart and just let the words flow. Don't intellectualize this exercise. When you think of these upsetting situations, do not think of forgiveness yet. For this step, you are just getting your feelings out on paper.
2. Once you have written out all your feelings about the situation, write out how you would have liked the situation to have turned out. For example, if you just wrote about a situation where someone said or did something that hurt you, I want you to write out how you wished the situation would have went.
3. After writing out how you wished the situation turned out, I want you to think about what may have caused the other person to act the way they did toward you. Remember, the only reason anyone would hurt another person is because they are fearful and experiencing pain themselves.
4. Using your understanding, write some reasons that this person may be fearful or in pain.
5. Next, reflect on the possibility that the other person did not intend to hurt you. Is it possible that your feeling hurt may be a misunderstanding on your part? Write all the reasons why this may be or may not be a possibility.
6. Your final step is to write down what you have learned from this experience and how you may have benefited from it.
7. Review your journal the following day and then five days after that. After reviewing your writings, did you experience any new insights? If you did not, that is okay. If you did get new insights, write those down in your journal as well.

Doing this journal exercise will help you process your experiences rather than keeping them inside you or acting out in a reactive manner. The next exercise can be used to change your beliefs about forgiveness.

Part 1 - Law of Attraction – Manifestation Exercises

Exercise
Belief Balance Sheet: Forgiveness

Do the following:
1. Get three sheets of paper. Select paper that is 8" x 11" or larger.
2. On the first paper, write down the beliefs that that are preventing you from forgiving. The following are examples:

    - If I forgive him, he will feel like he is off the hook.
    - If I forgive her, she may do it again.
    - If I forgive him, it means that it was never that important.
    - To forgive is to be weak.
    - If I forgive, I will open myself to future abuse.

3. Select the one belief that you believe is the biggest reason why you are unable to forgive.
4. Take the second sheet of paper and fold it in half lengthwise.
5. On the top of the paper, write down the belief that you selected.
6. Make a list on the left-hand side of the paper of all the ways this belief has cost you in your life. How has this belief cost you regarding how you feel about yourself? How has it affected your relationships, health, or finances?
7. When writing, keep in mind the following:
    - When writing this list, write down the first thing that comes to your mind, even if it seems irrelevant.
    - Write as fast as you can and feel the emotions that arise. This is a heartfelt exercise, not a cerebral one.
    - Keep writing until you run out of things to write.
8. Next to each item you write down, assign an arbitrary point value to how much impact the item has had on you. When selecting the point value, choose the first number that comes to mind.
9. When you have completed assigning the point values, find the total of all the point values and place it at the bottom of the page.
10. For the right side of the page, repeat Steps 6-8, except this time, write down all of the ways that this belief has benefited you.

When you have completed Step 10, think of a new alternative belief that empowers you. For example, if the original belief was, "If I forgive him, he will feel like he is off the hook," your new belief may be, "Forgiving him may lead him to feel that he is off the hook, but I will be free from this weight that I am carrying around."

On the third paper, repeat steps 4-9 using your new belief, with the following exceptions: Reverse Steps 6 and 9 by writing down all the ways that you believe that you would benefit from this new belief for Step 6. When doing Step 9, write down all the ways you believe it will cost you.

Part 1 - Law of Attraction – Manifestation Exercises

When you have completed the two sheets, do the following:
1. Immediately review your lists, allowing yourself to fully experience any emotions that arise.
2. Review yours lists every day, once in the morning and once before you go to bed, until you become fully associated with the emotions that you experience.

When you become fully associated with the costs for holding on to your old belief with the benefits of adopting your new belief, your mind will become programmed with your new belief.

Part 1 – Law of Attraction – Manifestation Exercises

As soon as you start to feel differently about what you already have, you will start to attract more of the good things, more of the things you can be grateful for.
– Joe Vitale

Appreciation

To understand the power of appreciation in manifesting, we first need to discuss energy levels and identification. Everything in this universe is composed of energy.

At the atomic level, there is just energetic potential. Our emotions are an expression of energy, and each emotion has its own frequency. Emotions such as fear or anger have lower frequencies, while love and appreciation are of a higher frequency level.

Our essential nature is that of energy as well, and as with emotions, we experience different frequencies as well. The frequency of our life force is dependent upon the degree that we identify with our minds and bodies. In periods of deep sleep, we lose all sense of identification with our minds and bodies. During these times, we return to our essential nature, which is pure consciousness or energy. During deep sleep, our vibrational nature is at its highest.

When we identify with our minds and bodies, our vibrational level is lowered. Our lower vibration leads us to experience a sense of separation. We see ourselves as being our minds and bodies, and everything else as being separate from ourselves.

Nurture great thoughts, for you will never go higher than your thoughts.
– Benjamin Disraeli

When we experience the emotions of anger or fear, it is due to the feeling that our sense of self is being threatened. We think things like "I will become angry if you take my money because that was 'my money.' If I lose my job, I will become fearful that I may experience unpleasant consequences to my lifestyle. In both anger and fear, I feel threatened by external events or situations, which I believe will lead to me losing something."

It is not just anger or fear that appears as a result of our sense of identification with the mind and body. Even the emotions of peace or happiness are dependent upon my external world meeting my expectations. If my life is being good to me, I will feel peace or happiness. My peace and happiness will only last as long as things go my way. As soon as life takes a turn, I will experience anger, fear, or any of the other lower vibratory emotions.

The emotion of appreciation is different from the other emotions in that we can experience appreciation without any expectations of receiving anything. It is for this reason that appreciation is considered second only to love in its vibratory level. Appreciation allows us to lose our identification, if only momentarily, with our mind and body, and focus on something outside ourselves.

Part 1 - Law of Attraction – Manifestation Exercises

Since we manifest that which is of the same vibration as our lives, living in appreciation allows us to manifest those experiences which mirror the same high energy level. Appreciation reduces resistance because we are experiencing a connection with something outside ourselves without expecting anything in return. The following exercises will help to cultivate your sense of appreciation:

Exercises

Appreciation Journal

Each day in your journal, write down all of the things that you are, or could be, appreciative of. For each item, write down *why* you are appreciative for it.

Real-Time Appreciation

Throughout the day each day, take the time to be aware of everything that you are, or could be, appreciative of. The more you do this in a sincere way, the more you will develop your appreciation "muscle."

When it comes to this or any of the other exercises, do not get hung up on looking for major reasons why you should feel a certain way.

Take appreciation as an example. You could be appreciative for the way the sunlight shines on the water of a pond. Such appreciation is just as powerful as having appreciation for having your dreams answered.

The sense of appreciation is what counts, for it is your connection to your higher self. That which you are appreciative of is but a stimulus that triggers your appreciative response. If you have trouble experiencing appreciation, the following exercise may be helpful.

Belief Balance Sheet: Appreciation

1. Get three sheets of paper. Select paper 8" x 11" or larger.
2. On the first paper, write down the beliefs that that are preventing you from feeling appreciation.
3. Select the one belief that you believe is most preventing you from experiencing a sense of appreciation.
4. Fold the second sheet of paper in half lengthwise.
5. At the top of the paper, write down the belief that you selected.
6. Make a list on the left side of the paper of all the ways this belief has cost you in your life. How has this belief cost you in terms of how you feel about yourself? How has it affected your relationships, health, or finances? When writing, keep in mind the following:
    - Write down the first thing that comes to your mind, even if it seems irrelevant.
    - Write as fast as you can and feel the emotions that arise. This is a heartfelt exercise, not a cerebral one.
    - Keep writing until you run out of things to write.

Part 1 - Law of Attraction – Manifestation Exercises

7. Next to each item you write down, assign an arbitrary point value as to how much impact this item has had on you. When selecting the point value, choose the first number that comes to mind.
8. When you have completed assigning the point values, find the total of all the point values and place it at the bottom of the page.
9. For the right side of the page, repeat Steps 6-8, except this time, you will write down all the ways that this belief has benefited you.

When you have completed Step 9, think of a new alternative belief that empowers you.
On the third paper, repeat steps 4-9 using your new belief, with the following exceptions: Reverse Steps 6 and 9 by writing down all the ways that you believe that you would benefit from this new belief for Step 6. When doing Step 9, write down all the ways you believe it will cost you.

When you have completed the two sheets, do the following:
1. Immediately review your lists, allowing yourself to fully experience any emotions that arise.
2. Review yours lists every day, once in the morning and once before you go to bed, until you become fully associated with the emotions that you experience.

When you become fully associated with the costs for holding on to your old belief with the benefits of adopting your new belief, your mind will become programmed with your new belief.
Another approach is to experience greater appreciation is to go inward through the use of meditation:

Appreciation Meditation
1. Find a place where there is minimal distraction and is comfortable. Sit down in a chair or on a pillow, whichever is most comfortable for you.
2. Close your eyes and place your attention on your breathing as you breathe normally.
3. Place your awareness on the sensations that you experience as your breath enters your body during inhalation and leaves it during exhalation.
4. Allow yourself to experience everything that arises in your awareness without any form of judgment or resistance. Greet every experience with complete acceptance.
5. Anytime you find yourself becoming distracted, gently return your awareness back to your breath.
6. Everything that you experience is an opportunity to express appreciation:
    - You can experience appreciation for a person, a pet, or for nature.
    - You can express appreciation for the fact that you can experience thought, sensation, sound, and mental images.
    - You can express appreciation for your breath, which flows through you without any effort on your part, and is essential to your survival.
7. Allow yourself to witness every experience that arises in your awareness without judging, identifying, or analyzing it. Can you find appreciation for the thoughts, sensations, or

feelings that you experience as being uncomfortable? Whatever appears before you, allow it to manifest in your awareness without any interference by you.
8. Should you find yourself reacting to any of your experiences, allow yourself to be a witness to your reactions without any form of judgment.
9. When you find yourself experiencing appreciation, try to intensify that feeling. Place your awareness on the feeling of appreciation. Does the feeling of appreciation have a color, texture, or sound? What happens when you focus on the feelings of appreciation? You can use this technique to intensify any emotion or feeling that you experience.
10. Allow yourself to experience the feeling of appreciation as deeply as possible.
11. If you have trouble with this exercise, keep practicing it until you experience the level of appreciation that you desire.

Part 1 - Law of Attraction – Manifestation Exercises

Take the first step in faith. You don't have to see the whole staircase. Just take the first step.
– Dr Martin Luther King Jr.

Humbleness

The value of humbleness in manifesting is, just as with appreciation, that you are creating distance between yourself and your ego. Appreciation causes us to focus outside ourselves. Being humble downplays the feeling of self-importance while being appreciative of the value that others offer.

Being humble is a position of strength. The humble person does not have to defend or prove themselves. Conversely, those who are connected to their ego exert a great deal of energy defending themselves or trying to persuade others to see their point of view. Anytime we attempt to persuade others to adopt our point of view, or become attached to an image of ourselves, we create resistance. We are creating resistance because we do not feel secure enough to allow others to hold an opposing point of view. We create resistance when we have to hold on to a self-image out of fear of being insignificant.

From an intellectual or societal perspective, the thing that we want to avoid at all costs is appearing insignificant. From the perspective of higher levels of consciousness, being insignificant is a victory over the ego.

With humbleness, self-importance is diminished. The ego is the source of resistance; being humble requires creating distance from the ego. If you feel that you have problems feeling humble, do the following exercise:

Exercises
Belief Balance Sheet: Humbleness
Do the following:
1. Get three sheets of paper. Select paper 8" x 11" or larger.
2. On the first paper, write down the beliefs that that are preventing you from feeling humble.
3. Select the one belief that you believe is the biggest reason why you are unable to feel humble.
4. Take the second sheet of paper and fold it in half lengthwise.
5. On the top of the paper, write down the belief that you selected.
6. Make a list on the left side of the paper of all the ways this belief has cost you in your life. When writing, keep in mind the following:
    - When writing this list, write down the first thing that comes to your mind, even if it seems irrelevant.
    - Write as fast as you can and feel the emotions that arise. This is a heartfelt exercise, not a cerebral one.
    - Keep writing until you cannot think of what to write.

Part 1 – Law of Attraction – Manifestation Exercises

7. Next to each item you write down, assign an arbitrary point value as to how much impact this item has had on you. When selecting the point value, choose the first number that comes to mind.
8. When you have completed assigning the point values, find the total of all the point values and place it at the bottom of the page.
9. For the right side of the page, repeat Steps 5-7, except this time, you will write down all the ways that this belief has benefited you.

When you have completed Step 9, think of a new empowering belief to replace your old belief. On the third paper, repeat steps 4-9 using your new belief with the following exceptions: Reverse Steps 6 and 9 by writing down all the ways that you believe that you would benefit from this new belief for Step 6. When doing Step 9, write down all the ways you believe it will cost you.

When you have completed the two sheets, do the following:
1. Immediately review your lists, allowing yourself to fully experience any emotions that arise.
2. Review yours lists every day, once in the morning and once before you go to bed, until you become fully associated with the emotions that you experience.

When you become fully associated with the costs for holding on to your old belief with the benefits of adopting your new belief, your mind will become programmed with your new belief.

Part 1 - Law of Attraction – Manifestation Exercises

Gratitude is an attitude that hooks us up to our source of supply. And the more grateful you are, the closer you become to your maker, to the architect of the universe, to the spiritual core of your being. It's a phenomenal lesson.
– Bob Proctor

Gratitude

In an earlier chapter, it was indicated that the emotion of appreciation was second only to love in vibrational level. Gratitude is ranked below appreciation only because we are normally grateful because we have received something. The state of gratefulness is dependent upon our external conditions. I may feel grateful because I have a job, my health, or because I received a gift. If I lose any of these things, I could easily move from gratefulness to fear or anger. On the other hand, losing these things may lead me to experience a sense of appreciation for what I once had, or what I may have learned as a result of it.

My sense of appreciation is not dependent on my external conditions while gratitude is. However, having gratitude is still important for manifesting. If we lack gratitude, we are experiencing resistance. We are practicing resistance because we feel that our current situation is not good enough. If I feel that my current situation is not good enough, then I am resisting the present moment. Finally, if I resist the present moment, I am in resistance to all that is, including myself.

The power of the spirit of gratitude is that it leads us to accept the present moment as opposed to thinking of how we want things to be. Focusing on what we want without acceptance of the present moment will lead us to manifest more of that which we don't want. Gratitude reduces resistance by causing us to focus on what we have. By expressing gratitude, we are focusing on the present moment versus thinking of lack or of greener pastures in the future.

Exercises

Gratitude Journal
Each day in your journal, write down all the things that you are or could be grateful for. For each item that you write down, write down why you are grateful for it.

Real-Time Gratitude
Each day, take time to become aware of anything that you are or could be grateful for. The more you do this in a sincere way, the more you will develop your gratitude "muscle." When looking for things to be grateful for, consider everything, not just the typical response that others give. In other words, you could be grateful that the sun is shining, for the kindness of others, or for your manifested form that allows you to experience life.

What counts is the developing of a sense of gratitude, because gratitude, along with the other higher frequency emotions, indicates alignment between our manifested self and our higher version. That which you are grateful for is but a stimulus that triggers your grateful response.

Part 1 - Law of Attraction – Manifestation Exercises

Belief Balance Sheet: Gratefulness

If you feel that you have problems feeling gratefulness, do the following:
1. Get three sheets of paper. Select paper 8" x 11" or larger.
2. On the first paper, write down the beliefs that that are preventing you from feeling grateful.
3. Select the one belief that you believe is the biggest reason why you are not experiencing the feeling of gratefulness.
4. Take the second sheet of paper and fold it in half lengthwise.
5. On the top of the paper, write down the belief that you selected.
6. Make a list on the left hand side of the paper of all the ways this belief has cost you in your life. How has this belief cost you in terms of how you feel about yourself? How has it affected your relationships, health, or finances? When writing, keep in mind the following:
    - Write down the first thing that comes to your mind, even if it seems irrelevant.
    - Write as fast as you can and feel the emotions that arise. This is a heartfelt exercise, not a cerebral one.
    - Keep writing until you run out of things to write.
7. By each item you write down, assign an arbitrary point value as to how much impact the item has had on you. When selecting the point value, choose the first number that comes to mind.
8. When you have completed assigning the point values, find the total of all the point values and place it at the bottom of the page.
9. For the right side of the page, repeat Steps 6-8, except this time, write down all the ways that this belief has benefited you.
10. When you have completed Step 9, think of a new alternative belief that empowers you.

When you have completed Step 9, think of a new empowering belief to replace your old belief. On the third paper, repeat steps 4-9 using your new belief, with the following exceptions: Reverse Steps 6 and 9 by writing down all the ways that you believe that you would benefit from this new belief for Step 6. When doing Step 9, write down all the ways you believe it will cost you.

When you have completed the two sheets, do the following:
1. Immediately review your lists, allowing yourself to fully experience any emotions that arise.
2. Review yours lists every day, once in the morning and once before you go to bed, until you become fully associated with the emotions that you experience.

When you become fully associated with the costs for holding on to your old belief with the benefits of adopting your new belief, your mind will become programmed with your new belief.

Service to Others

Regardless of the culture or religious teaching, the concept of service is a central tenant. In recovery groups, such as Alcoholics Anonymous, service to others is an integral part of the program. The reason why service to others is so entrenched in our society is that, like any other spiritual or ethical principle, it creates distance between us and our ego. By creating distance, we release resistance. When acting in the service of others, our focus shifts from our ego to the well-being of others.

Exercises

Journaling

1. In your journal, do the following:
2. Make a list of all the things that you enjoy doing.
3. Make a list of your skills, talents, and things which you are knowledgeable about.
4. Make list of all the needs that you are aware of that are being experienced by your family, community, state, or country.
5. Reflect on how you can integrate Steps 1-3 into serving those you indicated in Step 4.

For example, someone may identify relationship skills, artistic ability, and marketing as their strengths. They also may have identified neighborhood blight as a problem in their community.

This person could serve their community by organizing a group of people to beautify their neighborhood by removing graffiti or creating murals and other forms of artwork for people to enjoy.

Using their knowledge of marketing, they would be able to create partnerships with the business community for support and needed resources.

It is true that you could skip this exercise and just find a way to serve others. The advantage of doing this exercise is that by aligning your gifts and abilities, you can create even a greater impact for those you are serving, as well as for yourself.

> *Whatever the mind can conceive it can achieve.*
> *– W. Clement Stone*

Intention

Of all the factors that influence our ability to manifest, one of the most fundamental is intention. Being able to consciously manifest requires our intentions to be toward creating value or happiness for others. As long as our intentions are to serve ourselves, or harm others, we will continue to create suffering for ourselves and others. Such intentions are the result of fear, and the only things that fear manifests are more fear and suffering. Conversely, having intentions to create value or happiness for others brings a higher frequency to our lives, which will attract manifestations of like kind.

Exercise
Creative Intentions
Start checking in with yourself before making a decision that impacts others or the environment by doing the following:
1. Before making your decision, consider all of your options. For each option, consider its potential impact on all stakeholders, including you.
   - Does the option being considered benefit you at the expense of others?
   - Does the option being considered benefit others at your own expense?

The ideal option benefits all stakeholders. The problem most people experience during decision making is that they have not put enough time or creativity into coming up with options. We are very rarely restricted to only two options when it comes to decision making.

With thoughtful reflection and creativity, we can usually come up with a number of options by taking different elements of our initial options and combining them to create new options. Use this process to find an option that provides the greatest benefits for all involved.
By doing this process, you will move from a fear-based and limited perspective and toward a holistic perspective, which will lower your resistance.

Meditation
The following meditation can be practiced to use the body's wisdom when making a decision:
1. Sit down and make yourself comfortable.
2. Close your eyes and place your attention on your breath as it travels in and out of your body during inhalation and exhalation.
3. If you become distracted, return your attention back to your breath.
4. Continue focusing on your breath until your mind becomes calm and you are aware of the sensations of the body.
5. When you have reached the state described in Step 4, consider each option of your decision. As you consider each option, pay close attention to how your body responds when you consider the particular option. Examples of the body's reactions may include:
   - Tightening or loosening of your chest
   - Shallow breathing or breathing more fully.
   - Your body feeling heavy or light.
   - Tension or relaxation
6. The option that you want to choose is the one that gives you the greatest sense of well-being.
7. If you find that your breath is shallow, your chest is tight, or your body feels tense, then that option is not the option that you should choose.

8. It may be necessary to practice this meditation until you become more aware of the body's sensations, and you can determine how your body responds when contemplating your options.

How wonderful it is that nobody needs to wait a single moment before starting to improve the world.
— Anne Frank

Oneness of Existence

Oneness is often referenced in spiritual teachings. However, it remains just a concept for most of us. Our experience of life is anything but oneness, with all of its diversity. Besides diversity, we also experience ourselves as separate beings amidst all of this diversity. Unless you practice meditation or some other deep contemplative practice, the experience of oneness will remain conceptual.

A heartfelt understanding of Oneness dissolves the feeling of separateness. Though our sensory experience will continue to give the impression of separateness, our sense of personhood will dissolve as we merge with our experience of life.

In deep sleep, nothing is experienced because there is only awareness. To be devoid of experience is to encounter the essence of Oneness. If there is only Oneness, what is there to attract or manifest? We are projections of pure consciousness that have manifested for the purpose of being able to experience. It is through our experiencing that pure consciousness experiences itself. By moving toward the direction of Oneness, we can enjoy the best of both worlds. We can enjoy our manifested selves while tapping into our un-manifested selves.

In the next chapter, you will have an opportunity to engage in a powerful meditation to gain a more intuitive understanding of your un-manifested self. For now, here is a more intellectual exercise for understanding oneness. Before presenting this exercise, it is necessary to provide an example of how you can perceive oneness in everyday life.

If we look at a tree, we will most likely perceive the tree as being a separate entity unto itself. The tree is seen as being a separate entity from all the other entities. We do not confuse the tree for a rock, a bird, or for ourselves. We see the tree as being a fixed entity, and the tree will never be anything but a tree. Further, we will most likely believe that the tree is made of tree parts, those aspects that constitute the tree. The "tree parts" could be its leaves, trunk, bark, and roots. This view of the tree is a dualistic view in that we see the tree as a separate entity unto itself that is comprised of "tree parts."

Part 1 - Law of Attraction – Manifestation Exercises

Divine mind is the one and only reality.
– Charles Fillmore

If we reflect more deeply, however, we can see that this dualistic view of the tree is just an illusion. The sun provides the light that the tree needs to conduct photosynthesis. Without the sun, the tree could not exist.

The carbon dioxide molecules that are a component of the air are needed by the tree for it to conduct photosynthesis. Without the carbon dioxide molecule, there could be no tree. Clouds produce rain which the tree depends upon for its water. Without the clouds, the tree could not exist.

The nutrients in soil are absorbed by the tree's roots. Without the soil, the tree could not exist. From the perspective oneness, the tree is made of the sun, carbon dioxide molecules, clouds, and soil.

This is just a simplified example, and there are numerous other entities that make the existence of the tree possible. In turn, all of the entities that make the existence of the tree possible are themselves dependent upon other entities for their existence.

If there was no evaporation of water, clouds could not exist. If there were no electrical charges, the carbon dioxide molecule could not exist, and so on. Ultimately, the tree is not a separate entity unto itself. Rather, the tree is the composite of the entire universe. The entire universe creates the tree, and the tree is a testimony to the existence of the universe.

There is no such thing as a "tree;" rather, what we call "tree" is the composite of the totality of existence.

We believe in the Law of Attraction because we have a dualistic view of ourselves and our place in this universe. However, just as with the tree, you are the composite of all of existence.

Many of the elements that your body is made of originated from the stars, while your body has the same salt concentration as ocean water. Every aspect of who you are is the result of the existence of something else. Any sense of being a separate and distinct entity unto yourself is just an illusion. Any doubts or challenges that you may feel that you have in manifesting are just illusions. That which you are trying to attract is an aspect of you already. Instead of thinking that you are in the universe, it would be more accurate to say that the universe is found within you.

Part 1 - Law of Attraction – Manifestation Exercises

This statement will hopefully become more apparent in the next chapter. For now, try this exercise:

Meditation

1. Sit down and make yourself comfortable.
2. Close your eyes and place your attention on your breath as travels in and out of your body during inhalation and exhalation.
3. If you become distracted, return your attention back to your breath.
4. When your mind is calm, open your eyes and find an object to look at. The object that you look at can be living or non-living.
5. As you look at the object, refrain from engaging in any form of judgment.
6. As you study the object, ask yourself the following questions:
7. Is there any aspect of this object that is not subject to change? (Example: If you are viewing a flower, you know that the flower is subject to change due to the seasons and its life span.)
8. How is the object that you are observing impacted by the other objects in its environment? Example: Insects and birds make it possible for pollination of the flower to occur.
9. Meditate on how the object of your observation owes its existence to other seemingly unrelated objects.

Part 1 - Law of Attraction – Manifestation Exercises

When one door of happiness closes, another opens; but often we look so long at the closed door that we do not see the one which has been opened for us.
– Helen Keller

Chapter 3: Upper-Level Teachings

In this chapter, you will find exercises that are more advanced than those in the previous chapter, as well as more detailed information about the topic of resistance.

Resistance

Just as with guitar strings or electromagnetic waves, the life of each one of us has its own frequency or vibrational level. Our frequency is dependent upon on the amount of resistance that is in our lives. The less resistance we have, the higher the frequency of our lives. The higher the frequency, the more efficiently we can conscientiously manifest. The lower the frequency we have, the less ability we have to manifest that which we desire. The reason for this is that the resistance we hold receives a greater amount of our attention than that which we want to manifest. Since what we focus on is what we manifest, we attract more of that which we are resistant to. What is it that we are resisting? We are resisting our higher nature, which is pure consciousness. Anytime we resist anything, we are going against our essential nature.

We are simultaneously nonphysical and physical beings at the same time. As a physical being, we have forgotten our true nature. Because we have forgotten our true nature, we experience resistance to anything that we perceive to be threatening to our sense of self. If we realized that our true nature is that of consciousness, nothing could pose a threat to us. Since we would not perceive anything as a threat, we would not generate resistance. It is the lack of resistance that allows pure conscious to manifest as existence.

Whenever we do not accept the present moment, we create resistance. When we look toward the future, because we feel the present is not sufficient, we are creating resistance. When we lament the past, we are not accepting the present moment. When we are preoccupied with what may happen in the future, we are not accepting the present moment.

Nothing is, unless our thinking makes it so.
– Shakespeare

Resistance can even occur while manifesting, even when we have the best intentions. The following personal story will illustrate this. When I first practiced manifesting, I made the intention that I would see a certain book cover when I went to the library later that day.

To my pleasant surprise, I saw the exact book cover that I visualized upon arriving there. The following day, I decided to manifest something else. I made the intention that during that day, I would encounter a purple circular object with red spots. Throughout the day I looked for the object, but it never appeared. Why was my second attempt to manifest a disappointment when my first day was a complete success? There could be a number of factors. However, the primary factor was my own resistance. On my first manifestation attempt, I simply made my intention, forgot about it, and went on with my day. On my second attempt, I made my intention, but I did not forget about it. Instead of going on with my day, I kept looking for my manifestation to appear.

Every time I looked and did not see it, I started to experience doubt. My sense of doubt was a form of resistance. On my first attempt, I forgot about my intentions and just went on with my day. My manifestation appeared before me when I was not looking for it. The concept of detachment is frequently discussed in spiritual teachings. My first manifestation attempt was successful because I was detached from the outcome of my intentions, unlike on my second day.

The following are recommendations for becoming detached to your outcome:
1. If you are not already experienced in manifesting, start practicing your manifesting abilities by making your intentions about things that are inconsequential to you. If you do not have an emotional connection to your intention, your ego will not get involved. Continue creating intentions that do not have significance for you. As your manifestations take place, you can gradually make more relevant intentions.
2. Practice the meditations in this book until you start intuitively experiencing the understanding that who you are is the one that is aware, or the knower of all of experience. By reaching this level of awareness, your thoughts of doubt will lose their ability to influence you.

One of the most important practices to develop to be a successful manifester is that of meditation or mindfulness. Meditation and mindfulness practices allow us to develop greater attention to the present moment and to be less distracted by our thoughts. When we become less identified with our thoughts, we release our resistance to them.

Think of a time when you could not remember a person's name. At that moment, you were experiencing a thought, the idea that you had forgotten the person's name. This thought may have led to a sense of uneasiness, which was created by another thought, the thought that you should know their name. Because this feeling consumed your attention, you continued to struggle to remember their name.

It is attention that energizes our thoughts; thoughts within themselves are powerless. When we energize our thoughts, they become manifested in our life. The more you tried to remember their name, the more frustrated you became. You fully manifested the experience of forgetting the other person's name.

In your frustration, you may have given up on trying to remember their name. When that happened, you removed your attention from the chain of thoughts that you created, resulting in them losing their power. Because of this, your memory of their name returned soon afterward. Just as in my personal story about manifesting, I held no attachments to my outcome of manifesting on the first day, but became fully attached on the second day.

When a thought becomes the attraction point for similar thoughts, as described in the scenario of remembering a name, that thought becomes emboldened by the attention that we give it. The potency of these thoughts gives us a sense of certainty to their truthfulness. When we are confident that our thoughts are true, we have created what is commonly known as a "belief."

All that we are is a result of what we have thought.
– Buddha

Belief systems:
Our beliefs determine our experience of life, and our beliefs are like filters through which we experience the world. Beliefs are like tinted sunglasses that we have forgotten that we have on. Whatever color lens we have on will be how we experience the world. To not be aware of our beliefs, and not question them, is probably the single most important reason for us having trouble taking control of the manifestation process.

Our beliefs determine what we think, notice, do not notice, the actions that we take, and how we experience the world and ourselves. If a person has the belief that other people cannot be trusted, then that person's focus will be on all the reasons why other people cannot be trusted.
Not only will their focus be on why other people cannot be trusted, but they also will not notice any information that supports the contrary. Because of this, all of this person's actions will be based on the belief that people cannot be trusted, and they will experience the world as a risky place. Additionally, they will see themselves as being guarded.

Cherish your visions and your dreams as they are the children of your soul, the blueprints of your ultimate achievements.
– Napoleon Hill

It is the power of beliefs that prevent us from experiencing our unlimited potential to manifest. Holding the belief that you cannot be a successful manifester will result in your inability to manifest consciously, which will prevent you from taking charge of the manifesting process.

You will not notice everything that you are manifesting, believing that their appearance is the result of coincidence or luck. Similarly, you will attribute your undesirable experiences to bad luck, fate, or destiny.

How attached we are to our beliefs determines if we see ourselves as separate beings who are trying to manifest our desires or whether we come to the recognition that who we are is inseparable from all of existence.

What you radiate outward in your thoughts, feelings, mental pictures and words, you attract into your life.
– Catherine Ponder

When we identify with our minds and bodies, we cannot help but believe that we lack something in our life. It is this very sense of lack that leads us to the Law of Attraction or some other teachings.

When we learn to practice complete acceptance of all of our experiences, we release our sense of resistance. When we release our sense of resistance, we may come to the realization that who we are is beyond anything that we can experience.

When we realize that who we are is not what we experience, we may come to the realization that it is impossible to lack anything. Hence, manifesting and the Law of Attraction become totally irrelevant as we recognize that our true nature is that of unlimited potential.

Because the ability to manifest is dependent on how much we identify with our minds and bodies, the remaining portion of this book is devoted to techniques that can be used to move closer to the recognition of our highest self.

Exercise
Belief Balance Sheet: Releasing Intentions
To address any belief that you have that may be preventing you from manifesting to the degree that you want, do the following:
1. Get three sheets of paper. Select paper 8" x 11" or larger.
2. On the first paper, write down the beliefs that are preventing you from manifesting.
3. Select the one belief that you believe is the biggest obstacle to manifesting that which you desire.
4. Fold the second sheet of paper in half lengthwise.
5. At the top of the paper, write down the belief that you selected.
6. Make a list on the left side of the paper of all the ways that this belief has cost you in your life. How has this belief cost you in terms of how you feel about yourself? How has

it affected your relationships, health, or finances? When writing, keep in mind the following:
- Write down the first thing that comes to your mind, even if it seems irrelevant.
- Write as fast as you can and feel the emotions that arise. This is a heartfelt exercise, not a cerebral one.
- Keep writing until you run out of things to write.

7. Next to each item you write down, assign an arbitrary point value as to how much impact this item has had on you. When selecting the point value, choose the first number that comes to mind.
8. When you have completed assigning the point values, find the total of all the point values and place it at the bottom of the page.
9. For the right side of the page, repeat Steps 6-8, except this time, you will write down all the ways that this belief has benefited you.

When you have completed Step 9, think of a new alternative belief that empowers you.
On the third paper, repeat steps 4-9 using your new belief with the following exceptions: Reverse Steps 6 and 9 by writing down all the ways that you believe that you would benefit from this new belief for Step 6. When doing Step 9, write down all the ways you believe it will cost you.

When you have completed the two sheets, do the following:
1. Immediately review your lists, allowing yourself to fully experience any emotions that arise.
2. Review yours lists every day, once in the morning and once before you go to bed, until you become fully associated with the emotions that you experience.

When you become fully associated with the costs for holding on to your old belief with the benefits of adopting your new belief, your mind will become programmed with your new belief.

Every single second is an opportunity to change your life, because in any moment you can change the way you feel.
– Rhonda Byrne

Emotions

Our emotions are a mirror to the thoughts that we are thinking. The emotions that we experience are the sensory equivalent of our thoughts, both conscious and subconscious.
We cannot see or feel a thought; there is just an awareness that we are having one. Our emotions, on the other hand, are sensory since we can feel them.

If you are experiencing emotions that are empowering you, it is because you are experiencing thoughts of the same quality. By changing our feelings, we change our thoughts.

Part 1 - Law of Attraction – Manifestation Exercises

The Secret was valuable in introducing people to the Law of Attraction. However, it presented the Law of Attraction in a simple manner. Like many other Law of Attraction products on the market, the Secret focused on how we can manifest by the thoughts that we hold. While it is true our thoughts are the source of our manifestations, what is not explained is the role that our emotions play. Imagine that you are trying to manifest money, so you hold on to that intention. At the same time, you are holding on to deep-seated emotions from your past regarding scarcity. Because these emotions are deep-seated, you are not aware of them, except when they rise to the surface during times of uncertainty.

As discussed earlier, everything in this universe has a vibration. Thoughts and emotions become subconscious when we divert our attention from them. To keep thoughts and feelings at the subconscious level requires the expenditure of a large amount of energy. Because this expenditure of energy is greater than that which is being directed to your intentions, you continue to manifest scarcity instead of money. Our emotions impact our ability to manifest at the conscious level as well. While our intentions are powerful, what makes them even more powerful is when we become fully associated with the emotions that come from our intention. While the intention for manifesting more money is powerful, what would be even more powerful is for you to focus on the emotions that you would have if you had the money already.

See the things that you want as already yours. Know that they will come to you at need. Then let them come. Don't fret and worry about them. Don't think about your lack of them. Think of them as yours, as belonging to you, as already in your possession.

– Robert Collier

The following exercise is for employing the power of your emotions in the manifesting process:

Exercises

Harnessing Emotional Power

1. Sit down and make yourself comfortable.
2. Close your eyes and place your attention on your breath as travels in and out of your body during inhalation and exhalation.
3. If you become distracted, return your attention back to your breath.
4. When your mind is calm, bring forth the intention that you wish to manifest.
5. As you think of your intentions, imagine the thing which you desire to attract exists already in your life.

6. In your mind, visualize that which you want to manifest as clearly as possible.
7. Imagine what it would feel like to touch your manifestation.
8. Imagine what you would hear if your intentions were already manifested.
9. If you could taste your manifestation, what would it taste like?
10. How would you feel if your manifested intention was in your life right now? Allow yourself to experience your emotions fully.
11. When you can experience the emotions, intensify them by placing your attention on them.
12. Experience your emotions intensifying. You can stay in this space for as long as you desire.
13. Repeat this focus on your emotions as often as possible when meditating until your manifestations appear.

The following exercise will allow you to transform deep-seated emotions. This next exercise is more advanced in that it requires your willingness to experience unpleasant emotions.

Diving Deep into an Emotion
1. Think of a situation that is bothering you.
2. When you have identified the situation, ask yourself why this situation bothers you.
3. As you think about the situation, become aware of the feelings that you experience.

Continuing with this exercise, we will use an example. In this example, we will use the emotion of anger.

4. Allow yourself to fully experience the anger you feel. As you experience the anger, identify what anger FEELS like. I have emphasized the word *feel* because this exercise requires that you remain in the experience of feeling, not thinking.

You do not want to involve your mind in this exercise because it will just unleash a bunch of stories about what happened. Instead, ask yourself the question, "What does anger feel like?" When asking this question, pay attention to the first answer that comes to you. Again, do not think about it.

5. Continuing with this example, let us say your response to this question is that when angry, it **feels** like your face is tightening.
6. Your next step is to become fully associated with the feeling of tightening. Allow yourself to dive into this feeling.
7. When you become fully associated with the feeling of tightening, repeat the question by asking, "What does tightening feel like?"
8. Continuing with the example, your answer may be that tightening **feels** hard.
9. Become fully associated with the feeling of hardness; allow yourself to dive into this feeling.
10. When you become fully associated with the feeling of hardness, repeat the question by asking, "What does hardness **feel** like?"

11. Continuing with the example, you may say that hardness has a numbing feeling.
12. Become fully associated with the feeling of numbness; allow yourself to dive into this feeling.
13. Ask yourself "What does numbness **feel** like?"
14. Based on your response, you would continue to ask the question "What does (feeling) feel like?"
15. You would continue with this line of questioning until your start experiencing neutral or positive emotions.

What you accomplish in doing this exercise is the transformation of your feelings and emotions at the conscious and subconscious levels. By continuously placing your awareness on what you are experiencing, fully experiencing it, and identifying it, your experience of emotions and feelings will be transformed. You may experience a return of the original feelings or emotions, which is normal. If you continue to utilize this exercise when they show up, eventually you will gain the upper hand.

Earlier in this book, we discussed the role of separation as to how we experience ourselves. By seeing ourselves as separate entities that inhabit this planet, we create resistance toward those experiences that we find threatening. It is our resistance that interferes with our ability to manifest our desires. The following are advanced exercises to develop a new perspective on your sense separation.

Exercise
1. Sit down and make yourself comfortable.
2. Look at an object in your environment.
3. Determine for yourself how is that you know that you are seeing the object.
   Your first response to this question will probably be, "Because I see it!"
   But how do you know that you are seeing? The answer to that question is that you are aware of it. You are aware that seeing is taking place.
4. As you look at the object, determine for yourself whether the process of seeing ends at some point at which the object begins, or does the process of seeing and the object flow into each other?

Hopefully, you have come to the conclusion that the process of seeing and the object flow into each other. We cannot separate seeing from the object being seen.

5. Inquire for yourself as to where seeing takes place. Does seeing originate from within you, or outside of you?

How is that you know that the process of seeing and the object being seen flow into each other? How do you know that the process of seeing occurs from within you? The answer to both of these questions is awareness. You are aware of all of these things.

So far, we can come to the following conclusions:
- The process of seeing and the object being seen flow into each other. They are one in the same.
- The process of seeing occurs from within you.
- The realization of the previous two points was derived from awareness or knowing.

From these conclusions, we can surmise that the object being seen, the process of being seen, and you, the seer, are inseparable from each other. All of these things are known because there is an awareness of it.

We can take this process a step further by inquiring into the nature of who you are. You are the one who observed the object, but how do you know that you exist? You know that you exist because you are aware of that as well. The next logical question would be who or what is aware of you? The answer to that question is the truth of who you are. You can explore this further using the next exercise.

Part 1 - Law of Attraction – Manifestation Exercises

Exercise
Self-Inquiry
1. Sit down and make yourself comfortable.
2. Close your eyes and place your attention on your breath as travels in and out of your body during inhalation and exhalation.
3. If you become distracted, return your attention back to your breath.
4. When your mind becomes calm, allow your attention to roam freely. Do not try to control anything.
5. Allow yourself to become the witness to all that you experience. Receive each experience with complete acceptance. Do not judge, analyze, or try to modify anything that you experience. Let all of your experience come and go on their own accord.
6. As you meditate, you will experience thoughts, perceptions, sensations, and sounds. Notice how they appear into your awareness and then fade away. Observe how they change in their form or intensity. Nothing that you experience remains unchanged.
7. Notice how the mental phenomena you experience carry out their existence without any effort on your part. Thoughts, perceptions, and sensations happen by themselves.
8. Notice that, as the observer of all mental phenomena; you cannot be them. You are not the thoughts, perceptions, or sensations that you experience. You are the knower of them.
9. Who is the knower of your experience? Who is the one that is aware?

Remember that you are the witness or knower of all of your experiences. Any answer that you come up with as to the question of the identity of knower cannot be correct. How can anything that you experience be the knower if it is also known?

10. Keep looking for the knower, the one that is aware. Can you find it?

Our minds operate conceptually. In other words, our minds can only recognize that which takes on form. Thoughts, perceptions, sensations, sounds, and smells are all recognized by our minds as they can be conceptualized. The truth of who you are, the one who is the knower, the one who is aware, cannot be detected by the mind, for it is non-phenomenal.

Practicing this meditation will result in expanding your awareness to the truth of your existence and the illusionary nature of all of your experiences. Who you are is awareness itself, and as awareness, you are the knower of all experience. Experience owes its existence to you. How can you experience anything unless there is an awareness of it? By confirming this for yourself, you will go a long way to removing your sense of separation from the world around you. When you reduce the potency of your sense of separation, your level of resistance will be reduced. Finally, when you reduce your level of resistance, you will increase your vibrational frequency. The vibrational frequency will allow you to manifest into your life that which you desire.

Part 1 - Law of Attraction – Manifestation Exercises

Nothing external to me has any power over me.
– Walt Whitman

Chapter 4: Making Sense of it All

We have covered a lot of information so far, so in this chapter, we will discuss how to make sense of it all. Before we do this, let us do a quick review:

1. We are multidimensional beings who are both physical and non-physical simultaneously.
2. Our physical self is an expression of our non-physical being, which is pure consciousness.
3. Everything in this universe is of a vibratory nature. It is this vibratory nature that ultimately makes the manifestation process possible. Our physical being is the result of pure consciousness lowering its vibratory level.
4. As physical beings, we are constantly manifesting, though we may be unaware of it. It is this lack of awareness that leads us to attract both desired and undesired circumstances into our life. We attract both because we are unaware that we are the ones that are doing the manifesting.
5. We can increase our ability to manifest that which we desire by placing greater attention on our vibratory level.
6. Our vibratory level is determined by the level of acceptance or resistance that we have within our lives.
7. Resistance leads to a sense of separation, and a sense of separation leads to further resistance.
8. By learning to live with acceptance, gratitude, appreciation, service to others, and forgiveness, we raise our vibration.
9. When we hold on to resistance, we lower our vibration.
10. The quality of our vibration determines what we attract into our lives.
11. To become conscious manifesters, we need to lower our resistance.

Now that we have reviewed the past content, we will now discuss how to use the information presented in this book.

Part 1 - Law of Attraction – Manifestation Exercises

Preparing for Manifesting

As indicated at the beginning of this book, everyone is different in respect to their level of awareness as it relates to their connection with the greater self or the universe. It is for this reason that such a broad spectrum of exercises was provided in this book.

No one exercise in this book is more useful than the rest. What determines the effectiveness of any given exercise is how well it resonates with you. Further, the number of potential practices for raising your vibrational level is endless.

In fact, you do not even need exercises if you are intuitive enough to move beyond your mind and allow yourself to experience the present moment. Having said all of this, you should use this book similar to a buffet. Try the activities that seem interesting or enjoyable to you, but do not be afraid to try those exercises that seem too simple or esoteric.

Allow yourself to experiment with the exercises that seem to be right for you. Do not worry about how many activities you select to do; there is no precise number. It is important to state that there is an advantage of doing different exercises in that it allows you to experiment with different perspectives. All of the exercises in this book point toward the same thing, which is that you have the ability to take charge of your vibrational level.

> *A person is what he or she thinks about all day long.*
> *– Ralph Waldo Emerson*

Once you have selected the exercises, practice them until you feel comfortable that you have achieved the outcome of the exercise. The results of all of the exercises are the same: Lowering your resistance toward yourself and others and realizing that you can take charge of your vibratory level. How do you know your vibratory level? It is simple. The higher your vibratory level, the more you will experience peacefulness, acceptance, and centeredness.

This does not mean you never get angry, upset, or have a bad day, for all of these experiences are normal. What will be different is that these experiences will have less of an impact on you. The second thing that is important to note is that you do not want to let your ego get involved with the practicing of these exercises. It is natural to approach these activities with expectations or judgments. However, this will only engage your ego. When conducting these exercises, approach them as a blank slate, even if you do them daily. Each time you do these exercises; approach them as if you were doing them for the first time.

While doing these exercises, you may experience distracting thoughts, which is okay. Do not attempt to rationalize, deny, or resist any thoughts that may arise. Rather, allow them complete freedom to express themselves, but do not engage with them.

Part 1 - Law of Attraction – Manifestation Exercises

It should be noted that the Belief Balance Sheet occurs in many places in the exercise sections of this book. This exercise's sole purpose is to assist you in identifying the beliefs that may be impeding your ability to manifest and replacing them with more empowering ones. I recommend that you do these exercises in conjunction with any of the meditative practices, particularly for those in the last section.

Doing the Belief Balance Sheet exercises in conjunction with any of the other exercises will create an excellent foundation for manifesting. The Belief Balance Sheet exercises should not be done just one time, they should be done on an ongoing basis so that you are continuously rooting out any disempowering beliefs that you may have.

Unless you have experience in meditation and manifesting, I advise that you start off with the exercises in Chapter 2 before attempting the exercises in Chapter 3. All of the previous meditations in this book were intended to expand your level of awareness to reduce your sense of separation and resistance. The following is the last exercise in this book. It is by no means the most complicated in this book; however, all the previous activities will prepare you to get the most out of it.

Exercise
Meditation for Releasing Your Intention

1. Find a place where there is a minimal amount of distraction. Sit down in a chair or on a pillow, whichever is most comfortable for you.
2. Close your eyes and place your attention on your breath as you breathe normally.
3. Place your awareness on the sensations that you experience as your breath enters your body during inhalation and leaves it during exhalation.
4. Allow yourself to experience everything that arises in your awareness without any form of judgment or resistance. Greet every experience with complete acceptance.
5. Anytime you find yourself becoming distracted, gently return your awareness back to your breath.

With practice, you will be able to extend the amount of time that you can stay focused on your breath. With that focus, you will find your mind getting increasingly calmer. You will continue to experience thoughts.
However, they gradually lose their ability to impact you. Remember, your thoughts derive all of their power from the attention that we give them.

6. When you have thoughts, simply acknowledge their presence and then return your attention to your breath.
7. When your mind is calm, you will notice that your thoughts will slow down, enough that you will be able to recognize the space between your thoughts. In other words, there is a space that exists between the time that one thought fades away and the next one appears.

8. When you have found this space, release your intentions into that space.
9. Follow these steps with each meditation. You can release more than one intention during your meditation.

Practicing meditation and making an intention is easy, not getting caught up in self-doubt as we wait for our manifestation to appear is the difficult part. The key to manifesting is getting in a relaxed state, releasing your intention, and then becoming detached from your outcome. By becoming detached from your outcome, you will not think about it. When you do not think about it, you will not doubt that it will happen. When you do not doubt that it will happen, you will not experience resistance. When you release your resistance, your manifestation will appear when the conditions are right.

If you can dream it, you can do it.
– Walt Disney

Do not get fooled into believing that you can manifest without exerting any effort on your part. While it is true that manifesting without effort is possible, it requires removing your resistance to a minimal level.

Achieving such low levels of resistance requires intensive meditative practices. For most of us, we also need to get actively involved in making our manifestations come true. If you want to manifest a new sports car, and all that you do is meditate and release your intentions, your chances for success will be dubious at best.

The reason why is because most of us will experience resistance in the form of doubt. A sports car is a very distinct item, and it is expensive. Both the specificity of this intention, along with its cost, provides ample room for doubt to arise.

Conversely, if your intentions are to increase your income, that is an intention that is more general and can come from numerous sources. The intention to "increase your income" is more general than a sports car, and there are more avenues from which it can happen. For this reason, most people will find it an easier intention to manifest than a sports car.
With the intention of increased income, you have the opportunity to attract it through improving the way you handle your finances, getting a higher paying job, receiving an inheritance, starting your own business, and so on. All of these methods are recognized as available methods for increasing your income because that is how we have been socialized. Because these methods are believable to us, they generate less resistance from us. On the other hand, trying to manifest a sports car directly, without effort on your part, seems less plausible to our minds; hence, the sports car is harder to manifest.

You may be wondering at this point as to the previous comment that having a more general intention makes it easier to manifest than having a detailed intention. After all, we frequently hear that our intentions should be made as real and concrete as possible. In other words, having a vivid image of the person that you want to attract into your life is more effective than having an intention that you want to meet someone. Which view is correct, making your intentions detailed and explicit, or making them general? The answer is that both views are right; it depends on your level of resistance.

> *Whatever you create in your life you must first create in your imagination.*
> *– Tycho Photiou*

Imagine that you want to manifest a new job and you make your intention as detailed as possible. As you meditate, you create a particular intention of the kind of job that you want.

You know the salary you want, the people that you want to work with, and the distance of your commute. If you are not confident in your ability to manifest, you can quickly experience self-doubt as you wait for your manifestation to enter your life. You may start questioning your intention, wondering how realistic the idea of such a job presenting itself to you is. It is this questioning that will create resistance within you and prevent your dream job from manifesting. For this reason, you will probably be more successful if you are less detailed in your intentions and simply meditate on the intention that you want the job that will bring you happiness.

Until you become more confident in your manifesting abilities, it is better to make your intentions detailed for those things that do not have an emotional connection for you while making those intentions that have an emotional connection for you more general. As you gain confidence in your manifestation ability, you can become more detailed in all of your intentions.

From the perspective of higher levels of awareness, it is just as easy to manifest a multimillion-dollar mansion as it is to manifest a paper clip. It is only from our ordinary level of awareness that there appears to be a difference in difficulty when attempting to manifest these things.

Part 1 - Law of Attraction – Manifestation Exercises

Imagination is everything. It is the preview of life's coming attractions.
– Albert Einstein

Chapter 5: 30-Day Challenge

This 30-day challenge is offered to provide greater structure to the content that you have read so that you can apply it more effectively. Feel free to modify the 30 Day Challenge to your level of ability in manifesting.

Days 1-14
- Familiarize yourself with the exercises in Chapter 2 and choose those exercises that are relevant to you. If you are not familiar with the manifesting process, you may want to do all of them. If you have tried to manifest in the past but experienced obstacles, practice those exercises that you believe will address the areas that you need to develop further.
- Practice the exercises that you have selected for two weeks. This will allow you to gain confidence in your ability to perform them.
- It is recommended that you focus on no more than three exercises at a time. If you believe that you can benefit from doing additional exercises, take them on in Days 15-30.

Days 15-30
- Familiarize yourself with the exercises in Chapter 3 and choose the exercises that are relevant to you.
- Practice the exercises that you have selected for two weeks. This will allow you to gain confidence in your ability to perform them. Note: Due to its challenging nature, the exercise "Meditation on Self-Inquiry" should be done on an ongoing basis until you feel comfortable with it.
- It is recommended that you focus on no more than three exercises during this time. If you believe that you can benefit from doing additional exercises, perform these exercises after you complete Days 15-30. After completing Day 30, start the 30-Day Challenge over again by practicing these exercises on Days 1-14.
- If you still have exercises to practice from Chapter 2, perform these exercises during Days 15-30. After completing Day 30, start the 30-Day Challenge over again by practicing your selected exercises from Chapter 3 during days 1-14.
- Days 1-30: Refer to Chapter 4 as needed. Chapter 4 will provide you with guidance on how to deal with obstacles such as resistance and disempowering emotions.

Part 2 – Book 2

Self-Love Handbook
Magnified with Law of Attraction
***

Instantly Shift into Self-Love, Heal Your Life & Create the Abundance of Joy You Deserve

Introduction- Why Self-Love is the Only Way to Create the Life You Love and That Loves You Back

Are you ready to experience more love and light in your life?
Do you want to transform negative into positive?
Do you want to embrace the true, authentic you and let opportunities come to you? How about attracting people who care about you and want your highest good?
And what if you could almost instantly shift into self-love, magnify it with the Law of Attraction and totally transform your energy?

My intention behind writing this book is to help you unleash the true, divine you while enhancing your intuition and aligning yourself with the universal wisdom so that you can receive unlimited guidance on your journey.

While many people may mistakenly reject self-love as some kind of a buzzword, or an unnecessary ritual, we both know that you are here for a reason. You know that the answers you have been searching for are there for you, and the only gate you need to allow yourself to open is the gate of self-love.

I am here to guide you through the process that helped me on my journey and to offer you an invitation to become the master of your emotions, heart, mind and soul. Many people mistake self-love for self-interest, manipulation or even ego driven actions. However, self-interest and ego driven actions are not the same as self-love. Self-love is about stepping into your divine light so that you can inspire those around you. Self-love is the foundation that will help you experience higher vibrations, unforgettable experiences and a true abundance in all areas of your life so that you feel fulfilled. Self-love is the gate to your inner leadership. That divine, magnetic light that you are now giving yourself the permission to shine.

That light has the power to polarize your life in a very authentic way. You will feel empowered to say *no* to people, circumstances and events that no longer serve you.
People who try to manipulate you or to take advantage of you will not only lose their power, but they will also learn the negative consequences of their actions, which eventually will help them transform too. People who behave in ways that are designed to cause pain to, or take advantage of, other human beings very often operate from a place of self-loathing and are doing what they have been programmed to do.

Focusing on the negative, or turning down to those hurting, detrimental levels of self-hate is not the answer. Love and self-love are the answer. Stepping up and stepping away at the same time is the answer.

Part 2 – Self-Love Handbook

Becoming your own leader first, so that you can then become a meaningful, heart driven leader to those around you. Whether it's for your family, friends, local community, a company you work for or your clients.

In my case it's my beloved readers. This book is a passion project of mine and the lessons I am sharing are the lessons I acquired on my own journey of self-discovery, while learning about the Law of Attraction and holistic self-development.

The journey consists of patterns that I knew existed but even though I attempted writing this book many times, I found it very hard to express myself in a way that others could easily understand and follow. At first, I thought the answer was in taking more writing classes so that I could become a better writer.

I thought, *I probably have the writer's block. It will go away as soon as I learn a few "hacks"*. Yet I still felt very blocked. Finally, I decided to do an experiment, and focus entirely on self-love. I committed myself to getting rid of the resistance. I focused on letting go of the outcome and just doing exactly what I am sharing in this book, all over again. That helped me improve and internalize the process I am now fully ready to teach. As a bonus, it also aligned me into my intuition and to the Universe.

Now as I am working on the pages of this book, the process is very enjoyable and almost effortless. I can feel a nice twinging sensation in my head as well as in my heart and hands. It feels as if God, the Universe and the Divine part of me and you communicate with me and share the message that it is my mission to put down on paper.

That experience has helped me release the last "drops" of resistance and has given me clarity and empowerment.

I learned to forgive myself and step into unlimited self-love. This is the self-love that I live and breathe. This is the self-love that is my lifestyle, and my purpose. This is the self-love that I commit to full-time, not part time. Through that enlightening commitment, I am now able to share this gift with you, and I am forever grateful for the opportunity.

I totally understand that most people may be challenged with the idea of "self-love". I can totally understand that, because I have been there too. For years, I damaged my wellbeing with unhealthy habits and artificial masks, while stepping away from my talents and authenticity.

That negative pattern started when I was in high school where the English teacher used to laugh at my "funny" accent and at the grammatical errors in my writing.

Coming from a family of poor immigrants and living in a foreign country, I felt excluded and worthless. I remember that I only had one friend who wanted to hang out with me, but very soon, other kids convinced her to leave me. While everyone was getting ready for her birthday party, I was excluded. Someone even said, "The party is only for those who will bring some birthday gifts and Elena is too poor for that anyways so it's better if she stays at home."

If I'd had the self-love and empowerment, I carry in my heart right now, I would have respected myself enough to immediately say, "Don't react Elena, these are just triggers. People who say those hurtful words need self-love too." I would not now react (or over-react) as I used to.
But back then, I had no idea about self-love, the law of attraction or spiritual self-help.

It was back then that the feeling of being completely excluded and not feeing worthy led me to destructive habits and behaviors. Like, for example, going on a sugar spree. I would stuff myself with all kinds of bagels and ice cream. I wanted to go back home, watch TV, and eat all that food. In my late teenage years, I found a new group of "friends" who wanted to hang out with me, and they were all from a similar, poor immigrant background. We all shared the same fears and experiences. Unfortunately, that group got me into destructive habits of drinking, smoking and using other substances.

I had some illusional moments of belonging and feeling loved and enjoying the company of "friends".

However, I soon learned that they all laughed at me behind my back and just wanted to use me. I tried so hard to be like them, wear similar clothes, skip school and just be cool like them, so that they would love me and accept me.

Then I repeated the same pattern all over again throughout my twenties and thirties. Both in my personal life and in careers I had.

I would never listen to myself, I would never love myself and I would never approve of myself. Instead, I felt unworthy and wanted others to approve of me first. I had to experience the same pattern dozens of times until something clicked in me. I knew I had to shift my energy from being a victim to being someone who is empowered so that other people can feel this energy too.
You know what they say about people who fear dogs? The dogs can sense that fear and this may lead them to attack the person who fears them. And so, the vicious cycle carries on.
The same happens when a person is not feeling worthy and cuts themselves off from self-love. That vibration attracts people who also feel that way and their way of feeling better is, very often, to use, manipulate and hurt other people. The best way to avoid such toxicity in your life is to shift to self-love which will help you elevate your energy, feelings and actions.

Many people I had the pleasure to teach my self-love process to came to a simple conclusion: "Oh my God, the goals I was chasing for so many years were not really mine! I never cared about that career, job, client or business. For years I was wondering why I couldn't manifest this or that. Now

I understand that what I wanted to manifest wasn't even for me. Instead, I have always wanted to…"

Those "aha something clicked" moments are amazing. People are waking up to their true divine selves where they step into their passion and purpose while leaving self-judgment and judgment from other people. That completely erases self-doubt and helps align with meaningful inspired action.

There is no more pushing and fighting.

There is only empowerment. You wake up, you know your *why*, you know what to do and you do it while really loving the process. Your energy levels are much higher, because you no longer need to go against the flow. Instead, you go with it and you love who you're becoming.

I now love myself. I now treat myself with care.

This is true self love. It's not self-interest. Real self-love helps you unleash your full potential and gives you the courage to share it with other people. That gives you even more strength and motivation.

This book is designed to be read more than once. That's because each time you read it, you will go through a new shift while getting on a higher and higher vibration. You can also use it on a bad day. Just read a few random pages to help you shift. I also warmly invite you to have a clear intention behind reading this book. Perhaps you are thinking, "Will it work for me? Isn't it just another self-help book? Will I be able to transform?"

Let me get this straight. This is not about me and this book. I don't write to be famous.
I do it to share my message. Focus on yourself and your intention. The suggested intention for you should be, "Self-love will change me and my life." Trust the process. Some things may take longer. The journey never stops; therefore, it should be as enjoyable as possible.

Also, this is not just another "self-improvement book." While there are many amazing books in that category, I am not a big fan of the term "self-improvement" because it implies that we are not good enough and that we need to improve by constantly looking outside of ourselves.
However, the right self-love mindset should be this:
I am open to learning and grateful for people who provide books and materials to feed my mind with positive information and empowerment.
I am already enough. I am already good enough. I am already worthy.
All the answers are within me, I love diving deep to find them.
Reading helps me reconnect to the deep wisdom within me.
It's a real game changer and a great intro into self-love.

As I have mentioned, throughout my childhood and teenage years as well as my twenties and thirties I struggled with self judgement and very low self-esteem. I was chasing other people's goals and status and moving away from my light in order to get approved by other people. I was creating my own trap and constantly feeling pain. Eventually I got used to it. But deep inside I knew that there was some meaning to it.

I knew that eventually I could turn that pain into some kind of lessons or activities that could help other people. While most people never admit their pain, trauma and suffering (and it's not their fault because we have all been conditioned to wear masks), deep inside they know they need to heal. They understand that they deserve to access the healing power of self-love to transform and help their loved ones transform too.

During those years of suffering, I was still searching for that one thing that could help me. At first, I thought it was motivation, or productivity. I thought, *I could achieve more and be more successful. Then, people will look up to me.* And yes, back then I did have a couple of successful businesses, but those businesses eventually led me into a burnout.

At one point I was so sick that I could not work. I had to let go of my business to focus on my health. And then, again, most "friends" left me.

Don't get me wrong. Motivation and productivity are great. It's good to learn different ways to stay motivated and to organize our activities in a productive way. But...without self-love, both motivation and productivity can be traps. You can motivate yourself with inspirational speeches, affirmations and you can drink lots of coffee to "keep going" or "get the stuff done."

Superficial success like that doesn't make you happy. It can temporarily motivate you. But it's like building a house on sand. When it goes down it goes down. And it will go down quickly.
At the same time, motivation and productivity do make a difference if you take action that you really want to take. An action that aligns with your ultimate vision that is approved by the Divine You.

You pursue a goal, career or business that you are really passionate about and that you want to pursue. Or one that you think is good for you and you don't care about what other people think. That's self-love. And from that place- it makes total sense to learn motivational and productivity techniques.

Before my transformation, I tried everything to ease the pain. Aside from using destructive habits to quickly feel better, I also started researching self-development. I knew I could find my long-term answers in that field. At some point, I thought I needed more confidence. As a result, I hired a success coach and a confidence coach. I learned many useful techniques. I am sure those coaches had amazing intentions. Unfortunately learning more about confidence did not go to the root of the problem, which was a lack of self-love.

Instead, I learned to wear superficial masks and speak with authority, so that when I had clients on the phone, I could get more sales. But I did not enjoy working with so many of those clients. Often, we were not a good match anyway. So, the business wasn't going anywhere, even though I used to hit all my revenue goals every month.

I had what most entrepreneurs call "predictable income". Leads and clients. I knew that a certain number of calls would translate into a certain number of clients and money made in the front end. I also knew how many of those clients would stay with us and add more revenue to the backend of my old business.

Unfortunately, I was acting out of alignment. Don't get me wrong, we were doing a great service. The clients were happy. But I was unfulfilled and burned out. The money I made very often disappeared quickly because I was drinking as well as overspending on clothes and items I didn't need.

Okay, I just need to book another holiday. I need to post pictures from expensive hotels on social media. People will like that and comment on it. Then I will feel worthy and deserving, then I will love myself.

Oh...and if my old high school friends who did not want to hang out with me and my old teachers see how well I am doing, and how well I live, and how much money I make, then they will accept me. Then I will be able to love myself and feel at peace.

I could never relax on those holidays. I would look at my phone, my agenda and my laptop all the time. I was too afraid to lose my business to take a break.

At some point I hoped that would change when I hired an assistant. *Then I can relax, and she will take care of those phone calls,* I thought.

Okay, so I hired an assistant and it all went well. At first, I gained a bit more of free time. But, as always, negative patterns sneaked in again. I would either indulge in workaholism, thinking, *Okay, now that my assistant takes care of some admin tasks, I can focus more on strategy and learning.* I would take on more clients and more business just to feel worthy, and just to show I was okay, I was successful, and I was something.

During that time many bad things happened to me. I even attracted a greedy and unethical accountant who saw that I was easy prey and managed to "legally steal" some of my money. The same patterns manifested through unethical business associates, or clients who were a real pain in the neck. And, no matter how hard I worked, the money would always leave me. It was just spinning around.

I would constantly be on a spiral of self-destructive behaviors. Extensive partying, extreme workaholism or overspending on items and travels to relax. But I could never relax. Many of those travels would only make me drink more because I felt so scared to go back to the hell I had created for myself.

Heck, even when I learned about the Law of Attraction, at first I did not use it properly. I didn't have enough courage to go deep, to get rid of the old, negative patterns and destructive emotional layers that were driving my own behaviors.

At first, when I got into LOA, I would operate from a place of self-doubt and not being enough and I would magnify the bad.

I don't mean to be judgmental, but in a so-called spiritual community, you can find two kinds of leaders. Some leaders are really passion driven and their offerings are always based on the highest value and good to help people transform. Those leaders were the ones who helped me on my journey and got me onto the path of self-enlightenment. Unfortunately, there are also some individuals who, whether on purpose or unconsciously, create offerings that are designed to make people spin their wheels. The second group of leaders- well…they still need to heal. They still need self-love.

Luckily, when you step into unlimited self-love, you will be able to attract the guidance of good people who already love themselves and who love you too. People who understand the concept of "only for the highest good of the Whole." Your intuition will be enhanced to such a level that you will feel whether something is off or not. So, you will not feel like signing up for a seminar or a program if you feel that the energy of the people offering it is not the right energy for you.
You will be able to walk away from things that no longer serve you with a simple, non-judgmental approach. What does not help you may still help someone else who is still on a different journey and that is totally fine.

That is why, through this book, we will take a holistic approach. We will help you heal from the inside out. Some uncomfortable truths may come to the surface. You may even feel like crying but these are normal experiences on a path of self-healing.

Also please note that this book is not intended as a substitute for professional therapy with a qualified mental health professional. Throughout this book I only share my experiences and the step-by-step process that helped me, and I am always happy to answer readers' questions in private. However, in some cases you may want to speak to a professional therapist which is totally fine. If needed, give yourself the permission to do that, because it's also an act of self-love and being okay with sometimes not being okay and seeking expert guidance you need to make the next sacred step on your journey to inner peace.

Now, back to this handbook…Start with that commitment. Love and approve of yourself now.

Part 2 – Self-Love Handbook

Become aware of those voices in your head. Don't judge them as that is judging the fact that you have been judging yourself.

That voice that tells you that you are not worthy. That voice that says you are not good enough. These are voices that are not really yours. They come from social conditioning.

We need more magnetic, self-love warriors to help transform the world.
Pay attention to your thoughts. Are they in or out of alignment with yourself? Remember you can dismiss all the thoughts. You can easily let them go. They don't mean anything. You can put them into a balloon and release them.

Because you are lovable, you love and approve of yourself. Someone out there in the world is now waiting for you, another self-love warrior.

The side effect of self-love is unstoppable motivation. There will be much less self-doubt and eventually you will be able to powerfully erase it.

The process contained in this healing handbook will help you re-wire your brain. You will feel fully present, almost euphoric. Every moment will be magical. People will be curious to learn from you, they will be naturally attracted to you. And, at the same time, critics will melt away, as your light will be too much for some and the light will keep you safe.

Consciously choose to embody the here and now. You will shine more and more every moment. Whether you are working, driving, shopping or relaxing, every moment will be magical like it was meant to be.

You will realize when and how you're acting out of alignment and that will easily allow you to get rid of old habits. Your sense of intuition will be enhanced, you will instantly know the answer to the question: "Does it feel light or heavy?"

You will know what you need to let go of and as you get rid of those emotional layers it will really feel amazing. You will be naturally motivated to get hooked on healthy activities like meditation instead of browsing through your Facebook feed.

The way you interpret certain events or circumstances will change. For example, if, on some nights you will not be able to fall asleep, instead of stressing out about it, you will see it as a sign. "It means I need to meditate or do yoga or have a relaxing essential oil bath." As a result of that, you will never struggle with insomnia or anxiety again. You will know how to nip it in the bud and stop overacting once and for all. You will no longer feel jealous or feel as if others have or do this and that and you need to take their path too.

Because of your light, and being in full alignment with your purpose, you will get connected to your true gifts that the world needs. That will allow you to be of service while following your passion in such a way that you will find yourself attracting career opportunities you enjoy, doing work that is meaningful and, if that is your goal, leads to fame or appreciation. You will know which path will make you happy because your extra sense of perception will be enhanced.

Self-love is one of the most rewarding gifts you can offer yourself. Acting in a way you love and enjoy that is in the highest interest of all.

Perhaps you have some passion project you have been postponing? Maybe you want to change your job or attract your dream clients into your business? After reading this book, you will feel fully recharged and inspired to pursue your passion. If you don't know what your passion is, don't worry at all. The process outlined in this handbook will help you re-wire your brain and step away from limiting beliefs and mindsets. This will lead you to discovering your passion. (You don't need to search for it, it's already within you, you just need to discover it through self-love and self-awareness.)

All I am asking you to do is to make a commitment to yourself.
Take a piece of paper and re-write the following lines while saying them out loud. You can even manually create a few copies, and stick them in your wallet, in your office, in your fridge, on your wardrobe, etc.

I AM my biggest support.
I am committed to shining my truth.
I am committed to getting into alignment.
I am committed to making a difference in the world.
I choose to shift. I choose inner love.
I AM.
I CAN.
I am and I can love myself.
I love myself. I do.
I AM. I AM. I AM.

Through this book, we will follow a very specific process that consists of these steps:

Step #1 Emotional Peeling – We will dive deep to release self-guilt, low self-esteem and disempowering limiting beliefs. You will no longer feel like you have to constantly push because you're not feeling deserving and you need to constantly prove to yourself and others what you're capable of. Instead, we will get rid of negative emotions that are holding you back and that lead to habits that you know are not serving you on your journey. That step alone will help you feel so much lighter and you will never feel like a failure again.

Step #2 Why You Never Fail (removing fear) -This one is one of my favorites, especially when I get someone to do it via a 1:1 interaction. I can just feel that person's energy shift. However, I have the same intention for you, my reader. Wherever you're coming from and whatever obstacles you've had to overcome, I believe in you. And I know you deserve to love yourself more and give yourself more credit.

That step will help you look at your achievements in a totally new way. You will be able to make friends with your emotions and celebrate those little wins. You will also learn how to re-wire your brain in such a way that the word "failure" will be totally erased from your vocabulary.

Step #3 Control Your Precious Mind- This will help you to get rid of influences, people and marketing messages that don't serve you while attracting the exact guidance you need for your unique journey.

You will learn how to decide for yourself and that alone will help you make powerful shifts that are totally in alignment with who you are and what makes you happy. That step will help you get rid of ego that is designed to follow the masses.

You will ask yourself, *Do I need it in my life? Is it good for me?*

Many people who go through this step feel inspired to step into their unlimited courage, move to another city, or even abroad, or change their career or take on a new passion project.

You will no longer feel held back by, "Oh, but someone told me I would never be able to do it" or by someone who says it's not possible, or by what will others think.

Step #4 Hidden Tricks to Identify and Get Rid of Limiting Beliefs That Are Holding You Back from Loving Yourself- Live your life the way it was meant to be lived- full of joy. You will learn how to re-wire your brain, level up your self-talk and that simple trick to transform the *"I can't's", and "I don't know how's"* into meaningful action that creates the reality you want. Step 4 and chapter 4 will finish off with a motivational technique that will help you think beyond yourself, your mission, your purpose. The work you are meant to be doing. The work that gives you the abundance, not only financial but also an abundance of health, vitality and fulfillment. That will lead us to another powerful step that will help you re-balance your heart chakra, which is a very powerful chakra to help you feel loved, love yourself and love others.

Step #5 Expressing Kindness
Self-love and loving others are interconnected. By allowing yourself to be kind, in an authentic way, you also give yourself the permission to be kind and help other people.

This step will show you and inspire you. It's a very simple set of actions you can do daily to unleash the gate to love and self-love. It will instantly shift you to higher vibrations and you will be able to manifest truly amazing people, things and circumstances, totally out of the blue.

Step #6 Creative Self-Expression to Love Yourself
That step will help you awaken your throat chakra so that you can express love and self-love while continuing to attract more and more of it on a daily basis.

The flow of love and self-love will be abundant when you commit to sharing what you know with other people. It's a very powerful step that connects to the abundance mindset.

Most people overlook it and some fear that this information should not be shared. Some are worried it may reach people who have bad intentions. However, this information can only be used for the highest good. Love and self-love are the highest good and expressing them in your own unique way, exactly the way you desire will help you to keep magnifying the life changing benefits of self-love.

From there, your life will be transformed forever.

Oh, and don't worry. This step will offer many options, both for extroverts as well as introverts. Your personal preference will be taken into consideration.

This step may also connect you with a new career opportunity that is more aligned with your passion. Knowing how to step into your passion and turn it into something that helps other people while adding value to their lives is the best way to step into abundance.

Step #7 Creating Super Positive Reminders for Lasting Inspiration
This handbook is not meant to be read once and forgotten about. That is why Chapter 7 will show you multiple ways to create beautiful self-love reminders you can use to keep vibrating higher and higher while loving yourself more and more.

Through this step we will be diving deeper into Magnetic Attraction. After all, this book is called *Self-Love Handbook – Magnified with Law of Attraction*, right?
We have some work to do here, the most meaningful and fun work ever!

Step #8 Action and Attraction
After getting rid of negative patterns and destructive emotional layers and stepping into self-love and different ways of deepening and strengthening it, we will have a look at magnifying everything with LOA.

That is what makes this book different. It's a holistic combo of the Law of Attraction and self-love.

Each step amplifies and magnifies the previous one. And so, step 8 will take step 7 to a whole new level.

You will discover some missing pieces to manifesting and learn how to combine the Law of Attraction with the Law of Action in a meaningful and powerful way. You will intuitively know how to create balance between action and attraction. Thanks to that balance you will never burn out. For example, too much action and pushing never ends well, I can tell you that. I have already shared my story and how I ended up with a complete mental, emotional and physical burnout.

I am very excited for you. Aside from the reasons I have already mentioned in the intro, I know that the transformation and wisdom you will unleash with self-love will help you inspire those around you.

-Your children will be able to benefit from self-love and feel empowered at school. That power will protect them in such a way that they will not be affected by negative comments, unfair teachers or anyone who's trying to project their own self-hatred onto them. One of my personal goals is to help children and teenagers enjoy their school years free of judgment, bullying and negative patterns while unleashing self-love, creativity and motivation. That will allow them to step into amazing careers that they love and feel inspired about, careers that align with their unique talents, personality and vocation.

-If you are a manager or lead any group of people, your work environment will be radically transformed. Self-love connects to self-leadership. As a result, you will be able to become a truly inspiring and authentically charismatic leader that people will want to follow and who they will benefit from following.

-Your personal relationships will be improved. People will notice your inner peace and will feel inspired.

Part 2 – Self-Love Handbook

Chapter 1 Step #1 Emotional Peeling

It's time to dive deep to release self-guilt, low self-esteem and disempowering limiting beliefs. Thanks to this chapter, you will no longer feel like you have to constantly push because you're not feeling deserving and you need to constantly prove to yourself and others "what you're capable of". Instead, we will get rid of negative emotions that are holding you back and that lead to habits that you know are not serving you on your journey. That step alone will help you feel so much lighter and you will never feel worthless again.

You will also come to a conclusion about what people, events and circumstances could have made you feel like you were not worthy. You will be able to let go of them all while protecting yourself from similar circumstances happening again.

Just like with healthy diets…they usually start with some kind of a detox, right? Imagine a person who's constantly eating processed food and fast food and then once a week, tries to eat a salad and drink a vegetable juice. It wouldn't work. It's important to dive deep and follow a smart plan, like we are doing here.

At the same time, perfection does not exist. Just like with healthy diets and eating, you don't need to constantly torture yourself and deprive yourself. Because that is not healthy either. It all comes down to focusing mostly on clean food and having little "cheats" every now and then. They will not make a big difference as long as they do not form a part of a negative pattern that gets triggered by a lack of self-love or some emotional trauma that needs healing.

Your emotional and spiritual wellness is the same. It's not about thinking 100% positively or trying to be a perfect, enlightened and highly self-developed (through self-improvement, that by the way later in this book, we will be looking at closely and debunking some myths of this industry too).

First, you need to "detox" that's for sure. Get rid of layers that no longer serve you. It's like emotional and spiritual "juicing". Then, we get on a healthy and balanced emotional "clean food diet". We are not perfect, but we are super happy with any progress. And, if every now and then we have that piece of pizza as a treat, everything is fine. We do not feel guilty. We feel like we chose that pizza, the pizza did not choose us.

Same with our emotional journey. There will be some emotions that are considered negative or not healthy, and some days will be like that, but they will no longer lead to a downward spiral or destructive habits.

You will be reacting in a different way because you will be empowered by a healthy dose of self-love, feel balanced and totally in alignment with how you feel.

Negative emotions are just feedback. Through the chapters of this book, you will get so high on the vibration of self-love, that your perception will change. And that is a balance that we want to create.

So that was step one- a little detox and emotional peeling before embarking on healthy, balanced, emotionally clean food diet.

The biggest layer to get rid of is the one of self-guilt.
The question is, has your mind ever been exposed to any of the following lines or concepts?
- *Suck it up, it's all your fault.*
- *You are responsible for that.*
- *You are negative and because of that you always manifest negative things!*
- *Don't complain, just admit it's your fault.*

My reply is: Really?

How can people who say those lines damage someone's self-worth with those disempowering words? How can someone lead someone into a downward spiral of self-hate or self-guilt by making them feel worse and worse? Unfortunately, these lines are very often quoted in the self-help, spiritual and entrepreneurial communities. But...they are not helping anyone...they can only make things worse. While most people will blindly nod at their leader and say, "Yes, you are right, it's all my fault", and they will pretend it's now all okay, deep inside they will feel a huge pain and discomfort. They will feel judged and misguided. That hidden self-guilt will remain buried in the subconscious mind until one day it will come back to surface, typically triggered by something little and innocent.

Like you burn your dinner, and your kid, spouse or roommate says, "It's your fault, you didn't pay attention", or you get a fine because you parked your car wrong and a friend says, "You should have checked". Boom....and suddenly you start feeling guilty about everything just because five years ago some leader suggested you need to hide your emotions and pretend like it's all fine. Some people may even feel misled and then, again, they will feel guilty for following a given leader who got them on such a destructive path.

Why is the "it's all your fault, suck it up" approach wrong? And what approach can we follow instead?

Here's a simple example. It's just like a rebellious teenager. Yea, you can keep nagging them:
- *Why you cut your hair like that?*
- *Why do you smoke?*
- *Why this and that? Why can't you just be like other kids?*

Ask any therapist, or even someone with a minimal knowledge of psychology or compassion. They will all tell you that it's all about understanding how things work on a deeper level.

Unfortunately, we have all been conditioned to think the following:
- *I am always wrong.*
- *I am not good enough.*
- *It's my fault.*
- *Yea, I was there, I need to suck it up.*

We were mistakenly told that not admitting that it's all our fault means that we are in a victim mentality and because of that we will be pushed away. Whereas the opposite is actually true. We step into the victim mentality by refusing to dive deep and having the courage to question certain mainstream beliefs, opinions of certain communities and the brainwashing of certain leaders and authorities.

At the same time, some people confuse empowerment with entitlement. These are two different things. A person with an entitlement mindset refuses to learn or to step into any kind of spiritual growth or self- awareness. They don't want to do any work and they believe that everything should be given to them. Now, I don't mean to be judgmental, I used to have that mindset too. Especially when I faced extreme poverty and had to live on the government's money. So, this mindset is something I can relate to.

Luckily, self-entitlement is a state of mind that can be healed through self-love and self-empowerment.

What makes self-empowerment different to self-entitlement is that a self-empowered person has the courage to seek guidance. The feeling of self-guilt is transformed into self-awareness and self-discovery. The necessity to feel responsible is outshone by the feeling of gratitude and transforms "It happened to me" to "It happened for me."

(The concept of "It didn't happen to you, it happened for you", is something I learned from Tony Robbins. His teachings really helped me when I was struggling with depression and difficult moments).

In order to illustrate my point, and show you how you can easily shift to self-love while still maintaining a healthy touch with reality I want to share some real-life examples, from different friends and mentees of mine.

For example, Jerry spent many years feeling depressed which led him to drugs and alcohol. Jerry used to run a marketing company with two other business partners. The business venture sounded very lucrative and was aimed at helping small businesses with online marketing using

Facebook ads and SEO (Search Engine Optimization). It was when online marketing was still new, and Jerry was very excited to be starting a company in that field.

Jerry partnered with two business associates and invested lots of his personal money into the business. He had a lot of faith in that business and felt very positive about it, even though his wife felt skeptical and didn't like his business associates. However, Jerry had a vision of making lots of money, building a house and starting a family. For these reasons he decided to make a few "little sacrifices". He thought it would only be temporary and once the business was well set up, he would be able to create an abundant lifestyle for his family.

Jerry was mostly doing sales calls and customer service, while his business associates were supposed to deliver the marketing services for his clients. Every day Jerry drove 2 hours to their office and worked there for between ten and twelve hours.

Long story short- even though the business started off very well, the business associates took advantage of Jerry's trust as soon as they could. They got involved in some illegal activities, manipulated him into signing a few documents and disappeared, leaving him with a 100k debt. That left Jerry feeling devasted. Not only was he in debt, but he also felt deeply frustrated about the money and time he had invested into the business. He felt powerless and taken advantage of. That led him to drugs and alcohol. His wife left him.

Even though Jerry quickly managed to find himself a well-paid job, moved back with his parents and started paying off the debt, he still felt haunted by the failure of his business.
He attended a few seminars, seeking answers. And BOOM, that only made it worse. One seminar was related to a wealthy mindset and the guru told him, "Hey, you were there, you signed the documents, you invested that money, suck it up and move on! It's all your fault!"
Then, Jerry attended a spiritual LOA seminar where the guru told him, "You attract what you are, change yourself and you will change your life, don't be so negative, you are in a very negative, victim mentality place!"

And then Jerry went to a happy motivational seminar where he was told, "Hey, just be happy, life is so amazing, just be grateful!"

All of this left him confused and he decided not to seek help from the gurus. Instead he decided to do some research and turned to books and videos to see what other people, who have been through hard and destructive times, had done to heal themselves.

He turned to meditation, quantum physics and many other self-help fields. He kept going through all those materials, rejecting most of it, feeling very disappointed and let down.

One video he watched introduced him to the concept of self- love and the subconscious mind. That really helped him and got him onto the path of self-love. The path of self-love helped him change his self-talk and that led him to what I like to call "self-engineered thinking" (more on that and how you can use it too, in a second).

Today Jerry has a prosperous career as a life coach. He can now market his new business very well. In fact, he's also an expert in helping other people get more business. He has four beautiful children and a wife who supports him through the good and the bad. He also has a trustworthy team for his business. How did it happen?

It all started with a simple mindset shift that Jerry made. He kept asking himself, "What am I supposed to learn from all this? What is the path I am supposed to discover? What is my purpose? How can I transform my suffering into something meaningful?"

Instead of saying, "Why am I such a loser? Why am I such a moron? Why didn't I check those documents?" he switched to, "What is this situation telling me? Where am I supposed to go? Where does my new, bright future start? What do I need to do to transform?"
Every day he kept asking his subconscious mind:
-How can I love myself more? How can I forgive myself? How can I be at peace?
-How can I feel better and more empowered?
-What is the number one thing I need to change?

These are all empowering questions and our subconscious mind is a truly amazing tool. Please note that there aren't any specific questions you need to ask, it's all up to you. What's important here is to ask questions that are positive.

Instead of asking, "Why do bad things always happen to me?" or "Why do I always attract bad people?" better questions are: "How can I attract positive people?" and "How can I learn empowering lessons from the past?"

Instead of saying, "Why are all the gurus the same and just want to get my money?" you ask, "How can I manifest a person, a mentor, who can really help me?"
"Where can I find a mentor who will understand me and guide me on my journey?"
"How can I attract a woman/man who loves me for who I am and not for the money I make?"
"How can I meet that person?"

So, Jerry started playing around with that. He would write his questions down or say them out loud, very often while driving, or at home while looking at the mirror. As I have already explained, these are not entitlement mindsets, these are empowering self-love mindsets.

People with self-love and self-empowering mindsets step into Courage and Patience. Those people understand that deep manifestations take time and they are okay with that. They enjoy the process and they feel that something unexpected is bound to happen. That deep faith and belief keeps them going.

A person with a self-entitlement mindset is deep into resistance. By constantly claiming that it's all about them, that everyone is wrong and that they need everything as soon as possible, they put extra stress on resistance. Again, I have been there too, I was looking for quick fixes. I am not judging, so please interpret this paragraph as me talking to my younger self.

Your subconscious mind is like a search engine. Some research may take time. Not all the topics you search for on Google or YouTube immediately give you the answers. Sometimes you may find the piece of content or a product you were looking for on page five, while what popped up first in your research wasn't really serving you. Still, it may have given you an idea and an introduction to the topic.

So, in the case of Jerry, he started off with empowering questions and stimulated his "positive search engine". He did that while getting rid of self-guilt and "Yo, bro, just suck it up, you were there, you wired the money, you hired those scammers, you partnered up with them, it's your fault!" Jerry was able to step into self-love.

And yes, men deserve self-love too and that is why I am writing about this case. While it's mostly women who read and research the topic of self-love, men are also invited to explore this field. Self-love is empowering and can be used to enrich both feminine and masculine traits. I am getting off the topic a bit here, I know! Everyone deserves self-love and it can only help us unleash the best. It works both for women and men so if you are a man reading this, you should not feel ashamed nor you should feel like hiding this book. You should feel proud.

Like Jerry…
So, here's how his story ended.

As Jerry kept asking himself those empowering questions, one day, on a pretty random drive where he was exploring a new job opportunity, one simple idea struck him. He decided he wanted to quit drinking and drugs. Most people didn't know he had an addiction problem. After all, he had a full-time job in sales. He looked all right, like a normal working human being, not some homeless drunk in the park. But every night he would drink at the bar and on weekends he would resort to cocaine and marijuana. That was his way to ease the pain. To release the self-guilt. To stop thinking about the past.

So, after positively brainwashing himself with positive questions, he asked himself, "What if I could stop drinking? What if I could stop doing drugs?" His ego went like, "But come on. As the loser that you are, you deserve your treats. It's fun, you meet girls, you meet people. You have a good job. Soon you will be able to pay off your debt, move out of your parents' home and get your own apartment, you're good. Why not enjoy evenings and weekends?"

But that enlightened self-love voice went like, "But what if I could stop drinking? Would I save more money? Would I be able to take another job, pay off my debt faster and help my parents?"

There was a bit of an internal struggle going on. One day as he was having a coffee, he saw an AA (Alcoholics Anonymous) ad which inspired him to join the local AA meeting. Long story short, that was where he met his new wife. It was where he quit drinking and drugs. It was where he decided to take another job. It was where he got inspired to help other people and learned many valuable mindset lessons.

Today, if you ask Jerry how he got where he's at- a successful life coach with his own passion-based business- he will tell you, "I decided to become a life coach because of the inspiration I got from AA.

AA taught me a lot about mindset and self-reflection. I was able to set up a business successfully because of the extra skill I got from the second job I used to do to pay off my debt. That taught me a lot about work ethic and discipline and improved my sales skills. I was able to market my business because of the SEO and Facebook ads skills I acquired from my failed business. Even though it was mostly my ex-business associates' job, very often I would stay in the office late to follow up with clients, checking the quality and that led me to research. I didn't even know I had skills that were transferable until I started my new, passion-driven business. It turns out that my "failed" business, hadn't really failed.

I wasn't failing, I was practicing.
"Oh Jerry, and how did you learn to hire people and teach other people how to be successful?" Jerry said, "Well, because of the shady business associates who taught me a very valuable life lesson a few years ago."

"Oh, and what about your new wife, Jerry?
Jerry replied, "We met via AA, and we shared the same path, goal and journey to self-healing. We built our new selves through the power of self-love."
Wow, self-love, what a life-changing concept!
Now, here's a very powerful exercise for you.

Think of one thing you are very grateful for. It can also be an event or a person. Now, go back. What happened before that? And before that? And even before that? Go back to a certain painful moment from a few years ago. The moment that is no longer painful to you. Had you known what you know now, would you have felt pain?

Allow yourself to release the feeling of self-guilt. You were not failing, you were practicing!
Stop saying, "It's my fault, I need to suck it up."
Keep saying, "What can I learn?"
"What can I do to grow stronger?"
"How can I use my pain to help other people?"
These are all very empowering questions. Remember that your brain is a search engine, so be careful what you're typing in.

Fair enough, sometimes life gets hard and we don't achieve all our goals. Nobody has a perfect formula; some goals take longer. But there is always a meaning to that.

For years, I was told that the only way for me to share my message was by offering courses so I embarked on that path. I invested lots of money in coaching. One coach even told me I should never try to write, because nobody would read my books anyway. How dis-empowering is that?

Still, I learned how to communicate and how to organize my thoughts. When I decided to stick to my passion and go full time with my writing, it felt so light and so freaking right.

Firstly, because I finally felt like I was on my path. Secondly, because I realized how bad it feels when other people, aka leaders and authorities, talk down to you instead of understanding you, your unique gifts and talents and motivating you to follow your path.

I made a promise to myself to be a writer who shares empowering and uplifting messages and who focuses on unleashing the best in my readers without ever telling them what they should do. That is why I feel grateful for that ex-coach who wanted to get me on a different path.

I assume he's also under someone's negative influence and still hasn't broken free of them, hence his career and teachings are not authentic. Not judging, I have been there too. I know the pain. And I tell you what, self-love always leads to passion.

Talking of which, I have another inspiring, self-made, self-love success story to share!
Another friend of mine, Monica, is a passionate health coach who is helping people in her local community to shop, cook and eat organic, nourishing foods. She looks vibrant, fit and inspired. But it wasn't always like that.

Monica grew up in a foster home and never met her parents. As a teen she quickly got onto the path to self-destruction. It was when she was at her lowest that she started seeking information on meditation. She had a friend who had quit drugs thanks to meditation. As she was watching videos about meditation, she stumbled upon a video about self-love. That sparked her interest and she started asking herself empowering questions. For example, for years, she had been led to believe:

- "You are nobody, nobody wants you nobody loves you, your parents never wanted you."
- "It's because something is wrong with you, suck it up, own it, be responsible for it, right?"
But thanks to self-love, she decided to step into her light and look for her purpose. For years she thought that the only way that could take her out of poverty was winning the lottery, inheriting some unexpected money, or possibly marrying someone rich.
She discouraged herself with disempowering lines like:
-I never went to college, what can I offer?
-I am not educated enough.
-All the jobs I can get are low paid jobs.

Part 2 – *Self-Love Handbook*

-I can't save lots of money anyway, so what I have left, I am better off spending it on drugs. At least then I can hang out with some cool people and feel like I have something to look forward to.
Remember though, your brain is a search engine. Start typing in questions that will lead you to answers you are searching for. Don't close yourself off with negative patterns and questions.
So, Monica started asking empowering, self-love questions:
- How can I love myself more?
- How can I meet people who really love me?
- What do I need to change in my life in order to be happy?
- Who can I ask for guidance?

So, here's what happened. As Monica was asking herself those healthy, empowering questions, she started coming up with positive ideas. She decided that the number one thing she needed to sort out was her health. She decided to quit drinking and drugs. She figured out that her party friends were not the best influence for her. So, instead, she decided to find another part time job at the weekends, because that way, she would keep herself busy, save up more money, and stop hanging out with people who didn't really care about her.

And this is what she did. During the week, she worked 9-5 in a simple admin job, then spend her free time learning about self-love, reading positive books and listening to podcasts. She started exercising and eating healthily which led her to transforming her body. She started making new friends at a local gym.

Eventually she realized that she was passionate about health and wanted to help other people embrace self-love by helping them transition to a healthy lifestyle. She really wanted to become a certified nutritionist but the courses she was looking at were very expensive.

But she kept asking those questions. One night she could not sleep. She was filled with a weird excitement and a feeling of, "Change is near" mixed with a bit of fear, "What if I never make it?" That led her to watch some uplifting videos, and as she went into the internet rabbit hole, she came across a blog by someone who really inspired her. She stumbled upon an article that a blogger had finished off with a question: "What is your goal, and what is holding you back? Leave me a comment and I will help you."

She left a comment saying, "I want to be a health coach and nutritionist. I am already working two jobs to save up. My fear is that I will never be able to pay for my certification, and even if I do, it will be scary for me to leave my job."

Leaving that comment somehow made her feel better and she went to sleep. She woke up an hour earlier than her normal wake up time felling a bit anxious. She thought, *Oh no, I will go ahead and remove that comment, I probably come across as a complainer anyway*. She got up, started making her coffee and had a look at her phone only to see a notification that a blogger had replied to her saying, "What if you could start living your passion, in some way, shape or form, and feel

that vibration even before you get your official certification? You seem to be working hard and on a good track. Some things do take time. Like, it takes nine months to have a baby. Even if you tried to get nine women and gave them one month each, it would still take nine months."
That gave Monica a lot to think about. So, she started asking herself, "How can I help someone and live my passion now?"

A few days after, as she was driving back from work, she noticed there was a new smoothie place opening in her town, and they were looking for staff. Passion for health was definitely an advantage.

Monica applied and got a part time job there at the weekends. She let go of her other part time job at the gas station as she was more excited about that smoothie place.

That job paid a bit better and was more fun to do. Monica got to learn a lot about healthy smoothies and herbs. People who visited that place were all health-oriented.

A few weeks afterwards, Monica met an elderly lady who was looking for someone who could keep her company, clean her house and cook her healthy meals. She really liked Monica's story, her drive, passion and perseverance. Eventually, she hired Monica and offered her a really good salary. That led Monica to quit her day admin job. By taking care of that old lady, she could make almost the same money and free up lots of her time so that she could follow her passion and become a health coach.

I believe that old lady was Monica's manifestation messenger, her angel in a way. These always come to help us, eventually. Be patient and start asking yourself empowering questions. One day, all that pain and suffering will make sense. Stop beating yourself up.

Now, it's your turn. Give yourself some self-love. Think of a problem or an issue you would like to solve. Maybe it's a past trauma, or some feeling of self-guilt. It's time to let go of that now.
Think of your self-talk. What are the negative questions, negative affirmations and patterns you keep telling yourself? How can you transform them into positive questions instead?

Even if the questions seem out of the gate, and very high level, you deserve to love yourself enough to ask those questions. So, go ahead and do it now. Whenever your mind starts to wander, or you feel down, ask yourself:
What can I do to feel better now?
How can I raise my vibration?
What can I do to eat healthy food and enjoy it?
What can I do to let go of...?
What did I learn from...?
How can I attract someone who can help me...?

Chapter 2 Step #2 Making Friends with Your Emotions on a Deeper Level

I'll be really blunt here. You need to give yourself more credit.
Whatever it is that you're doing, you are not giving yourself enough credit. How do I know? Because I am "guilty" of the same thing. And it's something I am still learning how to get rid of, every day.

Why do we think it's bad to give ourselves credit? And why does it bother me to see people (myself included) who don't give themselves enough credit?

First of all, the real culprit here is mainstream society's brainwashing. You know, it goes like this: "Don't stand out, be like everyone else. If you excel at something, other people may feel bad about themselves."

The problem with that? People lose motivation to do anything or enjoy what they do.
Yes, I think it's very important to stay humble. And do the work you were meant to be doing while really taking your time to do it well, and with passion. Also, when you do the work that is really authentic and aligned with your highest calling and you take inspired action from the place of self-love (not self-interest), then what you do is also meant to inspire other people.
And that deserves credit.

However, before we start looking at the bigger picture and focusing on your work, whether it's pure passion, hobby or something you are doing professionally, it's good to start small. Why not have a look at all those little events and mini achievements when you reached your goal?
Go back to your childhood. Maybe it was your first swim (sorry, mine was traumatic I don't have any achievements there, but I am still happy I jumped into that pool).

Or that feeling when you rode your bike for the first time.
Or when you went on your first date. What about getting your driving license? What about your first vacation or a trip you enjoyed?

Finally have a look at all those little wins and moments of joy and happiness. How did they feel? Take a piece of paper and write them all down. Love yourself, and every cell of your body for those achievements.

Love yourself for even attempting to do something and taking action. Even if you didn't finish the project, please be good on yourself. At least you started.

Believe it or not, two years ago I began writing a book on confidence. The writing process was on and off because I was going through many emotional and spiritual shifts and when they happened,

I always felt compelled to go back to the manuscript and make changes. Eventually, I started beating myself up that one book project was taking so long. On one hand, I was beating myself up that I was so slow and lacked confidence in myself. Then I was beating myself up thinking:
If I can't even finish that book project about confidence, what kind of a person I am? Even when I put it out, I will feel fake.

And so, the book got forgotten somewhere on my computer.
Finally, I joined a group of other writers who also happened to have the same problem. One writer admitted he had dozens of book projects like this, half-finished and abandoned. Another one said, "Yea, that always happens if you are a self-help writer and you want to be putting out books that are authentic. So, get used to it. Most of your manuscripts will never be ready to publish, I hear ya Elena!"

It would go on and on. Now, while I do believe that most of my writer friends had very good intentions, and wanted me to feel understood, eventually I got very stuck in my own mindset. I was beating myself up for spending two years on writing on and off something I could not even publish or show to anyone. I started seeing that confidence book as a failed project and started feeling fake as well. In the meantime, I also began working with a mentor, who basically told me I should abandon that project and maybe focus on something else or simply focus on some main stream hot topics and put my writing in there.

That was even worse, because for me, if I lack passion for something, I am not productive. Where am I going with my story?

Well, it all changed when I began applying what I am teaching you in this chapter. Giving myself credit for every little micro step and action I had taken throughout my entire life.
I remember getting started on this exercise. I got myself a fresh journal (I am extremely hooked on journaling) and sat down in a coffee shop drinking a delicious matcha latte. And I began writing in that journal like a mad woman. Giving myself more credit, loving myself more. Believe me or not, I was there writing my thoughts down for at least a few hours. Focusing on having gratitude for every little achievement in my life, even things I no longer value, because I had taken for granted, for example, learning how to drive.

My nephew is just getting started on his learning how to drive journey. For him it's a big thing. Most of his friends are already driving around. That's all they talk about. Will he be next? Most of his actions, thoughts and what he talks about focus on driving. I was able to give him courage and help him, because I have been there as well.

That again amplified my gratitude for my achievements, and for every little step on my journey. Now please note, I don't want to come across as one of those authors who only write about themselves. Not my intention. I really want to illustrate my point and show you how one simple decision can totally transform your life.

As I began writing things down in my journal and giving myself more credit, my forgotten confidence book cropped up. And I got one more thought- *it was meant to happen*. I wasn't going to be a confidence author. That was not how I want to brand myself. I want to be known as a self-love and Law of Attraction author.

However, and this is a very big "however", when I got back home and began reading my old confidence manuscript, I realized that many of the concepts and thoughts I had written were something I could include in my other books. So, I did.

That is why I managed to write my book *Law of Attraction to Make More Money* very quickly. The confidence book was like a gym that had helped me grow my muscle and many of the mindset shifts I had originally written in my never published book on confidence, helped me tremendously as I was writing my last book.

Conclusion:

You don't fail. You succeed or you learn.

Learning may take much longer than you originally envisioned, and this is totally fine. But, by going back to all your achievements, and really feeling them again and again, you enter a totally new vibration of freedom and creativity. You feel empowered again and everything makes sense. Not only that, but you also enter the vibration of being resourceful.

So, even though I never published that book on confidence, many parts from the original manuscript formed the skeleton for my book *Law of Attraction to Make More Money*. What really made me excited were emails from the happy readers who read that book. The feedback like, "Thanks to your book I am learning to be resourceful", or "Thanks Elena, now I feel much more confident when it comes to manifesting money and abundance", or "The exercises helped me see things in a new light. I applied for a new job and I got it, I never thought that woo woo LOA book would help me feel more confident and motivated, but it did."

Exactly like I said in the intro. These are some of the positive effects of self-love (not self-interest). With self-love, there is no "pushing".

Also, whatever your occupation is, whether you are a business owner, work for the government, or are a student- when you give yourself more self-love and more credit, all from the place of the highest good for all, people will feel your transformed energy and they will be inspired.
That is why giving yourself credit, going way back to the past, and focusing on those little achievements will open another powerful gate to the best self-help tool ever- the tool of self-love. Don't hide your gist, don't hide your achievements. Don't be afraid of anything that you do.
I used to be guilty of that too, don't worry. For example, I can write pretty fast. One of the reasons is that I only write about topics I am passionate about and know can help other people. Very often

while talking to other authors or writers I felt a bit judged. "Really? You can write that many words a day? How is that possible?"

For a really long time, I didn't feel good about it. I even felt like hiding my gift. I felt like I would be rejected and ridiculed. Or that people would think I am crazy. However, going through this step of the self-love process made me realize that everything that we do must be celebrated. Using what we do to inspire other people in a positive way, always from the place of abundance and confidence, has a very transformative effect.

One of my mentors once told me, "People love motivation, but not from another motivational speech. What people really like and need is to see someone else do something they love and feel that energy. Because that energy helps them unleash their full potential and step into all their gifts that they can share with the world."

Everyone is different and everyone has different gifts. I stayed silent for a long time and I would allow myself to be a victim. A dis-empowered victim. I would allow everyone step on me and laugh at what I consider valuable assets I can share with the world through my writing.

For you, it may be something else. Please, don't hide it. Let it shine. There is someone out there who needs your gifts and your work. You are divine and what you bring to this world matters.

My motivation is to empower you to the best of my ability. I don't want anyone to feel the way I used to feel- forgotten, unappreciated, laughed at. Nobody deserves to be treated this way. I made it my mission and my purpose to help you step into your highest light for the highest good, for you and those around you.

Allow yourself to be you and only you. Because only YOU can be YOU.

Now, I warmly invite you to take a powerful decision- take a few hours off. It could even be the whole day, if you have the time and opportunity to do it. It's time for you to go on a date. With you! Yes, only you and your self-love journal.

Schedule your self-love date in. Allow yourself to enjoy coffee, tea or a smoothie in your favorite place. Or go to the beach, or a park. Or even book a massage. Whatever it is that you enjoy doing. Perhaps, you feel like staying in and listening to your favorite music, while having a bath, and using aromatherapy candles or essential oils and sipping on your favorite tea.

If you're a woman (I know most of my audience is women), you can even get a nice make up and do your hair differently. Enjoy and when you do that, keep saying to yourself, "I love you!"
(But I will stress it again, I never intend my writing to be only for women, I believe many men can also benefit from some of my ideas).

Part 2- Self-Love Handbook

Whatever your sex, origin, age or ethnicity is- Elena loves you!
Finally, whatever scenario you choose to do this step, be prepared for lots of writing in your journal.

Alternatively, if you don't like it, you can also record yourself on your phone and just share with yourself, what you are grateful for and all your achievements, both small, big and even the unfinished projects and attempts.

You will soon see they are not failed projects. They were valuable lessons that made you grow. Personally, I prefer to write it all down in my journal, and then read through it several times. Reading through my own achievements makes me feel very, very good.

Sometimes, I even go as far as recording what I wrote. You can easily do it using your phone, or by downloading a program called Audacity (it's free as of now). You can record all your achievements and even play your favorite music in the background. Call me a crazy woman, but I do it all the time. Then, I re-listen to myself while on a walk, or in a gym, before I go to sleep, or even when I have a bad day. It's really an amazing self-healing therapy you can do whenever you want.
So please, go ahead and do it now. Stop reading this book and take a few hours off to celebrate this step.

If you're ready with this "assignment" (that word makes it sound a bit stiff, while it's supposed to be fun), and would like to share your experience with other readers, be sure to post a review. Your review may motivate other people in our community to take inspired action and experience the healing benefits of self-love by giving yourself the credit you deserve.

Trust me, something will change for sure! Come back to this step whenever you have a bad day. Heck, a friend of mine even writes things like, "I know how to say a few words in French", or "I know one yoga pose and what it's good for", or "I know how to make a nice green smoothie". Everything counts. Everything matters. Whatever you have done is important and forms part of who you are and who you are becoming.

Part 2- Self-Love Handbook

Chapter 3 Step #3 Control Your Precious Mind As If Your Life Depends on It Because It Does

There is a reason why this step is step#3 and not step #2 in this process. You see, it's easier to own your mind and eliminate other people's negative influences and opinions when you already know how to respect yourself, give yourself credit and celebrate your little wins.

Here's the sad truth: most marketing messaging you see out there is designed to make you feel bad and make you feel like you're not good enough. Because you are not making this amount of money, you haven't traveled to all those places, your kids are not perfect, your job is not perfect, and you haven't lost that final pound this week...we can go on and on and on.

If your mind is not 100% owned and controlled by you, it's very easy to get distracted.
On a positive note, there are also many good people who use social media to share positive and uplifting messages using light and good intentions.

I am not meaning to be negative. In this day and age, it's hard to be living like a hermit. There will always be an ad targeted at you. And again, some ads are meant to be shown to you as this is what you are meant to attract because what you discover will help and benefit you.

The question is- what will help you and what will not help you? How will you know?
The answer is self-love. When you own your precious mind, you focus on yourself and you fully believe on yourself, you will not be prone to attracting people and messages who want to benefit from you without providing you with the value that you might be seeking.

By entering your sacred space of self-love, you enter a whole new vibrational state. The best way to go about it, is to keep asking yourself the following questions:
-Do those people (and messages) have good intentions?
-Where do I want to be in the next five years?
-What is my next exciting goal?
-Is that thing helping me get closer to that goal, or taking me further away from it?

Now, I am all for being positive. But you need to be positive in an authentic way and own your mind. You own your mind when you can think for yourself and make your own decisions.

When I was younger, I made lots of bad decisions because I didn't own my mind. I let my family and society tell me what to do. I allowed them to program my mind and then I was blindly making decisions that were not making me happy.

Then, I felt guilty. I wasn't happy, because I worked so hard for my "success", but it was only to realize that I worked hard to create a prison not freedom. In other words, I worked hard to create someone else's success, but not my own.

Things began to change a bit when I got on a path of self-help and began working with coaches and mentors. Unfortunately, I still wasn't in a self-love and *own your mind* mindset. As a result, I was easy prey for many of those people. I remember taking part in a small mentorship program related both to mindset and business. During one meeting, I felt compelled to express my intention about what I considered unethical and manipulative marketing methods that the course "mentor" we had was urging us to apply.

You know what happened? I was called a hater, and someone who has "a poor person's mindset". The "mentor" added, "Elena, you have many limiting beliefs you need to work through."
I managed to get my power back, and replied, "A belief is limiting if it's limiting you and your personal growth. However, if that belief empowers you, it's not limiting. You cannot have a belief that both empowers you and limits you". And I left that "mastermind". Needless to say, the guy who was trying to teach me and mentor me is no longer in business. Because of his unethical practices, several individuals reported him to the authorities, and he lost everything.
I am very glad I followed my heart on that day, because only God knows what could have happened.

What I am trying to bring your attention to are patterns.

For example, personally, I felt disempowered. I lacked self-love and I would just move around across different communities and industries with no sense of belonging. No matter where I went, I felt extremely lost and attracted people who also felt lost, but their way of dealing with it was to make me feel worse about myself.

Eventually, though, I started attracting amazing books, videos and resources that helped me.
I am very grateful for a YouTuber Aaron Doughty. Not only because of his amazing videos but also because he recommended the book called *Reality Transurfing*, written by a Russian author, Vadim Zeland.

I am extremely grateful for this author and his teachings which are very relevant to this step. In his book *Reality Transurfing*, he talks about the concept of pendulums. A pendulum can be any collective energy or organization that gets into your mind to control it. That is the simplest way of explaining what a pendulum is. I would recommend the original book (you can also look it up on YouTube as the author generously posted the audio version for free, at least for the time being as I am writing this chapter, his book is up on his official YouTube channel in audio format).

As I was reading his book, which to be honest I have read several times and will read again, I found so many answers I had been searching for. His writing really brought tears of joy to my eyes. I finally realized how to let go of other people's negative influences that no longer served me. On the other hand, there may also be positive pendulums, for example a community that brings joy into your life. Perhaps you go to a bookstore and you search for your favorite fiction author, because you know that thanks to his writing you will feel entertained and relaxed. Or maybe you listen to your favorite podcast or look for some specific and life changing information by following someone's blog, or a newsletter.

Whatever serves you, feels light and feels good helps you on your self-love journey. Self-love and self-awareness go hand in hand. By allowing yourself to make your own choices and walking away from things that no longer serve you, you stay connected to your inner wisdom and light.
Back to the concept of pendulums- a negative pendulum can be someone whom you perceive as an authority and who tells you to follow a certain path that is not good for you. It can be a mentor who's not offering the guidance that really helps you on a deeper level but is more driven by his or her own success and significance.

It can be doing something that everyone else is doing because you feel like it's expected of you. In those moments, be strong. Give yourself the courage to be yourself. That doesn't mean you should start attacking those "pendulums." According to the author of the above-mentioned book *Reality Transurfing*, fighting pendulums is futile and only drains your energy.

As I like to put it, the best way is to focus on yourself and your own path and shining your light with a strong intention of using that light to inspire those who need it.

The light can be any creative or passionate work you want to do, any professional work you would like to be doing to really feel fulfilled (this is like true ambition coming straight from your heart). It could be volunteering for your local community or taking up a new hobby. It could even be something as simple as walking around with an apple or a smoothie, because you never know, someone might be passing by and they may get inspired. Maybe that person had a bad day and as a coping mechanism had the intention of getting some unhealthy food and alcohol on the way back home. But now they have seen you and have decided to drive by a healthy food store and pick a salad instead!

All your actions matter, as we discussed in the previous step (step #2 – where you were asked to give yourself more credit). Through this step it is time to get honest with yourself and identify people, events, even social media platforms, or very specific programs, social media channels and other media that you feel are no longer serving you.

We have already done the emotional peeling to release self-guilt in the very first step of this process. Now, what about maintaining that and taking care of what you put in your mind?

At the same time, please remember that everything is a learning experience. I could have felt guilty of allowing certain mentors into my life. I could have started calling them out on being manipulative and what not. But that would bring me back to the victim mentality. Instead, a wiser thing to do is to realize the following:

-There was a reason I allowed that person into my mind. It was supposed to be a learning experience to make me stronger.
-I forgive that person fully. They need to love themselves more and they also deserve self-connection.
-I love myself and I forgive myself and others. I now send light and healing energy to that person and they can use it whenever they feel ready for their own self-love self-awakening. Until then, they can choose their own path and I no longer judge them.
-I allow myself to be me. I allow myself to choose wisely. I feed my mind with a healthy, natural clean food diet. This is for my highest good and for the good of my loved ones and my whole community.

Can you see and feel where it's going? It feels so much better to let go and feel empowered knowing that you can pick and choose what kind of messaging you decide to enter your mind. Now, it's time to finish this chapter with an exercise. It will take less time than the exercise in the previous step. In fact, half an hour is totally fine.

On one piece of paper, or on a new page in your self-love journal, write down all the messages, people and negative influences that you are now ready to let go of.
Take a look at the page and start drawing little hearts around what you wrote.
Now, place both of your hands on your heart. Say, "I love myself and I love you. I love you and I love myself."

Repeat a few times. Then say, "I am now ready to release, I am now ready to let go. And I am forever grateful."

Now, on a second piece of paper write down what you are grateful for and what those negative messages and influences taught you.

It can be something simple like, "I learned who I don't want to be. I learned which path is not for me. I get closer to my divine wisdom and light, it made me who I am".
Again, draw little hearts around your gratitude statements, then again say, "I am ready to release, I am ready to let go and I am feeling light and grateful." If needed and if it feels good and therapeutic for you, repeat the process several times and keep writing.

To finish off, rip off the pages, or if you were writing on a piece of paper, start tearing it up. You can also burn it. Whatever feels right. You are now letting go of the past, while being fully in the present moment where all the possibilities exist. Now you can open your beautiful mind to new opportunities.

On another piece of paper, describe exactly what your life will look like in five years' time. Write it, as if you were seeing everything and feeling and experiencing everything.

Whatever comes to your mind, remember that you are here and now in the present moment where all the possibilities exist. You are now on the self-liberating journey of self-healing and self-love. You are now totally letting go of the past and past experiences. You are feeling lighter and more empowered. So, allow your mind to think big. Write down all the details about what your life will look like in the next five years.

Focus on where you want to live, what you want to do for a living and who you want to spend your time with.

Do you live in house or in an apartment? Which city? Do you travel a lot? Where do you work? Who do you work with? How much money do you earn per month? What do you eat? Where do you eat? What do you wear? Who do you surround yourself with? Do you have children?

Allow yourself to see and feel all the details. We are definitely working with the Law of Attraction here.
Finally, on a new piece of paper, write down the following questions:
-*Who can help me?*
-*Who do I allow to enter my mind?*
-*Who inspires me?*
-*Who motivates me?*
-*Who loves me? (You love yourself, and I love you too and many others love you too!)*
-*Who can teach me?*
-*Who can guide me?*
-*Who can mentor me?*

If you already know your answers, start writing down the names of your potential guides, mentors and teachers.

Write down the books that you think can help you on your journey. Do you need to acquire new skills to help you tune into the new reality you are creating for yourself?

Whatever your vision is, self-love is an amazing amplifier, and without it, as you already know, it's very easy to get misled and start mistakenly manifesting other people's goals and desires. And you already know that the most important thing is to manifest your goals and your desires. That starts with self-love and authenticity.

Don't be afraid to let go of the influences that no longer serve you. They may have served you in the past, but if the next chapter in your life means you're ready for something new, it may also mean you are getting ready to let go.

Whenever in doubt ask yourself-how does it feel? Does it feel light or heavy?
Your gut knows the answer. Also, by installing your vision, the vision you now carry in your heart, the vision of you and your life in the next five years, you are connecting with your subconscious mind and your inner guidance.

You feel empowered to start asking yourself good questions, questions that heal your soul and guide all your actions.

Remember Jerry, whom I mentioned in the first chapter of this book? He mastered the art of self-love by asking himself good questions. Those questions helped him leave the path of self-destruction and got him on the path of self-love, self-gratitude and self-discovery.

Now that you have your vision, your vision that you know is yours, you know where you're going. Whenever you're in doubt, as for who to listen to, or which influence aka "pendulum" is right for you, ask yourself this question: "Is it helping me get closer to or farther away from my vision?" For example, if you set a vision for yourself that you want to be an actor or a writer, then mastering your craft is empowering and bringing you closer to your dream.

That means that in your free time, you naturally feel inspired to do what you love- acting or writing. It's who you are, and you love it. But, if a negative influence comes up, for example, your friends want to go out and get drunk, your inner mechanism might tell you this:

Is it really serving me? Tomorrow I will feel hangovered. Is it really worth it? What about signing up for those writing or acting classes?

That can allow you to connect with a new group of people who are exactly on the same journey as you are.

Likewise, if, on your vision, you prioritized your health and wellbeing and you said you eat healthy, nourishing foods and you love yourself, your weight and your energy, you will probably reject any kind of disruptive fast food marketing messages as negative influences or negative pendulums. Instead, you will naturally want to eat something healthy.

Finally, if your vision incudes a new profession, and deep inside you know it's a career that excites you, and a career that connects you with your passion, by asking yourself empowering questions you may get tempted to start saving up for college or any education or a diploma that may help you get closer to your desired career. Suddenly "sacrifices" will not feel like sacrifices because deep inside you will know you are making a good decision.

And even though everyone around you will be telling you, "It's not worth it, it's risky to change jobs, why not keep your old job?" or "It's hard to study and work full time," you will simply smile and reject those beliefs as negative pendulums that try to disconnect you from your truth and from who you really are.

I hope you're excited now. And it's time to dive into the next step.

I am also very curious to hear about your journey and experiences, so if you have a second, please share them by posting an honest review on Amazon. It will also help other people in our small community. Everyone loves to read about transformations. Other people's stories have much more value and motivation than just a pure *how-to* theory.

However, I will ask you to decide for yourself. If you're ready to share, please share, if not, wait for the right moment.

Chapter 4 Step #4 The Number One Self-Love Trick to Eliminate Limiting Beliefs and Self-Doubt

I am very excited for you, because in this chapter, we are going to re-wire your brain. We will cover that simple trick to transform "I can't do it" and "I don't know how" into meaningful action that creates the reality you want. You will feel positively surprised to see what you're capable of after going through this step.

Before we get into it, let's recall the process we have covered so far. I know for a fact that some of you have been doing the exercises diligently as you read each chapter.
But some of you just went ahead with reading, saying, "I will do the exercises later". How do I know? Because I am the second type of reader and I can totally relate! That is why it may be handy to go through a little recap.

If you did all the exercises after each chapter, you will be able to internalize the teachings on a deeper level. In case you skipped them-no worries. I don't want to interfere with your reading patterns. I know you will do the exercises whenever you feel ready and inspired to do them and you will know how to do them in your own, unique way. After all, everything happens for a reason.
In step #1 we learned how to get rid of self-guilt and how to move on and find the meaning of whatever negative happened to us. By erasing self-guilt, we release negative emotions and patterns and are ready for the new.

It's like the emotional detox. We also learned how to ask empowering questions and how to make friends with our internal search engine, that is- how to ask questions that connect us with our goals. That allowed us to shift away from being a victim to being a warrior.

In step #2 we learned how to value ourselves and give ourselves more credit. We dived very deep into all our accomplishments.

The transformative effect of chapter 2 is that we start to value any action we have taken, and we no longer see failure as failure. We succeed (on our terms) or we learn. That empowering mindset can instantly connect you with new habits and ideas to help you transform your spiritual life, your personal life and your career.

In step #3 we learned how to protect our minds from negative influences and why it's important to pluck up our courage and allow ourselves to let go of everything that no longer serves us. We even did a little ritual to release the last traces of self-guilt and through that ritual we felt lighter and lighter.

The ritual included listing all the negative influences and circumstances in our lives, finding something we learned from it, something we can be grateful for, sending them love and sending us love and letting them go.

Then, we created a vision for ourselves and where we want to be in the next five years. In alignment with that, we learned how to determine what actions, people and influences can help us get closer to that vision.

That helped us become more confident in taking meaningful and inspired action, totally in alignment with the Law of Attraction and fueled by self-love.

The best is yet to come. Because, in this chapter, we will learn how to erase self-doubt and limiting beliefs. A simple example: In the beginning, I struggled with writing this book. I kept saying that I didn't know how.

Even though I have written several books in the past, I felt stuck with this one. I felt so much resistance, and what you resist- persists.

If you keep telling yourself you *can't do* something, your subconscious mind will respond with just that and you will start receiving a "fake proof" of what you think is your reality.

You will start diving deeper and deeper into self-doubt and with that mindset, even if you see someone just like you doing what you would love to be doing, you might reject such an inspiration and say, "Oh but they had this and that, they had better connections, they had better education" and this and that.

How do I know? Because I was in that mindset for many years. Because of that I let many amazing opportunities slip by while witnessing other people's success stories.

I quickly realized they were doing something different and they were not really pushing that hard. They just knew what they wanted, really believed in it, and lived with the mindset, "I already got this, it's already mine". That mindset led them to taking small and inspired steps every day, and those actions didn't feel like work.

While it didn't take me lot of time to understand, it took me lots of time to be able to apply to my own life. One thing is to understand and tell yourself, yea, I know I need to do it, I really do. And another thing is to actually do it.

So, I went through a process of trial and error. One thing that helped me was my own self talk and internal dialogue. I was using the technique of empowering questions that I have already explained through sharing Jerry's story. Because of that I began eliminating resistance and I was able to start transforming all areas of my life.

For example, I had a limiting belief that living a healthy lifestyle is hard and complicated. That heathy food is very expensive, and that it takes hours to create healthy meals. I used to believe that working out and exercising are only for extremely motivated and fit people. I even thought that if I went to the gym I would be laughed at because as a kid, I had always been laughed at during the PE classes. Whether it was gymnastics, or a simple volleyball or basketball game, I had always been a victim there.

Knowing what I know now, I know why it was happening. Back then I was in self-hate and self-doubt and I would allow other people to create labels for me. I did not have the courage to obey, neither did I have the courage to transform on my own terms.

So, this is how it all started. My limiting beliefs about health and fitness originated from my childhood. In my family, nobody was healthy and many of my family members would laugh at people who jogged or got involved in any healthy activities. My grandpa would always say, "Oh those people have too much free time on their hands, maybe they are not working? When do they take care of their children?"

So, boom, my limiting belief got a strong consolidation.
If you work out, you don't take enough care of your family. If you work out too much you are not a good person. Working out is a waste of time. If you eat healthily it's too expensive and if you spend money on expensive stuff you are not a good person. Nobody will like you if they see how much money you spend. They will no longer connect with you. You will die anyway, you don't need to eat any healthy stuff.

That resulted in massive resistance. Several years ago, I still struggled with eating healthily and I could not lose weight. I tried different things but could never commit to a healthy lifestyle. My limiting beliefs and lack of self-love were a very harmful combination. I didn't know which direction to take, because wherever I went, I felt like a total failure.

It took me a while to understand where my limiting beliefs were coming from and why they were forming. It was because of the lack of self-love as well as allowing other people's opinions to enter my mind. And very often people with those opinions do not love themselves either or they just repeat what they have heard from others, acting like robots. If everyone is saying something it must be true, right?

Now, I don't mean to be judgmental, because I have been there as well. It was thanks to discovering the concept of self-love and going through all the steps I have already described, that I was able to identify the limiting beliefs that were holding me back.

The process I share in this book should be done in a certain way, exactly the way it is presented. Now, that you understand what self-love is and what is not, and how to use it for your and others' highest good, and how to protect your mind and ask empowering questions, this step will feel like a piece of cake.

However, had we entered this step at the beginning of the book, it may have felt a bit patronizing or even cookie cutter. Like a typical self-help book, yea, "Just get rid of those limiting mindsets that are holding you back and you will be fine."

But you and I know it's all a process. It's a deep work that we are doing here.

Back to my limiting beliefs. Once I had learned how to gradually get rid of them without feeling self-guilt and without feeling like a victim, I also understood that what very often holds people back is not the limiting beliefs themselves. Very often it's their feeling guilty about having them. Or creating another limiting belief: "I have a limiting belief, and this is who I am and I don't know how to get rid of it." The moment you start putting other "I can't" and "I don't know how's" on what is already stopping you from shining your light and reaching your full potential, you make it harder and harder.

However, once you understood the mechanism behind getting rid of limiting beliefs, you can easily apply it to all the areas of your life. This is exactly what I did. I started off with health and fitness. I realized that area needed most of my attention as I was transforming. I also knew that by creating a healthy lifestyle, I could resort to natural methods that would help me soothe the pain, feel less anxiety, sleep better and eat healthier.

Thanks to self-love, I quickly identified all those negative voices in my head as well as the limiting beliefs that were pretty much coming from other people and were installed on my hard drive. But here's the caveat: you cannot just remove a limiting belief and hope for the best. You need to replace the limiting belief with an empowering belief.
For example, the beliefs I got from my family:
- "If you work out you don't have the time for your family."
- "Eating healthily is only for rich people."
- "Eating healthily doesn't taste good anyway, come on, you gotta have something good in your life. Life is already hard enough."
-

I began replacing these with self-love and empowerment, one by one. For example, instead of, "If you are always working out, you don't have the time for the family", I said, "You can both work out and hang out with the family and friends".

I began organizing hiking trips that were fun. I could get some of my friends and family members and we would just walk in nature, burn calories and have fun. We could still catch up, but instead of going to a bar, we would get some fresh air, admire nature or even join a yoga workshop. Then, eventually we felt inspired to combine our hikes with eating healthy food.

Aside from that, I realized that health is the most valuable asset we have. I can still remember what it felt like when I could not get up and felt absolutely powerless. The doctors would just prescribe antidepressants, but the truth is, my body lacked a healthy, clean diet and exercise. Now, I have never been a gym person. So, I decided to focus on other activities, mostly in nature, like hiking, for example. Then I also joined yoga and Pilates classes. I added more positive changes gradually. I kept track of my progress. I still allowed myself to get off track every now and then. That is absolutely fine. You don't want to be too strict on yourself. It's better to focus on your long-term vision.

Eventually, I started enjoying my hikes so much. Getting outdoors in the fresh air just felt amazing. I loved my hikes so much that I decided to take them to another level and I began jogging. Another change and shift added gradually. Had I vowed to jog every day at the beginning of my journey, I wouldn't have had any success with it. I would have worked on will power alone. And that can only last so long.

A friend of mine, who was going through the same process, decided to transform his health and fitness as well. Aside from that, he became very inspired by what I was doing with my writing. His challenge was time, because he had a full-time job and a family to support. But he managed to do it anyway. He started small. He started waking up ten to fifteen minutes earlier and doing some simple exercises that required no equipment. Just watching YouTube videos and following online fitness courses and DVDs.

He made a small commitment that only took fifteen minutes a day, every day, first thing in the morning, before things became too hectic.

His old limiting belief had been that if you had a full-time job and a family to support, and you wanted to be a good dad, you had to give up on your passions because continuing with them would be egoistical. He had heard it from his dad, his uncle, and his grandpa.

But the new, empowering belief, fueled by self-love was this:
"As a good dad, I need to take care of my health and fitness and set a good example to my family. This also allows me to be more productive at work and increase my chances of getting a promotion."

So, he kept going. Eventually, he started waking up even earlier and added more exercises to do in the morning because it felt so good. His wife also became inspired to do fitness training.
Then he decided to add another habit. While at work, he had a one-hour lunch break. He didn't need a full hour to eat anyway. He could enjoy his lunch within twenty minutes, and then instead of browsing through his phone, he decided to focus and write. He soon realized that half an hour a day can be easily turned into a thousand words. That's thirty thousand words a month which can be a short novella or a smaller size nonfiction book.

That got him on a writing path which quickly became an extra source of income.
His old belief that "you are not a good dad if you follow your passion," is no longer there. His new belief is this: "Thanks to my passion I can take better care of my family. Passion is perseverance. Passion is manhood."

And of course, as a kid he had been told that he would never make a dime from his writing. Then he was told that because of his corporate job, it would look unprofessional for him to become a writer. But it doesn't matter, because he is not writing for fame, but as a passion project which easily turns into extra income for him and his family. It also helps him relax and destress from his day job.

Think beyond yourself, your mission, your purpose. The work you are meant to be doing. Who did you allow to enter your mind and why?

Now, look at your vision, the one we created in the previous chapter. Are there any voices in your head that you feel are preventing you from taking action? Perhaps you fear it will be hard or that it will take too long, or that you will get laughed at.

What if there was a magical power that could totally erase those voices from your head? What if I told you there is a magic pill you can take, a pill you can use to erase self-doubt? Wouldn't that be helpful?

The good news is that pill exists, and it's called self-love. Do not allow other people's beliefs to become yours. Also, very often their beliefs are not even their own in the first place. Once you start seeing how disempowered and easily influenced most people are, you quickly realize how necessary it is for you to transform so that you can set an example, shine your light and inspire others. Not by bragging and not by making them feel inferior. That stuff never works long term. You can help other people by becoming the best version of yourself starting right here and now. You don't need to wait for the perfect moment. Be yourself and shine your light. Also, give yourself permission to follow your own pace. Remember, you don't fail - you succeed, or you learn.
Now, it's time for yet another awesome exercise...

Write down all the negative thoughts and everything you have been told you cannot do. Yes, I was told I should not be writing this book and that it was a waste of time. I was told many things that I decided to walk away from. And I am so happy I can finally be myself. I want to share it with other people.

Take a piece of paper and write down all your negative beliefs, negative self-talk and everything you think is a limiting belief. By now you should be able to spot them easily. If you still don't know how, here's the trick- if there is something you really want to do, and you think about it and you really feel light, but then you think about what you need to do to get there and you immediately start feeling heavy, it is a sign that there is some kind of a resistance showing up on your path. If the goal feels light, it is definitely for you. But then somewhere, somehow, you begin blocking your own way.

It's time for another emotional peeling!
On one piece of paper you will be writing down all the negative beliefs and opinions you realized are stopping you.

Then, start drawing hearts on them. Take a few deep breaths. Place your hands on your solar plexus.

Keep breathing. Say to yourself, I am ready to let go! I love you, I love me, I love me, and I love you.

You can also say, "Elena loves me".

Keep that piece of paper in front of you. Take another piece of paper and start rewriting negativity into positivity.

For example:
"Eating healthily is not for me, I can't eat this way, I don't like the taste."

Becomes:

"I have been watching some videos and reading eBooks about healthy recipes. The authors of that content all used to be overweight and unhealthy. But now they say they love eating healthily and can teach me how to do it as well. If they can do it, I can do it too. I can easily learn at least one new, healthy recipe a week. I can also learn healthy meal plans. There are many delicious recipes I can find and enjoy, and I can skip the recipes I don't like."

Be creative and repeat this process with all your limiting beliefs.

Once you have rewritten all the limiting beliefs into positive and empowering ones, allow yourself to destroy the first sheet of paper, where you write all the negative beliefs. While doing it say, "I love me, I love you. I love me I love you, I let go of you limiting beliefs, because you no longer serve me, but I am grateful for you because thanks to you, I was able to create my empowering beliefs instead."

And remember- Elena loves you! You are an amazing human being and you are here to follow your heart, your light and your passion. I am here to help you and guide you on your journey the best as I can.

Good stuff may take some time, but you're on your way. By aligning yourself with your actions, no matter how small they are, you are also aligning yourself with the infinite light of self-love. You are allowing yourself to take care of your body, mind and soul.

Self-love is very often depicted as self-care or doing some "girlish" stuff like getting your make-up or nails done.

But, in reality, self-care forms part of self-love. It's all interconnected. Taking care of your body helps you take care of your mind and soul. Taking care of your mind and soul helps you take care of your body.

Everything starts in your mind. Your precious mind. Own it, it's yours. Do not allow other people's opinions enter it, unless their opinions are helpful for you your journey.
Still, don't beat yourself up because there will always be some negative voices entering your mind. But now, you have the power. Now you know how to respect and love yourself enough to get rid of those limiting beliefs.

Stay strong and enjoy the cleansing benefits of re-writing your negative beliefs into the positive ones.

Part 2- Self-Love Handbook

Chapter 5 Step #5 Expressing Kindness

Self-love and loving others are interconnected. By allowing yourself to be kind, in an authentic way, you can massively speed up the process of transforming your life.

I remember that when I first got started on the path of self-love, I was very excited because I had seen this huge power and potential, something that could really change my life on a deeper level. However, there were a few things that were holding me back.

1. Lack of patience
2. Relapsing back into negative patterns
3. Losing motivation

That's a "nice" mix, isn't it?

So, let me tell you what exactly was happening in my life back then and how you can protect yourself from those negative patterns.

Lack of patience, relapsing into old habits and losing motivation are all interconnected. Seems pretty obvious right? You get impatient, you get pulled back into old negative patterns and then you lose motivation. But the real issue is not lack of patience, relapsing into old patterns, and losing motivation. The real issue is how you deal with it and how those relapses make you feel. The way most people react, and I used to be there too, is to feel guilty and develop some new negative beliefs on that foundation. You know, things like, "I can't stick to anything"; "Other people can do it"; "I lack discipline"; "Something is wrong with me".

No, nothing is wrong with you, in fact everything is fine. The above-mentioned reactions are normal and human. You will be pulled back into them many times, and so will I and so will be any spiritual gurus.

Of course, they don't talk about it, because they are just perfect and everything what they say is perfect! That is the perfect world. But in the real world, things are different, and we live in the real world not in an ivory tower.

Our reactions are human and normal. Sometimes, our minds make us relapse a bit into negative patterns. One thing we can control is our reaction. The reason that we very often get pulled back into negative patterns of self-hate, self-guilt or addictions can be also because we don't allow ourselves to focus more on others.

And I am telling you- the best motivation is to think outside of yourself. And the best way to think outside of yourself is by performing random acts of kindness.

Part 2- Self-Love Handbook

This is the concept I learned from an author, John Magee and his book, *Kindness Matters*. Following the inspiration I got from his book, I quickly discovered that, by setting up a simple daily goal of for example:

-Sending out five genuine messages to people I am grateful for and appreciate
-Volunteering to help my local community
-Walking around and expressing my kindness as soon as I see something or someone I like. (Okay. That sounds weird, I know, I will elaborate more on that later.)

We are talking about authentic kindness not artificial kindness. You can walk away from things you don't like, it's fine. You are not a hater because of that. People have different tastes.

But...think of three or five people who inspire you. Message them and express your kindness and gratitude. It can be someone you know personally, or it can be someone you follow online, maybe a blogger or someone who shares their wisdom via videos.

Message them or comment on their work and express your kindness. How does it feel?
Another way is to volunteer to help your local community. You will immediately start putting your focus and attention on other people and by doing that you will be stepping into love and light. By loving others, you love yourself and by loving yourself you love others.

For me, volunteering for my local community was an amazing experience. I also discovered some of my hidden gifts and met people who I truly believe were what I like to call "Manifestation Messengers". Those Messengers connected me to many amazing ideas and encouraged me to follow my passion in a meaningful and empowered way.

Had I not decided to volunteer back then, I wouldn't be where I am right now. Quite probably I wouldn't be even writing this book.

Another thing that you can immediately implement are random acts of kindness or compliments that you offer as you walk around your town. It can be something simple as offering someone a ride or helping them with their shopping. Or knocking on your old neighbors' door and asking if they need help around the house, or maybe if they want some fresh fruits and veggies.
At the same time, if you see someone wearing a nice dress or looking great in that new haircut, then tell them. Express your kindness and compliments: "Wow, I really like your new hair!"
Do it in an authentic way. It's not about forcing yourself to pay compliments to everyone. It's more about allowing yourself to express your positive thoughts with an intention of lighting everyone up.

The world needs more of those local, empowering leaders. Think about it. There are many people who wake up feeling miserable. They walk around feeling depressed and they go to bed feeling sad. Don't you think that they deserve an act of kindness? An authentic one. The one that will make them click. The one that will initiate their own journey of self-love.

The world doesn't need another "guru" from the ivory tower. The world needs us, small self-love leaders who are in the trenches, working on ourselves and living in the real world and overcoming real obstacles.

Now, it's your turn. Which act of kindness are you going to perform today?

Please let us and other people in our community know how this step worked out for you. Did you feel this instant vibrational shift? Didn't it feel good to be able to help someone, or even to make someone smile?

Share your experience related to random acts of kindness as well as your self-love journey and honest thoughts you have about this book so far, in the review section on Amazon. Your feedback can inspire and enlighten other readers on their journeys.

Finally, now that we have covered the importance and the healing power of random acts of kindness as well as thinking beyond yourself and helping people in your community, it's time to dive deeper into self-expression. This is one of the concepts very deeply connected with self-love.

Part 2- Self-Love Handbook

Chapter 6 Step #6 Creative Self Expression

You are here for a reason. You are here to leave a legacy. You are here to inspire other people. "Oh, Elena, but what if I don't want to be famous?"

Well, self-expression is much, much deeper and it doesn't have to be about becoming famous. Fame in itself is not bad at all. You can become famous in your field thanks to your work that is passion-driven and value-based.

It means that it consists exactly of those two components. You are passionate about what you do, and at the same time, you put that passion into creating value for other people.

Creative self-expression can be accomplished by social media or blogs. And, if you have that passion that driving force to help other people, something you have been wanting to share with the world for a while, don't wait to be perfect. Don't wait to be a perfect writer or speaker. Start now, start today, because you will get better and better as you go.

At the same time, creative self-expression can also be done through art, or even cooking. For example, if someone is passionate about smoothies, and they open their own smoothie bar- it's also creative self-expression.

The intention behind creative self-expression is always helping and inspiring other people while performing a meaningful action from a place of love and abundance.
Self-expression is deeply connected to self-love for multiple reasons.

One of them is that it helps rebalance our throat chakra in an authentic way. You see, if you have something valuable you know you need to be sharing, but you allow other people tell you what to do and what not to do and you suppress your wisdom, you are depriving your throat chakra of joy. Your ideas may very well disappear. The question is, will it be worth it?

For example, when I first got started on this writing journey, it was hard. I sometimes got hate emails or very rude reviews. I am not referring to honest feedback, where someone says, "Here is what I liked/ this could have been better/ I would have liked more information about..."
I am talking about nasty troll reviews. Like, "It's a scam that book only has one hundred pages." (The product information is there for you to check before you order. I could go to a vegan restaurant and complain that they don't do meat, or I could go to a steak house and complain they don't do vegan burgers.)

Those things happen. People who post those comments need self-love. To be honest, last year I took many months off writing and was going to quit at some point. My fear was, "What if it really takes off and I start getting more of those comments?"

I was feeling really upset. Finally, I reached out to a mentor who was a successful writer and she told me this:

"Really? Why do you think you should stop? Isn't it the trap of your own perception? Nasty negative comments show only one thing. Those people need more love and self-love. Those comments are just a reminder from the universe that the world needs you. What happened for you, happened for a reason. A person who leaves nasty comments very often comes from a dark place. Who knows what happened in their lives?".

"On the internet they feel safer and they can say whatever they want without showing their face. In real life they may be very shy people and they wouldn't even talk to you. Who knows what is really happening there?"

"At the same time, hate is not the answer. Love is the answer. Do you think it's really worth stopping? Think about your vision. Your vision is to be writing every day and connecting with your readers. Your vision is to be getting emails from people whose lives were transformed thanks to your writing and what you share. What you have created so far is just a warm up. The signs you are getting from the Universe are amazing. Start by loving yourself more and then teach others by sharing your gifts and wisdom."

Wow, that gave me lots to think about and I decided to change my perception. Now, my question is- what about you? What is blocking you from expressing yourself?

Remember, you don't need to go public with it. Maybe you just want to take those dancing classes. That is also self-expression. Maybe, you want to learn a foreign language? Maybe you want to write children's book? Or perhaps you want to start a personal blog, just sharing your thoughts? How about drawing and doing your art? Or maybe learning to play the piano or guitar? Music is a very transformative power. It's therapeutic both for the creator and the receiver.

At the same time, maybe you feel you have many valuable thoughts you can share with other people? Well, start a new social media account where you can share and connect with like-minded individuals. Become a thought leader. As a thought leader, you can even write your own books, have a blog and start creating courses or retreats.

Traveling and exploring new places, as well as photography also form part of creative self-expression. Maybe you always wanted to be a travel blogger?

Whatever your choice is, the time is now. You know what it is. There is always something.
If you still struggle with finding your channel or form of self-expression, go back to your vision, the one we elaborated a few chapters ago. Ask yourself, "What does the new me do every day? What does the new me enjoy doing? What does the new me crave to be doing every day?"

Then, ask yourself, the new you from the future- and how did it all start? It started with one tiny decision, one tiny act of self-love. When I decided I am going to move forward. When I decided to love myself enough to get up and brush myself off and keep moving forward. It happened when I decided I would be a self-love warrior. That is when it happened.

Now, it's your turn. Think where you will be in the next five years. Feel it. And tune into that vision with your meaningful action. Your self-expression.

Part 2- Self-Love Handbook

Chapter 7 Step #7 Positive Reminders and Your Own Magic Pendulum

It's time to have some fun! Your mind is stronger and much more powerful than you believe. And you already know you can actually control what you put in it. While there are many negative influences and opinions as well as detrimental messages out there, messages designed to get you off your self-love journey, you know your power. You know you're much stronger than that. You can easily design your own positive reminders and messages.

This is what we will be doing in this chapter, and yes, it does connect with the previous one, because we are embarking on creative self-expression again. So, just in case the last chapter felt like, "Okay, sounds great but I still don't know how to express myself", you can easily express yourself now.

All that can be easily amplifying your self-love.
So, let's do this! This process consists of three simple steps.

Step #1
Choose your place or places.
Ask yourself where you hang out most and what objects do you look at?
Think of your phone, your office, your computer, your book shelf, your fridge, your washing machine, dishwashing machine, your Kindle, your wardrobe, your bathroom.

We need to be very strategic here because the self-love reminders we will be planning will be very, very strong! While I am a big fan of small baby steps, in this case there will be no baby steps. We will be flooding the heck out of it!

So, write down all the places or objects you look at or happen to be at often or even multiple times of day.

Done, okay? Let's do the next step.

Step #2
Create a list of your favorite quotes and messages.
You can write down your own affirmations and thoughts or use quotes from people who inspire you.

One of my favorite quotes I like to use is by Tony Robbins, "The past does not equal to the future", or "It didn't happen to me, it happened for me."

Then, I also use a bunch of other reminders, such as, "I love you", "I love myself", "I love the person who I have chosen to become."

Now, it's your turn. Write it all down in your journal or on a piece of paper.

Step # 3
It's Shopping Time!
Whether from your local store or online, get some colored paper, stickers, or even beautiful postcards, and have fun with them.

Play your favorite music while you put your self-love messages and beautiful quotes on papers and stick them all around your house and other places you have chosen.

If you share your home with roommates or family members, you can either choose to put your self-love reminders only in your personal place like bathroom, or wardrobe or office, or you can choose to get them on the journey and go all in with self-love reminders and decorations.

As always, I am very curious to hear what you have come up with, so be sure to shoot me an email or post an Amazon review and let us know how this part of the process went and what you got out of the book and this particular chapter as well.

Many people simply reject this idea as childish. Or a waste of time. But thinking this way is very detrimental. We are always thinking. We think both consciously as well as subconsciously. The conscious thinking, for example, can be something like:
"Follow the to do list for today."

The subconscious thinking can be some kind of a trauma we decided to hide, because a few years ago someone told us something rude.

By choosing to use positive reminders we are inspiring our subconscious mind with tons and tons of positive messages. That creates the balance we need to step into the light, truth and alignment. Choose to inspire and control your precious mind. Very often those reminders can save your day or turn a negative trigger into a positive thought and action. For example, in my kitchen I have lots of health self-love reminders, like "I love my body", "I choose to fuel my body", "I love who I am becoming", "I love health", "health is wealth", "health is life" and similar beautiful thoughts. In my office I choose reminders like, "I am on my mission". "I am aligned to my purpose", "I write daily", "this is who I am". I also print out some emails I get from happy readers and look at them constantly because they definitely help me get rid of the writers' block.

Don't skip this step. Get creative here. I would even advise you to take a day off to do it. Combine it with some decluttering and cleaning if you want.

Chapter 8 #Step 8 Magnifying LOA Combine Action with Attraction

It's time to finish off with positive and inspired action. This handbook is not meant to be read and forgotten about. I want you to put the teachings into practice.

It's very important to track your self-love activities. Don't worry, we are not talking about some complicated rituals, or exercises that take lot of time. We have already done the hard part.
What I want to show you in this step is a very simple process I use daily to align myself with my vision and make sure I keep taking positive and inspired action.

You can transform this process to whatever you need to do or choose to do. You can create your own journaling practice as well.

That being said, in the morning, start off with writing down a few things you are deeply grateful for. It can be something related to your health, work or family. Whatever area of your life you want to focus on. You can even do a detailed gratitude ritual where you divide your gratitude journal or piece of paper into different columns or sections.

For example, health – what am I grateful for? You can list one or several things, depending on your time.

For example, I am grateful I am alive. I am grateful I can smile. I am grateful for all my senses. You can even go deeper and be grateful for things you haven't received yet, but you know are coming. So, in the case of health, wellness and fitness, perhaps you are giving yourself more self-love by eating a healthy, clean food diet? Maybe you start off your day with a little walk or workout?

And you know that by doing it every day, you will transform your body, or lose weight if that is your goal. That feels really amazing, because you know you are following a process that serves and you really trust that process.

On top of that, you are already grateful for the result you are looking to achieve but at the same time you are on the state of flow. And when you flow, you are free to eliminate resistance.
So, love yourself enough to be grateful even for things, results and circumstances that you still haven't received.

Like I said, you can focus on one area of your life that needs the most attention, or you can go ahead and write down a few pages where you express your gratitude for all areas of your life. You can even switch it up depending on how you feel. Most people start off with just one area of their lives, the one that requires the most attention and self-love. The reason is that holistic success is all about creating balance. My balance may be different than yours because we have different goals, ambitions and preferences.

If you are feeling stuck in your life, chances are it's because of one area of your life that requires attention. The strong imbalance that manifests in one area of your life, very quickly will transfer to others causing havoc and imbalance.

So, love yourself enough to be honest with yourself and identify that one area of your life that requires the most attention from you, at the present time.

Whenever you have some free time, for example days off or weekends, you can allow yourself to journal and ground yourself for longer, simply by expressing gratitude for all areas of your life. Health, career, family, spiritual etc.

Now, the next step in the journaling process is to connect yourself with your vision for life, something that really excites you. Write down a few powerful and affirmative sentences that align you with that vision. There is no need to write a lot about it if you don't feel like it. Better to write a bit less, but really focus on your feelings and let go of all those negative voices in your head like, "I will never get there, I am not worthy, this is not for me."

No, no, no! You deserve all the good stuff. Self-love will get you there, trust me on that! Close your eyes, breathe, you can listen to some music if you want.

Finally, it's time to plan your day. You already feel aligned to your vision, now ask yourself, "What kind of frequency do I need to get on today?" Again, don't force it. Just let it be. Some days might feel a bit less energetic, that's fine.

But you can still allow yourself to take meaningful and purposeful action to get closer to your vision. So, identify three simple mini actions to take today to give yourself the self-love you need to get closer to your vision. Embrace the here and now, the present moment where all the possibilities exist, right here and right now.

By starting off with gratitude, you get onto a higher vibration. Then, you connect with your vision and so you know where you're going. Now, ask yourself, "What can I do today? What kind of action, even imperfect, can I actually take today?"

Here's a simplified process that I have just explained in this chapter. Again, feel free to remodify it and turn it into a process that you will enjoy. It's something I recommend you do every morning (fifteen minutes should be enough). You can also do it in the evening, before you go to sleep, so that you plan ahead for the next day.

You can even go through the process twice a day if you really need it.

Step #1 Express deep gratitude, even for things you still haven't received but know are on their way. Really feel it.

Step #2 Align yourself with your vision by either writing it down, or meditating on it, really feeling, smelling or visualizing it.

Step #3 Plan out three simple mini actions for today, actions that are self-love based and can get you closer to your vision by helping you get to the new, more empowered you.

It's all about taking that meaningful, inspired action that comes from a sense of purpose, abundance and...yes you already know this – unconditional self-love, for your highest good and for the good of those around you.

Part 3 – Book 3

Law of Attraction to Make More Money

12 Hidden Truths to Help You Shift Your Mindset and Start Attracting the Abundance You Deserve

(without Trying So Hard)

Introduction

If you have ever tried to use LOA to make more money but found yourself frustrated and with few or no results, you have come to the right place. Perhaps you have read other books, taken courses and tried everything under the sun, including affirmations, meditations and visualizations. You have seen other people on the same journey get results and you were wondering what you are doing wrong.

If that's how you're feeling right now, don't worry, I have some good news for you. Believe it or not, I have been in the same situation. Not only that, but I have invested tens of thousands of dollars both in courses and mentorship related to the Law of Attraction and Spirituality as well as Self Help and Business. I have experienced lots of failure and frustration in my life, and it was only on my 42nd birthday that I began to change my life.

You see on that day, my 42nd birthday, quite by accident, I met a mentor, a mindset mentor who was able to help me. I did not expect that day to change my life at all. In fact, it was my birthday and I was feeling so depressed.

I had been through a tough divorce. I had lost my job. I had been diagnosed with adrenal exhaustion and had to start taking medication. I was putting on weight. I was living off my savings and doing some freelance work on the side. I was simply getting by. That day, my 42th birthday, I didn't feel like seeing anyone.

All my friends were married. Showing off their children and loving, caring husbands.

Some of my female friends chose to live a different lifestyle and have corporate or entrepreneurial careers while enjoying frequent vacations in exotic locations. Showing off their healthy fit bodies, enjoying great friendships, getting affluent clients and huge appreciation for what they were doing. Some of my friends were successfully living off their passion and art.

In other words, they all seemed happy and successful. Yet it seemed like I was the hardest working one. The one who invested so much money in courses and mentors. With zero results. So frustrating. Little did I know that it was meant to happen.

It was a part of my journey, as you will later see through this very book. All those years of pain and rejection. Working hard and studying from different mentors eventually exploded into a life I am blessed to be living today.

That is why I am writing this book. I believe that everyone deserves to have this information and that flow of abundance. Not only financial abundance, but also an abundance that spreads and circulates to other areas of life. That may sound a bit woo-woo to some of you. I get that. I used to be very skeptical about everything. I will tell you this- this book is more science and mindset that will help you use LOA to your advantage.

This is exactly what happened to me...
So...on my 42nd birthday, I had nothing to show for.
My plan was to get drunk all by myself while watching TV. A typical night for me at that time.
I was absolutely fine with that as I had lost hope.

I had moved to a smaller and cheaper apartment, the cheapest I could get. I was counting every penny. Honestly, I did not even have the money to invite friends over. I just wanted to be all by myself and cry. I felt so numb so lost, it was like I didn't even feel my body anymore.

I was in so much mental and emotional pain that even the mere thought of picking up a spiritual or self-help book or watching a LOA video would make me cry. I would think:
Why are the creators of those materials successful and I am not? Why it's working for them but not for me?

In the morning, I did my super-cheap shopping...and yeah, I had that plan to stick to...go back home, drink cheap wine and just hope everyone would forget about me and my birthday. I didn't want anyone to ask about me. I had lost contact with most of my friends and family anyway and they all thought I was a loser.
1. I lost my job.
2. My ex-husband was cheating on me with another woman.
3. I felt scammed. I had purchased so many courses that had promised me a better future. Both LOA as well as business courses. Nothing had worked. I no longer felt like learning and investing in myself and wanted to go completely offline. Whenever I would switch on my social media accounts, I would just see other people who were happy and successful, and it was very painful for me. I could not take it anymore. I feel very ashamed to admit it now, but I did have some suicidal thoughts during that period of my life. I was questioning the meaning of life and everything.
4. I had put on weight and felt moody and ugly. I had been diagnosed with a disease that, as all the doctors would tell me, required medication and strong hormonal therapy until the end of my life. That would affect my emotions and make me put on weight. I felt lost and confused, I didn't even feel like myself anymore. Friends and family suggested I get a boyfriend, but I just felt like staying at home.

I was thinking, *Man...if I could only afford to fly to another country and just stay there. Detach myself from the past. Disappear. Start all over again.*

So, on that particular day I was just about to switch off my phone when I received a call from a cousin of mine. A cousin I haven't seen in, like, fifteen years. He lived abroad in tropical countries. And yeah, he would always call or text on my birthday.
So, he called me and asked, "Hey, how are you? Guess what? I am going on a quick conference near your town. A friend of mine got sick and he transferred his ticket to me. It's a three-hour drive from the hotel I am staying at, but it's not a problem at all. I really wanna see you. After the conference I can drive to your place or we can meet up somewhere. I am with some friends, they are very cool people, what do you say?"

Needless to say, it took some time for him to convince me.
As kids we always used to play around and had a good connection even without words.
His mom is my stepdad's sister, but I was raised by my stepdad. I never even met my dad. So, we were always like a family. Cousins.

My stepdad was always very into the system (get a degree, get a job, marry and have kids), however, his sister was more like a hippie and had brought up their kids in a different way. I always wondered how my cousin could afford to travel all the time and meet all those cool people.

Long story short, we decided to meet in a small bar at the town center. I forced myself to go there with a smile on my face.

When I arrived there and saw my cousin, I just felt like crying, which is what I did. I explained how I felt and I couldn't stop crying.

He said that the friend he was with for the conference was a mindset coach. He added, "I think he may be able to help you work through the issues you are feeling now."

I said, "Mindset coach? How will that help me? I need a career coach, a relationship coach and a health coach."

But, after a few drinks, I was like, "OK, let's see what he can do." I really had nothing to lose.
So there appeared Mr. Mindset coach. At first, I was thinking he would try to sell me his service or program, but he didn't. Yet, I really felt like it would be amazing if he could offer me some coaching. I really got a lot of value from what he told me and our conversation kept on for hours and hours, It all came down to a very simple pattern around my mindset and my perception. Eventually, I decided to invest in his coaching even though, knowing about my poor financial situation, he didn't want to charge me.

But I had this feeling...*Elena...this time you will invest in yourself and it will be different. You will take action. Things will change.*

He told me that my self-image wasn't really matching the goals I wanted to achieve along with many other things that came as a result of our improvised session at the bar.

From then on, we ended up working together, and through this inner work that I did my life was forever transformed.

Finally, I was able to distill the best information and divide it into powerful mindset steps that you too can do to start making more money. Whether it's through your job, business, other ventures or something unexpected.

Also, if you are already familiar with what I like to call traditional LOA techniques, whether it's old school LOA (classic visualizations, affirmations and meditations), or you are more on a New School jump wagon (here I refer to the *Reality Transurfing* school of thought), this book will help you shift your mindset and that will allow you take any LOA action from a totally different angle. The angle of being the boss, the owner, the producer of your life and never worry about being a victim.

I can assure you that it's a fresh approach, and if you are coachable and willing to change (aka become the most empowered and divine version of yourself) then this book will help you.

In fact, if you read it with attention and start analyzing patterns from your own life, you may start manifesting from a completely new perspective as soon as you start reading this book.

Some people may want to read this book several times. It's a short read so there should be no, "But I don't have the time" excuses.

Some people may want to focus on one specific step for longer. It all depends on you and your vision. While reading, please don't judge yourself.

Be an observer of your own reality. Use constructive self-criticism rather than judgment. Some truths may be a bit painful. However, every transformation requires change.

That is how I view my life now and I was really at rock bottom.

Now, I don't like bragging about my income and I like to protect my privacy. It's something I really resonated with after reading the book *The Reality Transurfing*. Just like the author of that book states, he achieved certain levels of success but is not planning to show it off as it could affect his privacy and flow. I feel exactly the same way.

However, I can tell you this. I was able to triple my income within three months of using the strategies I developed after working with a mindset coach. Then, I tripled it again.

I was able to move abroad and change my environment too. I still ask myself, *how did it happen?*

Currently I am using a similar system to help people transform their health and love life too. However, money is not evil. Not at all. It's freedom and abundance you deserve, and I will show you the best and ethical mindset hacks to help you transcend your current situation.

An interesting fact- after diving into and internalizing the 12 mindsets I am sharing in this book, I was able to go back to the books and programs I invested in earlier and have success with them.

It all made sense to me and I felt like part of a bigger system designed for my needs and vision. Many of my friends and confidential mentees had the same experience. Especially my mentees who are in business. Suddenly after going through the 12 mindset shifts discussed here, they were able to successfully apply the information they had invested in previously.

In my case, I was able to go back to dozens of LOA and quantum physics courses I have taken and books I have read and make them work for me.

However, in alignment with what I have previously mentioned…it's not how many books you read, how many courses you take and how many seminars you attend.

It's not even how much action you take or don't take after going through the materials you study. It's about how you take them.

While most LOA enthusiasts would say, "Ah, right, it's about the state you're in and your energy", what I want to show you through this book is there is much more to that. Yes, your energy is also very important, and I have written a few books related to LOA that focus mostly on your energy to help you manifest faster.

However, this book relates mostly to your mindset because that can affect your energy too.
One thing I have always been curious about is why there are people who don't really meditate. Yet they always manifest! They've never studied LOA yet they do something that allows them to manifest. How is it that whatever they put their hands on is a success?

It wasn't until I met my mindset coach that I began working through the issues that were stopping me not only from success but also from taking advantage of the numerous LOA resources I had studied. (These are proven to work because they have worked for many other people.)

It's very important that you don't just read passively. Even before we start diving into the tools, I want to teach you that you must have a curious mindset and do whatever it takes to be excited. This isn't a book based on plain gratitude (although gratitude is extremely important).

It's all about deep transformation and stepping into the more empowered version of yourself that will allow you to create the life you deserve. In many cases you may even realize that you have not been able to manifest certain things as they were not really for you anyway and would not have made you happy. That can be a massive relief if you ask me, and it leads to replacing self-guilt and frustration with gratitude.

The strategies from this book have been designed specifically for the finance area of your life. Still, the mindset shifts and mechanisms I will teach you can also be applied to other areas of your life and can help you become what I like to call a manifesting high performer on your own terms. By tapping into your unlimited potential, you will be an inspiration to your loved ones. It is my deep desire that you internalize my teachings by applying them to your life so that you start getting results. Then, you can use your experience and knowledge to help other people too.

I believe in abundance not scarcity. If everyone followed the mindset shifts outlined in this book, the world would be an amazing place. There would be a flow of abundance, no complaining and everyone would just be happier.

While it would be childish of me to believe that such a collective shift could happen overnight, I believe in the compound effect, both on an individual as well as on a collective level.
So please, share this book and the teachings in it.

I am not on social media, and I don't have a podcast or a YouTube channel. I have nothing against people who use all those channels that modern technology offers. However, I know myself well enough to understand where I need to put my energy so that I can be effective in my mission and passion- helping people transform with what I have learned from LOA, all in a very practical and doable way, using one of the most popular mediums of learning- books.

I am blessed to be making a living from my passion which is art and design and I am also grateful that I get enough free time to pursue my writing career.

It allows me to share my stories and lessons learned with other people without affecting my flow and making me feel unfocused and even shattered like most of the social media channels I tried did. For me, it's always been a passion to help others and express myself through my art as well as writing.
For you, it may be something different. I truly believe you will be able to discover your passion and tap into the flow of financial abundance by getting rid of emotional blocks that are holding you back. You will also eliminate what I like to call *LOA Short-Sightedness*. This is something that accounts for the fact that so many people give up and reject LOA as a concept that doesn't work for them.

Just like I don't do social media in order to be able to put my energy where I need to put it to be able to shine and help others shine, I do not organize any workshops or courses, although I know many people who do, and there is nothing wrong with that. They are very good at what they do. It's a good path for them and many people need to invest a lot of money in themselves to be motivated to apply the information they learned. That was my case.

Again, there is nothing wrong with that. I invested tens of thousands of dollars into both LOA, mindset as well as professional courses related to my passion and now career (art and design). Whatever your situation is, this book will "unstuck "you and will get you on the right track. I can't wait to receive an email or review from you and witness your transformation on this journey with the system I will be sharing with you.

There are different ways to use this book, depending on your time and lifestyle:
Option #1 Read it in one sitting. Then, re-read each section and do the exercises.
Option #2 Assign a day for one mindset shift and after reading through each section, do the exercise. After twelve days (that is going through the twelve mindset shifts) evaluate and ask yourself which shift is the most important for you at this stage.

Now, back to the book- I highly recommend that you focus on just a few mindset shifts you believe are the most important for you.

How will you know?
Ask yourself – when thinking about the new me with this new mindset, do I feel lighter and more excited? Would that help me change my life and manifest faster?
If the answer is *yes*, focus more on those.

Now- time to take some meaningful action here to help you transform!
Let's do this!

Mindset Shift #1 Is Your Desire Good for You?

If you have ever consumed any success, self-help, business, high performance of even classical LOA materials, you probably already know that in order to be successful with your goals, you need to know what you want.

It's not hard to make a vision board.
It's not hard to write down what you want.
And it's not hard to record what you want and turn your desires into affirmations and meditations. All the above-mentioned techniques are amazing if you actually know what you want, and it comes from you, from your core.

The problem? Most people don't know what they really want, even if they intellectually think they do. Very often people get into spirituality and LOA because they are looking for something else out there. Maybe they got burned out in their corporate jobs, or careers. Or maybe they spent years trying to achieve their goals and when they did, they ended up feeling miserable and unhappy.
The same question appeared: Was it worth it?

So how do you become clear on what you want? How will you know whether what you want comes from yourself?

First of all, you need to be very careful about what you put into your mind.
Then, you also need to accept what I like to call "temporary chaos". You don't need to have it all figured out in five seconds.

The #1 mistake that most people make with LOA is that instead of diving deeply into this step, they create their vision really fast, without even checking if that vision truly comes from their hearts.
Then, they try hard to manifest. Another mistake. Trying too hard sends the following signal to the Universe: "I don't have it, it's not for me, I need to work harder because I don't have it".
Then, there is frustration: "I can't manifest. Maybe I am not worthy. Let's try another course. Anyone up for a new guru and their secret methods?"

And again, no matter how good the next course is, without clear vision we can easily get lost.
My number one recommendation when it comes to creating your vision is this:

Take a weekend off. Only you. Book a hotel you have never been to, drive to another city or go somewhere unknown. Ideally, you would want a solo vacation for seven days, but that may be not doable for most people. That is why two days may be a good solution to start off with.

Another thing to optimize your efforts with, again are your vision and your core exercise. And yes, you can always change your vision and what not, that is fine, but why not dive deep now and get it right from the get-go?

Think about it. By constantly changing your mind, you are only confusing the Universe. Especially when it comes to your financial goals. These goals make most people add a ton of emotion and stress, because most people associate money with a lack of money and therefore stress, and not feeling worthy.
It should rather be associated with offering value, living your passion, creating a life of freedom and becoming a more empowered version of yourself which is amazing.

But... it all starts with focus. Very clearly defined vision that is detailed but attached to one specific transformation you are looking to achieve. You also need to remember that what you want already exists. It's not that you are creating it. It already exists just like the more empowered version of yourself exists too. It's a different reality and you need to apply this mindset- I simply need to tune it with my thoughts, actions and energy.

One of my early mistakes with LOA was that out of fear, I created a dozen of different vision boards that did not really connect to the same vision. Different vision boards with different houses and lifestyles.
I was thinking that any of them would be good for me. I guessed that by doing a shotgun approach I would at least be able to manifest something. Eventually something will materialize?
Wrong, wrong, wrong! A shotgun approach to manifesting will only make you burn out. A sniper approach works so much better, more on that later in this book.

Not surprisingly, during that time, I tried different business ventures. All of them failed. I invested a ton of money and never made any money. I could never commit to one idea.

Instead of creating one business, one client base and one strong asset, I was jumping all over the place. Thinking- *well, something will work eventually*.

(Oh, and I will also tell you this- I tried the same with diets and nothing worked. I could not lose weight, even though most of my vision boards had pictures of slim models and women that looked exactly the way I wanted to look.)

To make it worse I would journal every day. What Elena? But journaling is good, isn't it? Yes, it is, if you do it the right way.

But in my case…oh boy. I would just randomly add a ton of different goals and tried to visualize a bit of everything.

Now when it comes to creating your LOA abundance vision and manifest the income level you want, the focus you need to adopt is the same kind of focus that the best businesspeople apply. Don't diversify too early and focus on creating strong assets. Better to have fewer assets but strong ones. You want assets that will work for you. In our case, assets that will lead to our ultimate manifestations that leave us speechless. How is that even possible?

In my career, I was blessed to work with very successful entrepreneurs (we are talking seven to eight-figure level entrepreneurs). They all told me the same thing. Most of them used to be stuck at the same income level. The money that would just allow them to pay the bills, business expense and taxes. They suffered because they could not grow, have the impact they wanted and have the sense of freedom and security that their businesses would not only survive but also thrive and change the world.

Their stagnation was due to the shotgun approach. Too many different projects and ventures, in the hope that something would take off. After all, the more the better, right? Why not diversify?

The more I studied money, and the law of attraction, the more patterns I saw. There are certain rules of both meaningful entrepreneurship/successful career and quantum physics that are basically the same. It's just that the human brain interprets them in a different way. The law is very simple- <u>the less you focus on the better</u>. Then you give it your full attention and it's really amazing!

Think about it…certain companies don't like employees who get a second job at their competitor company.

In my case, I used to run two unrelated businesses where I was trying to serve two different groups of people. It felt as if nobody would trust me because they didn't see me as an expert. Instead they saw me as someone who "tries to get their money" by doing a bit of everything.
Bad idea.

So…I started working with the mindset coach and got rid of the limiting belief that I am not good enough. I also stopped creating a ton of different vision boards and a ton of weak assets in the hope that something eventually would work. I just used to believe I wasn't at all worthy.

The moment I learned about my limiting beliefs, I was able to change my vision.
Like mentioned in my suggestions above, I booked a hotel in a new town for a few days. I disconnected from the internet.

I was all by myself in silence and spending lots of time in nature. I gave my brain a rest. I wasn't reading anything or listening to anything.
It was just me and my notebook.
Taking deep notes from my heart.

No stimulants, no caffeine. No alcohol. I also gave myself some time to meditate, get a massage, and eat healthy plant-based foods while also drinking fresh juices and clean water.

First two days I still didn't know exactly what I wanted. I had so much going on in my mind. But I knew one thing- I had to focus on ME. What would make ME happy.

ME. My feelings and my emotions. Not what I want or my desires.
You see, what you want is really a reflection of your feelings and emotions. Most people don't focus on their core but instead they just jump straight to creating a vision board. Using what I like to call a "rat race strategy".

Ok, lemme see. The Joneses got a new car, so let me go on Pinterest and find something and put it on my vision board and manifest it.

There is nothing wrong with wanting to have a nice car, I also like nice things. The question is- do you really care about that car? Maybe what you are really looking for is sense of freedom and wealth? Knowing that you have enough to get a nice "toy" when you please? But at the same not being too attached to it?

A former client of mine had a vision board with a beach house on it. I asked her, "Why did you put it there, how do you feel about it?"

She said, "Well, I guess my parents would like it."
I asked, "What makes you think so?

She said, "Because it's a house of someone who is successful and has a secure career. My parents would be proud of me if I had such a house."

Can you see where it's going?
After a deep talk we realized that she didn't even care about such a house. What she really cared about was establishing a stronger bond with her family and feeling accepted for who she is.

Keep asking yourself:
-*Why?*
-*Why do I want it?*
-*How does it make me feel?*

The second round of questions is:
-*Does it make me feel light?*
-*Does it make me feel heavy?*

In most cases, when you start off feeling heavy that vision is not your vision but someone else's. Other people may be quick at manifesting it, and maybe you thought you "could try too". Yes, you could, but is it right for you?

A friend of mine had different travel boards in her apartment. However, after a deep talk she realized that she wasn't really passionate about traveling but since many of her friends traveled a lot and knew a lot about different cultures and languages, she felt a bit unworthy. She felt that her knowledge about all those countries they would talk about was close to zero. She felt out of tribe. But honestly, she had no passion for it while on the other hand her friends were very passionate about languages and traveling. What she really wanted was to feel appreciated and that she was an expert at something. She just liked spending time with friends in her local area and would always be the last one to leave a bar while helping those who were going through relationship problems.

Today, that woman is a very well-paid relationship coach.
After diving deep, she changed her vision boards and aligned them more with her goals and visions instead of her friends'.

She kept visualizing the joy she would feel after helping people with their dating and relationship issues. She imagined getting "thank you" emails and text messages from people.

Finally, she decided to go all in to become an actual relationship coach. To this day she hates traveling! She loves connecting with her clients in person, in local cafes and bars. She has no problem attracting affluent clients and is creating a strong manifestation momentum really doing what she loves instead of just trying to chase other people's dreams.

Another former client of mine had vision boards of famous entrepreneurs and he thought he wanted to be like them. He tried so many businesses repeatedly. Why did he do it?

One of the reasons was that he thought that being an entrepreneur means you get famous and go on different podcasts and travel the world while meeting people. He also wanted to make money. However, once he learned how lonely entrepreneurship can get and about the sacrifices he would have to make, he realized that what would really make him happy was becoming an actor. He did. He gets to travel a lot, be interviewed on shows and he makes great money too. His first vehicle- entrepreneurship- did not really align with his vision but he had mistakenly believed that was his only way, to success.

After connecting with his emotions, he realized that he needed to change the vehicle as he was really spinning his wheels pursuing other people's dreams.

So, here's the task for you:
-Allow yourself some time off and get connected to your true feelings and emotions.
-Start off by asking yourself what would make you happy. Materialistic goals are fine if they are coming from you because you feel joy while being surrounded by the objects you want to manifest. However, if the root of your goal comes from insecurity and not feeling worthy or trying to impress the Jones' then I recommend you redefine your vision.
-After you have built those fundamentals in your imagination, set the intention to create a very simple and basic vision board, with just a few basic images that will not confuse your conscious and subconscious mind.

-Does it make you feel lighter or heavier? Of course, lighter should be the answer.
-Take care of your emotional state. Have an Epsom salt bath or get a massage if you have been having a stressful day. It's hard to align yourself with your vision if you're feeling stressed out and there is no point in creating vision board just for the sake of doing it.

Part 3 Law of Attraction to Make More Money

Mindset Shift #2 Grow Your "No" Muscle

After going through the first step and creating your new, simple yet revamped vision board, you will know what to focus on in terms of people and opportunities.

After that first step, most entrepreneurs I know get rid of certain projects to be able to focus on the one thing that truly aligns with their vision and passion.

People who seek a more exciting career opportunity suddenly get clarity about which company to submit their CV too.

Action doesn't feel like action because you are not forcing anything. It doesn't feel like hustle or hard work. It feels good and you are taking it from the place of abundance and confidence that you and your vision are one.

Suddenly you feel energized and empowered.
One of the early mistakes I made with LOA was the classical, "Let me just think about it and it will happen" mistake.

What I mean by that is that some people believe that it's enough to think and what they think about is just something random circumstance or object they wish they could manifest but nothing ever happens. As you already know, one of the reasons is because it wasn't truly theirs in the first place and deep inside, they don't care about it or think it will help them get rid of their insecurities. (Mindset work that we do here in this book will help you shift many of those insecurities and limiting beliefs so have no fear, my friend, I am with you.)

Another reason that it fails is that they think about what they want, but they act from a place of lack and scarcity. Because of that they soon lose motivation and don't do anything.

The best way to manifest is by what I like to call the Fused Alignment Method:
1. Your vision is your own and makes you feel lighter and super-happy.
2. You center your mindset around this belief, please repeat after me: *What I want already exists and I take a meaningful action to fuse myself with my vision and I love it.*
3. You take care of your energy and focus. The Universe is putting you to the test....
4. You take action in a powerful and meaningful way. Just don't do a mad shotgun approach, it will only spread your energy too thin. Instead feel like a powerful designer of your life. Maintain singular focus.
5. Let your emotions guide you. Listen to your gut. Are you making another logical decision? Because, you know, it makes sense and is the next step that you feel you are supposed to take? Do you feel as if it is being expected of you? Remember- if you're feeling heavy, and it doesn't feel right, chances are you are pushing your manifestations and deep desires away.

6. Learn to say *no* – when you decide to transform and to shift your mindset, you really need to control your mind and be very mindful of your time. That is why you need to learn to say *no* to people. Ask yourself, *can I afford it?* Your time is very valuable especially now that you are embarking on this new journey that later will allow you to help other people too. (Trust me, when you master the process I am teaching you thought this book, you really will feel like sharing it with other people.)

You want to be proactive and promise yourself to take care of your energy and focus. You really need to help yourself first.

Now, let's carry on…I know what you're thinking…
"Oh, Elena, but I still don't know how to manifest more money."

That's the thing…you need to let go of that thought for now.
For now, you need to focus on the clarity and vision.
It may come as you read this book a few more times.

You can empower yourself by controlling your time, focus and energy.
Simple example- I am a writer. I help and inspire people through the writing channel of creative self-expression.

I very often get asked by other writers, "Elena, how do you get ideas?" or "Elena, how do you get rid of writers' block?"

My answer is simple. I set an intention.
I never know exactly what I am gonna write, I just feel it.
I am not in the mindset of just sharing some information. I am in the mindset of providing you with tools for your transformation.

When I write, I manifest by creating, but that creation comes naturally. I don't need to try hard. Some may call it a *flow* or a *zen* state of mind. I am in motion. That motion helps me manifest. I forget about me and my desires and myself. I just focus on writing. I am aligned, and it feels like I am nowhere, but I am also somewhere. It just flows.

I did used to struggle with so-called writers' block. A negative review or a hate email would affect me and my writing.

Then, after doing some inner work, I began noticing patterns. Our minds very often repeat what we have learned through an environment that shaped us. So, for example, in the case of my writing, I remembered that the first lesson I ever got, the teacher would talk about the writer's block all the time and so did other writers. Because of that, I was in a mindset of "it's normal to feel blocked, all writers do".

Then I realized that it was not empowering me or my message. And I made a new decision: **I have a writer's flow.** So, I basically swapped *block* with *flow*. It has served me very well.
I focused on the bigger picture and on my mission. A part of me detaches from my writing so that I can transfer all my energy into the message that I am sharing. It's a very liberating flow and something that can be achieved in all areas of life. In fact, this book will guide you on how.

Why does it flow for me? I am not a talented writer. My vocabulary is basic, and I need an editor who heals my grammar when needed to make sure I create a quality product.

But I take care of my focus and energy and I am proactive.
I disconnect from the outer world and social media.

First of all, if my preferred channel of expression is writing books that can help you on your journey, I stick to that. I know people who organize workshops and that's great. Some people create a webinar and then offer coaching or a course, and that is fine too.

Imagine though if I tried to do all of it at once. I would not be aligned. I know people whose favorite form of self-expression is video or a podcast. For me, it's writing so I stick to that and I say *no* to anything else.

Also, every day I get some offer or other from a digital marketing company wanting to help me with this or that, but I don't want to lose my focus. People who find me through my books naturally enjoy this format of consuming content. It's as simple as that.

Same with health and fitness. I don't do any complicated diets. I eat a clean, mostly plant-based diet.
I jog every morning, five times a week and then I do yoga. That's it. I don't overcomplicate things as it would make me lose my focus. I would feel too stressed out with things I have to do.
And now I just focus on what I do, and it is my second nature.

The point of this is- learn to say *no* to things, circumstances and even people who do not align with your vision. You can still be kind and nice. There's no need to be arrogant as that's bad energy.

I usually say *no* with, "Dear…thanks for your offer. I really appreciate your time. As much as I would like to help, currently I need to stay focused on the projects I have already committed myself to. I am sure you will do amazingly well anyway. Love, Elena".

Mindset Shift #3 The Biggest Mistake Behind Finding Your *Why*

You have probably heard many self-help gurus talk about the importance of *why*. And yeah, it's totally true, but most people miss this point just like they miss the point of a truly aligned vision board.
So how to find your *why* specifically for the purpose of manifesting more money and abundance? How to get in a state of mind that will allow you to create your own template? So that with that template you can not only maintain your increased income but also keep manifesting more and more while feeling fulfilled.

The best exercise you can do is to think about your current income goal. Also, for most people, I would start off by doubling your current income as your goal. Not that I don't believe in unlimited abundance or tapping into your true potential. It's just that for most people coming up with huge goals when it comes to their income usually eliminates all their manifestations as their subconscious mind just doesn't get what is going on.

For example, if a person makes a minimum wage and sets a goal of making 1 million dollars a month, it's just a number and a goal. Your mind can't fully comprehend it, and not only your subconscious mind but even your conscious mind goes like- *ok time to go back to earth, this is not for me.*

And that makes you go back to the same old, same old. No matter how many millionaire vision boards or visualizations or affirmations you produce, your inner mechanism will rebel against this number.
That is why as a general rule I would start off with a goal that is your current income multiplied by two.

In some cases, you can make your current income tripled as your goal.
Is that it?

Nope. Because again your mind doesn't care about the numbers.
It cares about the feelings and experiences and about you already feeling as if you were in that reality. The trick? You must feel that way at least 80% of time. That is why you need to be aware of any negative voices, fear or self-doubt.

Your brain will try to put you off even setting your manifestation goal. The classical ways of it include making you look for excuses like:
-Oh, but when I make more money, I am gonna have to pay more taxes and get an accountant and that will be expensive.
- BOOM- a scarcity mindset sneaks in and you are basically done.

So here is the exact process I have used myself and I am always using to reach the new levels in my manifestations. Manifestation may take time. If it takes longer than you expected, the trick is to stick to your vision. Do not allow your behavior or negative thoughts pull you off track. Staying on track should not feel like a chore either.

1. First, you set a simple income goal. For example: your current income is 5 k a month and your goal is 10 k a month.
2. Now, since your mind doesn't really get the difference between those numbers, you want to take another approach. This is what I like to call Perfect Manifestation Fusion Method.
3. The Perfect Manifestation Fusion Method requires that you place all your focus on the experiences and feelings that earning 10 k a month and therefore doubling your income will give you.
4. As you go through this process remind yourself to be aware of all the negative patterns and self-sabotage that will sneak in. In case you find yourself with any negative thoughts that tell you are not worthy or deserving, make sure you spot the pattern and re-frame it.

For example:

Limiting belief:

But if I make more money, my friends will leave me.

New, empowering belief that will help you manifest faster:

My friends will be inspired by me. I will be able to help and support those around me. I am very grateful for who I am becoming.

Same with- *Oh, but I will need an accountant and it will be very complicated and taxes are expensive in my country.*

New belief:
There is always a solution and I deserve to be making 10 k a month or more. I believe in the flow of abundance. As I manifest more and more abundance, I spread it around by hiring people who offer me their help.

Or:
My new income is aligned to the new me who I am becoming right here, right now. The new me already exists and will take me to a new place a new country where I will be able to enjoy more abundance freely.

You see, you may be stuck in your old mindset. Many people worry about taxes, but in reality, the fact that you'll be paying more means that you'll be making more and contributing more. Think how your country can benefit from what you will be offering and you will see it in a different light.

Part 3 Law of Attraction to Make More Money

Then, I have also worked with people who, as soon as they started manifesting more money, decided to fulfill their dreams of moving abroad and setting down in a country with less taxation.
Either way, this is just a limiting belief and you need to center your mindset daily to make sure you are not sabotaging your manifestation.

>Ok, so now the next step- the most important one.

5. Now that you are making 10 k a month, what does your life look like? What do you feel, hear and see?
How do you design your day?
How do you help those around you? What clothes do you wear, where do you live? How do you contribute to your society? How does it feel to make your first big manifestation come true?

Now, what you want to do is to anchor to the feeling of manifesting and detach yourself from the amount of money you want to make.

The number is just a tool to temporarily help you shift to a new reality that you now believe it will help you create.

Be as specific as possible. What food do you eat? Where, and with whom? What do you do for a living? What does your work look like? How do you relax?

So again, instead of defining yourself as a 10 k a month earner you define your reality by feelings, emotions and experiences.

Later, as we go through many fascinating success stories of people using the system from this book, you will understand why feelings are most important than numbers.

I can still remember my disappointment after doing daily journaling and affirmation with the "I am making...a month" and nothing ever happened because of that. I was just spinning my wheels and focusing on lack, not on abundance.

Now center your mindset by aligning yourself with that scenery you have just created. Do it twice a day. Ideally, you want to do it early in the morning as you are just waking up and before you go to bed.
If you are too busy, or you feel burned out because you have tried a ton of LOA rituals in the past and found yourself spinning your wheels, or maybe you just like simple solutions, you just got one. Link your morning "feeling-visualization" practice (again both are great and if you are not a visual person, just feel it and don't worry about not being able to visualize as that puts too much stress on you and totally disconnects your manifestation).

So…link this new manifestation practice to your usual morning routine such as making and drinking coffee. I always do that.

You make your coffee and you align yourself with that new scenery you created while thinking what it would be like to double your income. You can also hold onto that feeling on your morning shower. Repeat in the evening. Personally, I like to have some herbal tea and do a short meditation before I go to sleep and so I link it to my vision.

One mistake that many people make with manifesting is that they get too attached to their income goal and don't focus enough on the feelings and lifestyle they believe it will give them. There are a few dangers of that:
-No manifestation or very slow one
-A quick spike in income and then plateau back
So, you basically do what I like to call a *quick buck manifestation* which is not bad. Everyone can do with more cash but…rather than instant or unexpected manifestations I prefer long-term secure manifestations that are deeply rooted in my vision. That allows me to make them a permanent lifestyle.
-Achieving the income goal and then getting stuck there. It happens to many entrepreneurs who start off with, "I want a 6-figure aka 10 k a month or more business". They write those goals all the time and hustle and grind.

(Now, I am not against the hard work. In fact, I work pretty hard myself, but I love what I do and it's not work at all, it's my flow and my passion… but if it kills your energy and flow and health, it can only lead to manifesting disease and anxiety rather than long-term wealth and happiness.)
Finally, they get to the desired 10 k a month. But since they programmed their minds for that number and linked so much emotions to it, they stay there.

To double their income to let's say 20 k a month using the same strategy they used before, it will take forever and will go together with lots of pain, anxiety and frustration.

I am not implying that I have a formula for some get-rich-quick manifestation or a spike. I am all for constant progress that keeps your energy where it needs to be in your particular case so that you don't burn out. That is why I always preach patience, belief and slower but constant growth and a more conservative approach compared to other LOA writers. Yes, I could manifest a quick spike in income by writing a book called *Instant Money Manifesting- Win a Lottery in 7 days or Less* but writing such a book and putting it on sale would be totally against my personal values and against my vision and would eventually turn against me.

When it comes to my teachings, I focus on long-term happiness. First, you need to set up a good foundation and re-connect with your truth. I am sure that with this book you will have many *aha* moments and discover a series of patterns that have perhaps prevented you from manifesting the fully abundant life you were meant to live.

Can you see where it's going?

You will not see me write any quick-buck manifestation book because none of these things is beneficial for the long-term (with the rare exception of someone needing money to help someone in need etc.) Then it's a different energy.

That being said- money is just paper.
So, the final step in this mindset shift and this chapter is very simple. Reconnect with the new you again, the you from another reality. The reality that already exists. The reality where you are making twice as much as money as you are making now.

At this stage you should be already detached from the number. Really, it doesn't mean anything.
Let me give you an example. A friend of mine went through this exercise. She was living on 3 k a month and her goal was 6 k a month. She kept stuck for years and she always had that 6 k or even 5 k in her mind. The way she was living was very close to poverty (according to North American standards).
She went through the exercise and saw herself with that desired income and the way she wanted to feel and live.

She wanted to wake up, do yoga and eat healthy food without worrying too much about having to save on food. Move to a sunnier part of the country where there is no depressing winter and where she could enjoy the beach. She was very specific in creating that vision and kept re-connecting herself with it twice a day just like I suggest in this book. She would even play a song with that, so it all seemed like a beautiful video she was watching on YouTube, something that really got stuck in her mind.

Finally, she completely forgot about the numbers, focused on being grateful for her humble living and had the courage to carry on doing the exercise from this chapter.

Do you know what happened? Something that had never occurred to her before. She fell in love with a man who was moving to Thailand and she moved with him. They started an online business together and now she's approaching a much bigger income than she originally wanted.

But you know what the best part is?

When she first moved to Thailand, all she had were some savings. While there, building an online business with her partner, she was able to live well and do exactly what she had intended to do in her original vision.

Wake up, do yoga, eat healthy food, swim in a nice pool and enjoy the beach. And she was doing that for only 1 k a month. That's the best part!

Before she started transforming with the methods I am sharing with you in this book, she was too fixated on that 6 k a month goal. She believed it was the only way for her to enjoy what she wanted- the yoga, healthy food, more freedom but also security, sunshine and the beach. She believed it would only happen on a holiday anyway. She manifested so much more though.
I could write an entire book filled with stories like hers which I might do if you ask me to (let me know in the review section of this book as the stories alone could be the second part).

Now this is supposed to be a short read, so I want to keep it to the point!
I hope that by now you understand how it works.

So, how to use that process to find your why? A truly compelling why.
Re-connect with that vision again. Your feelings and emotions of you making twice as much as you are making now.

This is happening right now.

Now ask yourself- *Who am I?*
Why do I DESERVE to be living it?
Answer (example):
I deserve to eat healthy food.
I deserve to live a peaceful life.
I deserve to feel aligned on the beach every day.
I deserve to be able to contribute to my community.
I deserve to be wearing nice clothes.
I deserve to be dining at nice, healthy plant-based food restaurants.
I deserve to have a personal chef.
I deserve to be a good leader.

Etc. etc.
Whatever you put on that statement is your why and the new more empowered version of yourself. It's who you are and so in alignment with it that you are already living that reality and taking actions that connect you to it.
Another why?

People you care about...
So again...re-connect with that feeling and emotion and start with:

My family deserves to travel to new countries at least twice a year.
My children deserve to eat healthy food.

Keep going! If you start crying don't worry. It's a good sign and it may actually help you get rid of some blocked emotions.

Now, that super strong and compelling why is a real why.

The real why.
Your why is not: *"Oh because I have to manifest this amount of money a month."*
That is just some illusion that will keep you away from manifesting.
So, center your mindset and emotion on your feelings and use it to re-connect with your why. Your why. You will be surprised by the results!

Part 3 Law of Attraction to Make More Money

Mindset Shift #4 The LOA KISS Method

Honestly, most people overcomplicate LOA...and I am not judging as I have been there too. I was a victim of way too many pretty much redundant rituals that led to nothing as far as powerful manifesting goes.

Now, you already know that you can link your daily visualization and feeling practice to an already existing habit you enjoy, for example- drinking coffee or having a nice, relaxing shower or bath. Live your experiences with your mind and already feel grateful.

In case your mind starts going with negative questions like: *What if I fail?*
Turn it around to: *What it will feel like when I succeed?*

Be aware of any negative patterns, thoughts, and circumstances as well as people that may appear in your life to test you.

Promise yourself to be stronger than that, after all... now you have your *why*. You know what is already yours and what you deserve.

Also, while it's good you share what you learn with those around you, in fact, it is my intention for you, I also recommend that you avoid sharing this process with people who are toxic or negative. Don't judge them, send them love and be kind, but make sure you protect yourself and your manifestations from negativity whether intentional or unintentional.

At the same time, if you are feeling guilty about having to hide from some people instead of being open and transparent about what you do, let me tell you this- some people come to your life for a reason, and eventually, they will learn from you.

However, the way those people will learn is through Indirect LOA Inspiration.

They will witness your transformation, and they will get inspired. They will need no words or explanations. They will then come to you and put themselves in the position of students rather than skeptics or critics.

Trust me, it happened to me many times, and each time it gets better.
At the same time that mindset shift will help you get rid of any negative emotions and the feeling of being a victim or feeling judged. (This distracts many people from abundant manifestations too).

Part 3 Law of Attraction to Make More Money

Mindset Shift #5 The Most Powerful Word for a Bad Day (aka Your Manifestation Bridge)

What we are working on right now is your own Manifestation Bridge.
A bridge between where you are right now and where you want to go. Now, here's the thing- that bridge is you, and you need to take good care of yourself, both physically and emotionally.
At this stage, you will be put to the test on a pretty much daily basis.

There will be many negative voices in your head. Some people around you also get negative. It is now your mission to protect your vision and construct the bridge, and that bridge is the new you. The latest version of you. Stronger and more empowered.

The one word you need to remind yourself of whenever feeling you're are sliding down to the path of self-pity, guilt or any negativity is *Courage*.

I have that word written down on my vision board, and I have a courage card in my wallet. It's also a background for my phone and computer. I get reminded of that word many, many times. *Courage. Courage. Courage.*

You need that courage to create that great bridge and be able to repeat the process so that you are continually moving to new levels of manifestations.

The first times are always a bit harder, and there are more fears and doubts. Your old self will try to fight it back. You see, I won't lie to you, we are our own biggest obstacles when it comes to our manifestations. I was, yet I was blaming everyone else (more about that later).

Manifestation is not a linear process. All you need to be doing is continually aligning yourself with the feeling and emotion of your vision. The feeling can be backed up by affirmations, journaling, and meditations as well as visualizations. But these are just tools. You already know that your vision and the emotion you attach to it is the most potent thing you need to focus on. In fact, sometimes you need to go back to this very first step in this process.

Then there is also patience. Whenever you are getting impatient make sure to re-align yourself to the feeling of your vision. And the best part is: going through those feelings with a smile on your face is what helps you manifest for the long-term.

Courage, courage, courage.

Remember my friend? The one who was making 3 k a month and had a "goal" of 6 k a month?
By the way, the money income goal is now out because we know that it's just a number and a part of setting up the initial process of reconnecting to your vision and emotion.

So, as you already know my friend was going through the practices and methods described in this book.
And she had that particular freedom-sunshine vision, right?

On a conscious and linear level, if someone had asked her back then, "OK, so how do you think you can earn more money?" She would have said, "Well, get a better job. Maybe invest in my education so that I can get a better job. Maybe learn about creating my own business. Or keep my job and start a side business to make more income. Or maybe, win the lottery, or perhaps some unknown relative leaves me money."

These were all that I like to call *conscious clues*, and while these are all legitimate vehicles to earn income, the best way that will be your ultimate and long-term manifestation that will really change your life is never that simple to express.

It appears eventually after going through the initial *Build the Bridge Phase*. One of the crucial elements is what I like to call *The Taste of Manifestation*.

Let me give you an example because at this stage it's probable you may not be following me, and I don't blame you for that.

That information may be hard to swallow at first.

My friend followed precisely what I am teaching in this book. She created a vision that would make her happy and kept aligned and re-connected with that vision, twice a day. Morning and evening. Also, she did it very often during the day too as she was so excited about it. At the same time, she kept saying the word *courage* whenever negative thoughts would sweep in, and this would help her shift from frustration to gratitude and from fear to courage.

At that time, she didn't know that within one year she would be in another country, living her dream life on less money and in addition to that living with the man of her dreams. (He came as another manifestation due to her being courageous as you will soon find out.)

And...she could never have expected that within two years of her getting started with this process she would be running an online business, together with her partner. A company that eventually took them to multiple six figures. She had no idea about those opportunities back then, but one thing would lead to the next.

I call it *the LOA Domino Effect*. I love it.

You see, you need to pay close attention to what is happening around you. The best way to do it is to start testing your dream reality. Why? It's like a test drive. During those tests, as you examine

your dream reality while still in your old one, your state and emotional wellbeing shift even more, and you start attracting what I like to call *Powerful Manifestation Messengers*.
Now, those messengers may be ordinary people who don't feel like they are on a mission. For them, they are in their default reality doing their own thing. But the Universe aligns them with you for a reason.
My friend spent the initial three months with no significant changes or manifestations in her life.

Still, she religiously stuck to the process I have described earlier in this book and also in this chapter. She was still technically at the same income level. But deep inside she already believed and felt her new reality and felt ready to test it. At the same time, she completely detached herself from her income goal and focused on her feelings instead.

Please note - I am not saying you should forget about the money, stop paying your bills or don't file your taxes. Needless to say, because of the dimension we live in, you need to keep an eye on that.
I am referring to your emotions and to your emotional attachment to numbers. In most people that attachment is not healthy because it comes from a place of scarcity, lack, and insecurity.
I am not good enough now at my current income. But when I manifest this level, then I will be good, and everyone will love me for it.

That is a dead end, my friend. It's a vicious cycle that will never lead to fulfillment. What happens then is endless hustle, fear, and scarcity.

So back to our friend. She knew she had to taste her ideal reality. To do that, she decided to go for a quick solo trip for a few days to the south of the country and enjoy the beach.

At first, she came up with an excuse:
Man, I can't afford it. It's expensive. Yeah, I can get another job or extra shifts at work, but then I will run out of money.

Luckily, she quickly reminded herself of *Courage*.

And so, for a few weeks, she took an extra job as a babysitter and saved up money to be able to go on her short solo trip, taste the sunshine, beach and healthy food and participate in a yoga workshop.
Many of her family and friends thought she was crazy.

"If your goal is to make more money, it's better for you to save that money and use it for a college or certification so that you can later get a better job." This was the most common advice from family and friends.

That was also what she heard in her head and was stuck with for an extended period. She tried that route before. She'd tried different professional courses yet could never find the passion or fulfillment she needed to keep her going.

"Stop wasting money on travel. It's almost Christmas, can you afford to waste so much money now?" her mom kept saying.
But...My friend kept saying to herself, *Courage. Courage. Courage.*

Don't get me wrong. Her family and friends were worried about her and were giving her a piece of solid advice that they believed was the best. And yeah, it makes sense if you employ a linear way of thinking. *I need this to get this and that to go there and then I will be happy, whole and complete.* (Very often it doesn't end that well even if a person manages to earn the desired income level. It usually ends with burnout, some chronic disease or anxiety that take at least a few years of intense work to heal.)

Ok, back to my friend, off she went to the south and guess what?
It was there that she met her partner. Love at first sight.

A few months after, they both moved to Thailand. After tasting her dream reality, the *Manifestation Messenger* appeared. (In her case, it was her true love). I always tell her that was like a second manifestation.

Maybe it was because of all the courage she put in at the beginning?

You already know how the story ends. By totally immersing herself in her dream reality (even though at first her income dropped because she quit her job and lived off her savings and while in Thailand teaching English to make some money). But it was a temporary "sacrifice." Giving up the old to be ready for the new.

I use inverted commas for the word "sacrifice" because again, amongst us "manifesters" it's not really a sacrifice, but someone coming from a linear world would not get it.

If your goal is 6 k and your job pays you 3 k, and now you quit, how will you ever reach that goal? Goal. Hustle. Attachment. Strong emotional attachment and carrying too much of other people's opinions.

Also, please note, this is an unusual story. And yes, a person with children and family obligations may not be able to move overseas. That is not the point of this chapter. That story simply illustrates an example, and everyone is different and will have a different story.

By being courageous and sticking to your vision that you already know is yours and then really feeling it, you feel ready and entirely worthy and deserving to taste your dream reality even before you are prepared.

From there, you attract *Manifestation Messengers*. In some cases, they are not people but simply circumstances (and in some cases, they may be perceived as bad, for example losing your job may lead you to get a new better one or changing your career while aligning yourself with your passion).

Still, the *Manifestation Messengers'* goal is to show you the new reality you deserve and make sure you get there as soon as possible.

Another example- another friend of mine had a goal of making a certain amount of money that would allow him to have a nice sports car. He just loves cars.

He had this vision. He drives a car with his wife they go to beautiful places together, and he feels sunshine on him. Again, he was living in a pretty cold part of the country. For years he "tried to be successful" and "do whatever it took" and "hustle" to get that dream car.

In reality, it wasn't just about the car. He wanted to feel free, be creative, live in a warm climate and have a job that would give him the flexibility of time to spend with his wife.

He worked in the software development department of a big company that always kept him on the brink of getting that promotion. Yet something would always happen, and they would give it to someone else. He worked harder and harder. Long hours and business trips that felt very lonely. He did not feel worthy or appreciated and felt envious of guys who not only had a nice car but also had time to enjoy it with family and friends.

When he came to me for help, he was on the brink of an emotional breakdown. Still, we worked through the process and created his vision. Because of his technical, logical background at first he had difficulty with focusing on his feelings and emotions.

Eventually, he was able to allow the manifestation flow to kick in and just feel courageous. He gave up linear thinking altogether.

It turned out that his technical career did not excite him at all. Years ago, he had chosen that route as he felt he could get a secure engineering job and make his dad happy.

What he was passionate about was creativity, marketing, organizing events, having fun while meeting new people. He also really enjoyed writing, and that was a helpful tool for him to reconnect with his vision. I have noticed that different people prefer different tools. Some like to sit and visualize, some want to sit and write out their vision every day, in the present tense and feel grateful for it. Some people like affirmations.

Some people go hardcore and do all the techniques. Which can be great if it's done from a place of passion, joy, and curiosity but never works if a person does it because they feel impatient and want to desperately speed up the whole process to impress themselves or other people.

Back to my friend. He religiously kept going through the simple *reconnect to your vision* exercise, morning and evening.

Eventually, he felt ready to taste his dream reality.

He took his family on a short vacation to the sunny south and rented his dream car for taste rides. One of those rides led him to meet someone who invited him to a business conference. At that conference he met the CEO of a very creative marketing company where they were looking for someone with software development experience to help them develop a new product.

He took that job which led him to move to a more beautiful, sunnier city. In his new career he felt much more appreciated although the pay was a bit lower at first than in his old job.

Still, he was already testing his new reality.

The new company he worked for really admired his dedication and work ethic as well as other talents and skills he demonstrated outside of his primary field of expertise. Now he's an Executive Marketing Director, and aside from an excellent salary and benefits he also has a company car. This is what happens when you abandon linear thinking and understand that long-term manifestations do require some courage and sincere belief.

The initial transformation may also require some sacrifice and the leaving of your comfort zone. Now, this is a taboo topic among most LOA teachers and writers. Honestly, though, the old model where you just focus on the techniques (meditate, visualize, affirm) without getting to the root of the problem is not effective at all. It's all about understanding why you want what you want. Then you can focus on the feeling and the root (the reason why you really want something) and you transcend the desire with peace of mind. That peace of mind comes from knowing that what you want is already yours.

For example, I am writing this book, and in my writing, I may go against some societal norms or even what many LOA gurus or writers teach. That requires courage. I know that someone may send me a hate email. This has happened before and probably will happen again. But I don't focus on that. Instead, I reconnect with the feeling of joy and happiness I get whenever I get a *thank you* email or review from a happy reader. That feeling helps me overcome a bad day when perhaps I don't feel like writing.

Yet I drink my coffee, I reconnect with that feeling, I meditate, or if I happen to travel, I just have my coffee on the beach and then write from a coffee shop or a hotel.

When I am on that track, I can already taste my New Reality. In this case, it's the new reality of the creation I am bringing to life which is this book.

I am not focusing on what could go wrong. That would stop me from taking meaningful action. Instead, I keep aligning myself with my vision and my new book is also getting aligned with its original vision and mission. I think of it as a separate entity that I am teaching this process to even though it's my creation.

However, to create it, and to enjoy the process, I need to take care of my energy and detach myself from the vanity of metrics and numbers.
Last week someone wrote to me and asked me how to launch a bestselling book with a certain number of reviews.
I politely replied that it's never been my goal. When writing, I focus on creating value for my readers. I detach myself from the time too. I don't stress out about writing less on a given day. When I write- I write, and it flows. Some days I write more and, on some days, less. I do not impose any artificial goals and get stressed out about all those vanity metrics.

Of course, these are vanity metrics for me. Other people may genuinely enjoy setting their own goals in their own ways and aim to have a certain number of ratings and reviews on their book's page. Maybe they want to write a certain number of words each day and stick to that. That's fine if it suits them. My goal here is not to judge.

Your manifestation starts with your awareness. Ask yourself, are you too busy with the linear process and vanity metrics? Can you really align with them? Where do they actually lead you?
Finally, I highly recommend you do what my friends did:
1. Center your mindset daily, preferably twice a day, by focusing on your feelings, that is, the feeling you get when you align with your vision.
2. Ask yourself- what can you do to taste your new reality right here right now? Treat it as a temporary mini manifestation that is entirely under your control. Some people may call you crazy, that's fine, it's their opinion, opinions are not objective. Stay aligned with your vision.
3. When you do allow yourself the taste of your dream reality, it's quite possible you will come across your *Manifestation Messenger* or *Messengers*. In some cases, they may manifest as objects, circumstances, animals, or something you will merely feel is a sign.
   In some cases, it may be even something that always happens, yet you never valued it or never perceived it as your *Manifestation Messenger*.

Tasting your dream really is a fantastic step, and there is no reason you should deprive yourself of it.
Get back to the earlier pages of this book and read the inspiring stories of my friends and clients if you need to. At this stage, though, you should focus on yourself, your long-term vision and ultimate manifestation.

Part 3 Law of Attraction to Make More Money

Mindset Shift #6 Own Yourself

When it comes to manifesting, most people focus on what they want to manifest and how to go about it.

However, the most often overlooked point is – *what place are they manifesting from?*
What about you? What place are you manifesting from?
A place of abundance or scarcity?
A place of confidence or fear?

A place where you are already feeling whole and complete or one of *"I will be happy when…"*?
For me, personally, it was a big pill to swallow. I used to feel like a victim all the time. Whatever happened to me, it was always someone else's fault.

It felt more comfortable and, as the years went by, I became addicted to feeling like a victim. It became my pattern. I would apply that pattern all the time to all areas of my life.
I would sabotage my health thinking, "Yeah, I may try this diet but what's the point if in my family everyone puts on weight easily?

And yeah, I had hypnosis for weight loss, some healthy cookbooks, a ton of meal plans, a gym membership and more guided hypnosis. I was thinking I was doing everything, and I would even brag that I take the holistic approach. But it did not work, so I blamed my family and their genes and also the creators of the books and courses I purchased.

It was only when I realized that I was in a victim mindset and decided to switch to an owner mindset that I was able to transform. I suddenly felt grateful for all the years I had been overweight because they had allowed me to understand and shift my victim mindset and create a grateful owner mindset instead.

I know people who have been through much more pain, rejection and suffering in their lives than I have.

Yet they have managed to turn that suffering into something meaningful, something that helps other people and at the same time helps them become abundant creators and owners.

I was also a victim in my relationship, and it was always someone else's fault. And yeah…if you have ever been in an abusive relationship, I know how you feel right now. I totally understand it's hard. The thing is, you may technically be a victim, but you can choose to be an owner instead. Whatever happened to you happened for a reason. You can transform it into something positive. The book I would recommend for this matter is *Man's Search for Meaning* by Viktor E. Frankl.

Now back to manifesting money and abundance...why do you need to switch from a victim mindset to an owner mindset?

As Tony Robbins once said, "Life doesn't happen *to* you it happens *for* you."
Challenge yourself every day to center your mindset around it. Whenever you find yourself thinking- why is it taking so long, why am I not manifesting yet? Why am I always stuck in a traffic jam, why this and that, ask yourself- why is it happening for me? What is it trying to tell me?

Oh, yeah, it's taking so long because I am supposed to master the process. Makes sense. Actually, I am grateful for that. I will master the process. I am learning.

Traffic jam? Ah, right, it's a sign that I need to start waking up earlier. I was thinking of allowing myself to go through a fantastic LOA morning ritual where I can meditate, align with my vision, workout to lift my energy and vibration and even make a healthy plant-based breakfast. I can be up early, leave for work early, be at work early, and when I am there I can inspire others and attract new opportunities. I have a friend who started doing that after changing his perception of traffic jams and thanks to that he got a promotion and a pay rise. The boss was on the fence about choosing him or somebody else, but the other person kept coming in late and blaming traffic jams.

My friend would be ahead of time and ready to shoot off and work with full focus at 9 AM when the work would start.

Promotion led him not only to get a pay rise but also learning new skills. Eventually, he quit his job to start his own business with his own team. He now successfully leads that team, and the business he has is much more aligned with his passion than his old job. While in the job he was grateful and showed up ahead of time and set an example to other colleagues. He stuck to his rules. He also discovered that he had so much more energy after waking up earlier.

Look, if you're like me and you were born into a poor family, don't feel like a victim. It's your advantage and competitive edge. You are the owner.

You are a fantastic human being and thanks to whatever happened to you, you feel stronger and more aligned with your vision. Be grateful for your past. It led you to where you are now and on this journey of amazing self-development. Right now, you are reading this book because of the reason. That reason is whatever happened to you made you who you are (or who you're becoming). Had your life always been perfect you would not have bothered to progress and develop your consciousness and awareness.
To finish off this chapter ask yourself:

When do I feel like a victim? Has feeling like a victim prevented me from manifesting in the past?
How can I shift to the owner mindset today?

Be aware of what thoughts you are thinking. Reframe them. That will allow you to stay stronger and more aligned with your vision. The suffering was just a little step to make you stronger. It was just a test. You are on a long-term manifestation journey- remember that!

And let me quote Tony Robbins again: "Life doesn't happen *to* you, it happens *for* you".
In case you still feel like a victim or find it hard to get rid of negative addictive emotions and thoughts I would recommend you check out Dr. Joe Dispenza's books and meditations. They helped me tremendously.

The exercise for this step is to write down all the situations where you have felt like a victim. Then, rewrite them in a more powerful way. First, focus on some experience from the past and then move on to your current situation and the circumstances that you feel may be blocking you right now.

Example:
Old belief:
I got fired from my job.
I had to degrade my lifestyle.
I felt horrible. I mean who does that? I studied hard and I worked hard.
All companies are the same. They don't care about human beings.

New belief:
Losing my job was the best thing that ever happened to me.
I got inspired to change my career, and in between even though I had to degrade my lifestyle and went through some financial difficulties, I found myself with lots of free time.
I used that time to focus on my passion and align myself with my new vision.
This eventually led me to get a new job, and I manifested some unexpected commissions.
It did happen for me, and I am so thankful.

Old victim belief:
All men/women are the same. I gave it my all in my last relationship. I gave up my family and friends, and I completely changed my lifestyle and schedule to fit in my ex-partner's. I can't believe he/she left me. Who does that? They did not appreciate me at all.

New empowering belief:
At first, it was hard to understand why my ex-partner broke up with me but eventually it led me to learn a ton of things about myself.
Yes, the initial break up stage was hard, but it inspired me to re-connect with some old friends, and I also began working with a therapist. I now understand that I can't sacrifice my own happiness to make other people happy. I felt like it happened to me for a reason and I am so grateful for it.

Now I am in a fantastic relationship, and I communicate better while making sure there is a healthy balance, and nobody feels like a victim. Full trust.

Oh, and congrats! You are halfway through, and the rest of the steps in this manifestation method will be shorter and more straightforward.

The first part of the book was definitely the most challenging one, and it's where you were supposed to experience the greatest number of breakthroughs.

However, if you are still feeling like you may be lacking clarity for your plan of action, I recommend you re-read all the previous steps.

Part 3 Law of Attraction to Make More Money

Mindset Shift #7 The Resourceful Method

The best manifestation success story from this book is the double manifestation my friend experienced. Not only money but also the love of her life.

However, to get where she got, she had to be resourceful. For example, she wanted to test her dream reality by making a short solo trip to the south of the country, and she had no money for that. Well, what she did was to offer a cleaning service in her area. It wasn't the best long-term solution, and she had to use her spare time to clean other people's houses to be able to afford that dream trip. However, as she was going through that process, she felt happy, grateful, aligned and centered. A few days after her doing two jobs, she manifested a mini bonus payment from her main job, which was the first time it had ever happened at the company she worked for.

Those things always take place when you are grateful, center your mindset daily and commit yourself to be resourceful. That means no moaning and no complaining!

You already know that EVERYTHING happens for you, not to you.
You already know that the opportunity is abundant.
So now, it's your turn. How resourceful are you?
What are you willing to sacrifice?

Do you feel like you may be wasting your time on activities that do not align with your vision?
Do you feel like there are certain activities that even though are not super-sexy at first glance, may help you get closer to your vision, or can help you to test your dream reality faster?

Are you willing to accept certain temporary sacrifices while enjoying them, with a smile on your face?
Remember- it all happens *for* you. The opportunities around us are very abundant and have always been that way. The problem is when we overcomplicate things with our conscious, analytical minds. It's time to say *no* to that craziness and negativity and focus on your manifestations.

In my case, for example, I knew I wanted to work with a mindset coach, and I had to invest some money in his coaching.

You already know what my situation was.... broke.
But I knew I needed his guidance to help me break through my own limitations and I just had the feeling that this was the missing part on my journey. I spent a weekend with a pen and notebook looking for ideas to generate extra income.

Here's what I did:
-I sold some old items on eBay.

-I organized a small workshop for children, teaching drawing (everyone has something they can teach in their local community).
-I offered a simple design service online.
-I offered a few Spanish classes to a friend who was moving to Spain and needed to polish up his Spanish.

While none of those mini side jobs made me manifest large amounts of money, they allowed me to gather some side income and focus on my next step which was deep inner work with a coach.

I did not moan or complain like I surely would have before I began experiencing my transformation. Plus, I genuinely enjoyed all those mini jobs and felt good about offering a quality service. I did not care at all about what other people were saying: "Elena is losing her mind. She is now unemployed, and obviously she can't find a real job anywhere."

I just focused on what made sense to me. Again, opportunities are abundant. When you stay aligned with your vision, going through temporary sacrifices makes total sense.

And you know what? This is REAL gratitude. You stay in motion, and you move forward. You show up. You also show the Universe that you are committed, and that you really want to taste your dream reality while at the same time having faith in the Universe to offer you the best solution for your situation.
Now it's your turn. How can you move to a more resourceful mindset?

And, most importantly, how can you become more aware of the situations where you give up or complain and become a resourceful manifestor instead?

Mindset Shift #8 Your LOA Stamina to Keep Believing & Achieving

Those who don't manifest give up too soon.

I know it's harsh...but any investment takes time and so does re-programming your mind. What I recommend you focus on at this stage of your journey are even more alignment exercises. Stay aligned with your vision and that feeling. It's already happening. Right here. Right now.

Set a series of reminders on your phone and use them to re-connect with your big vision at least a few times a day.

Long-term manifestations do take time and consist of a meaningful combo of the law of attraction with the law of action.

Do not allow anyone to distract you. You need to stay extremely focused, and it's thanks to the focus that you will be able to develop what I like to call your LOA muscle, and that is amazing.

It's one of the intentions I have for you. I want you to master the process and feel confident about it.
As an exercise for this short chapter, I highly recommend that you do the following:

Ask yourself, when was the last time you really wanted something to manifest but eventually since it was taking more time than you originally envisioned, you decided to quit? Or maybe, you were even feeling like, *that may not be for me.*

Remember, you are a remarkable human being. Never ever allow yourself to settle for less than you can be, do or have.

Your potential is unlimited. To fully unleash it you need time and clarity. If you already know what you want and have a vision you can align to via your feelings, emotions and actions, not by some meaningless numbers, vanity goals or empty promises, then you are already on your way to manifesting whatever you want.

Any challenges and obstacles are just a test created by the Universe to, first, see if you really want what you are asking for. It's also a LOA gym to help you grow that LOA muscle. That way, next time you can create an unlimited manifestation momentum that will create real miracles in your life. Another thing I recommend you do is to start asking the Universe for patience. Do it at least a few times a day. Ask for endurance, energy, and strength. That is the sign of alignment, surrender and a deep belief. At the same time, be sure to take this action from a place of abundance and confidence, not from a place of a scarcity. Don't be like, "I am not good enough SOS Universe do something for me ASAP".
Make sense?

Mindset Shift #9 Abundant Mindset Mastery

How do you feel when you spend money?
For example, when you pay for a car repair, or pay your bills or buy food. Do you feel like, "Heck, why is it getting more and more expensive?"

If that's you, it's time to change this mindset.

From now on, whenever you pay for something, whether it's paid by cash, credit card, bank transfer or any other means, on or offline, swap the feeling of scarcity with the sense of gratitude.

"Wow, it's great I can just buy food. It saves my time. It's great I can buy clothes, I wouldn't even know how to make my own. Oh, and I am so grateful I just paid the water and electricity bill. Thanks to that I can live in a comfortable way. Many people on this planet can't even experience such a luxury so why would I complain about it?"

Exercise 1- go through the same process yourself.
Remind yourself of at least three situations where you recently spent money, even on some basic stuff. Now ask yourself how you can be grateful for that while practicing an abundance mindset.
Here's another mindset shift. From now on, it's absolutely prohibited for you to say, "I can't afford it." Now, you only want to say, "How can I afford it?" The best part is that now we will re-modify the first exercise and practice gratitude for the items, objects, and experiences we haven't technically purchased yet.

Exercise #2
Think of three random items or experiences (for example, some trips) that you currently want. Imagine that you buy them, pay for them, feel the money or the credit card in your hand and be grateful. Feel it.

Now make sure you add that feeling to your daily alignment that you know is the best practice you can focus on, at least twice a day.

Finally, ask yourself- how are you taking action? Is it from a place of abundance or scarcity? For example, my friend took a second job cleaning people's houses, but she did it from a place of absolute bliss and abundance. She not only felt grateful as she was getting paid that extra money that allowed her to go on a short vacation and unexpectedly manifest the man of her dreams. She also felt grateful while doing the job. Again, it wasn't her passion, but she knew it was a part of the process. You can be always passionate about the process, accept it and surrender to it fully while taking inspired action from a place of abundance.

She did not take action from a place of being a victim, saying, "I am a loser. I's not fair that I need to work two jobs to be able to go on a holiday. It's not my fault that the university is so expensive.

My parents could never afford to pay for my education. I can't believe my wages are so low I need another job."

Can you see a difference? How does that apply to your situation?
Are you taking action from a place of abundance or scarcity?
Whatever LOA practice you are doing…are you acting from a place of abundance or scarcity?
Remember- you are good enough now. Make sure you re-write all your story right here right now to make sure you are taking action from a place of abundance.

Fill in the gaps:
I ………am feeling whole and complete right here right now.
I take meaningful action from a place of abundance.
I deserve to live an abundant life.
Life happens for me, not to me.
I am grateful and proactive. I am and so I can. I unleash my full potential.
Money is abundant and whenever I have the opportunity to offer cash for someone's product or service, I feel aligned with my vision and ultimate joy.

Enjoy this one, it's a real game changer!

Part 3 Law of Attraction to Make More Money

Mindset Shift #10 Be on the Other Side

Give, give, give and be kind while giving.
That one used to be very challenging for me. I had those voices in my head...*Elena, how can you give more if you don't have enough yourself? You're on the verge of going on unemployment benefits. It's scary...*

Yes, it was, but I did not let that feeling get me off my vision. First, I looked at some items I had around the house, some things I could just donate to a charity. Then I decided to create a simple micro habit and started giving money to causes I wanted to support. Whenever I could do that, I felt so grateful.
As Bob Proctor says, "Money must circulate."

I wholeheartedly agree with that statement. The more you give, the more you receive. By giving you are sending out a signal to the Universe that you are already feeling whole, complete and abundant and are no longer on a scarcity vibration.

While you don't have to donate everything you have got, be sure to assign a certain amount of money, weekly and monthly and stick to it. As you start making more money- raise it. For best results, be sure to combine your donations with random acts of kindness. Do something to put a smile on other people's faces. Right now, you are stepping into the higher, and more divine version of you. You will feel like a different person.

What you can also do is take some spare food or make sandwiches and give the food away to your local homeless shelter or give it away to the homeless people you may encounter on the streets. Never stop giving. When you stop giving you stop receiving.

Be proactive. There is always a way to give something to someone even if right now you cannot do it directly by sending money to someone. Just focus on the abundance mindset and ask yourself how you can be a better giver.

Add it to your prayers. Now you ask the Universe for energy, patience, focus and you also ask how to be a better giver. Enjoy!

Part 3 Law of Attraction to Make More Money

Mindset Shift #11 The Invisible Force That Makes You Fail or Succeed (and how to use it to manifest what you want)

Aside from the word *courage* I warmly invite you to get into an empowering habit of repeating *I can, I am* as often as you can.

You see, the manifestation process is connected to your self-image. If deep inside you think that wealth and abundance are not for you, you will not be able to attract what you want. Luckily there are certain mindsets and even lifestyle exercises you can start applying to help you transform your self-image:

-Keep reminding yourself of *I can, I am* throughout the day.
-Remember that you are already feeling whole and complete.
- Consciously decide to do things differently as if you were a new person. Go to a party you usually wouldn't go to. Do your hair differently.
-Every day look yourself in the mirror and remind yourself of how grateful you are to be you.

Finally, take a piece of paper, or use your LOA journal and write down your name with 2_0 next to it.
Example: Elena 2_0

Now, re-connect with your vision. Get into that fantastic feeling because the reality you want to manifest already exists.

Now ask yourself- *Who am I in that new reality*? Have an objective look at the new You. Imagine you are a stranger and look at the new, transformed version of yourself.

How do you behave? What do you wear? Who do you hang out with? What do you eat? Where do you live? Where do you travel?

Now ask yourself- *What action can I take to fuse myself with that new, more empowered version of myself?* Right now, you are getting closer and closer to the art of meaningful manifestations. You are moving way beyond your current reality and massively increasing your vibration by merely changing your mindset and tuning into your feelings and emotions. You are transcending your old self and your old reality. As you keep going through these steps, you may attract more *Manifestation Messengers*. Things will be different. By aligning yourself with the new more empowered version of yourself, you are experiencing similar heights as when tasting your dream reality. Enjoy!

Mindset Shift #12 Your Net Worth Starts with Self-Worth

Please note that this step may be a bit uncomfortable, especially if you are like me and you are coming from a poor family where money was scarce, and everyone would always look for the cheapest option out there and the most discount.

If that is your case, it may take some time to go through it. But here's what you need to understand: your buying behaviors will always reflect in your money attracting abilities.

I know, I know, you are probably wondering- *But Elena, what must I do if I am really broke right now? How can I afford to buy more expensive items instead of living on the cheapest things possible?*

It's simple. If that's your case, create just one simple ritual. For example, allow yourself that once a week, or once a month, you will break away from old patterns and buy a more expensive item, just to experience the feeling of being a premium customer.

When you do that, get back to the abundance mindset and think- *Wow, someone on the other side had a fantastic money manifestation idea and they are not afraid to charge higher prices.*

I used to work with an entrepreneur who came to me feeling very frustrated about his business. He said that everyone in his industry would do better than him even though he would always charge the lowest prices possible. His goal, however, was to have premium clients.

After having some deep conversations with him, I realized that he was still afraid of money. Then I asked him, "How much would you like to charge your clients?"

He said, "5 k for a full package service I am offering."
And I wondered, "Have you ever invested 5 k in a similar service?"

He said, "No." At the same time, he was looking for sales and marketing "hacks" to learn how to attract more money to his business. Yet...nothing would happen.

Finally, he decided to change his buying behaviors and started experiencing the feeling of an abundant, premium client. That helped him get into the mindset of wealthy people, and what they really value in a service he was offering. That one simple action changed him, and he totally re-designed his business.
"Oh," someone might say, "that's not fair, how come he only wants to serve wealthy clients?"

Well, aside from his business he also runs his own charity helping hungry kids. He's in the cycle of giving and receiving. He understands the game by now.

Now, I hope that you have gotten a simple yet profound understanding of how LOA, mindset, and self-image can work together to help you manifest more wealth and abundance by getting to the root of the problem and helping you transform on a deeper level.

As a final exercise ask yourself:
"How do I react when I see higher prices? Do I judge and criticize people who set them up for people who pay them? Do I think I am smarter for always spending my time looking for the cheapest items possible?"

Again, there is nothing wrong with that at all if that is your choice.

If you are driven by scarcity however deep inside you would like to be free to buy whatever you want without checking the price tags and at the same time you judge and criticize people who love to order premium products and services ...well chances are you are sending out a very misleading vibrations to the Universe which may result in you feeling stuck for years.

How do I know? Because I have been there too, and it took me years of LOA, mindset and deep self-development work to re-create my beliefs and start aligning myself with abundance.

It is my intention that you do the same while enjoying peace, freedom, and fulfillment.

Part 4 – Book 4

Law of Attraction for Motivation

How to Get and Stay Motivated to Attract the Life You Have Always Wanted and Be Unstoppable

Introduction

Thank you for taking an interest in this book. It really means a lot to me. My name is Elena and I am a Law of Attraction nerd and author with a passion for holistic self-help.

Even though right now I am blessed with a life I love, as well the opportunity to share my passion and knowledge with others, it wasn't always like that.

My life used to be a mess and it was a vicious cycle of pain, rejection and addictions. I was desperate for answers for myself because I wanted to create a better life for myself and those around me.

That got me on a path of never-ending study. I started devouring self-help and spiritual resources and working with all kinds of mentors, from business and success coaches to energy healers.

I became committed to transforming my life. As I was going deeper and deeper into the materials and seminars I was learning from, I quickly realized that some resources were very superficial and mainstream and were not helping me at all. After reading a ton of books about success, motivation, productivity and similar topics, I knew that I even though I had learned a ton of new concepts, something was missing. Something was missing because I got to a point where I felt stuck and confused. It felt like I could never make a long-lasting change. I would witness other people's success and transformation and it seemed like they were motivated and unstoppable, but I felt like a dumb turtle (no offense to turtles, I think they are very cute).

To sum up, I felt like the mainstream world of high performance, business mindset, and strictly financial success self-development world was not providing me with the answers I was searching for.

My main question was, *How does one become truly unstoppable?* What is this invisible force that can keep you going but at the same time, when not used properly, can wear you down? And finally, I wanted to know how to unleash my full potential, but from a place of self-approval and authenticity. I got sick and tired of pursuing careers just to make those around me think I was something special while I was feeling empty and drained inside.

I knew I was going to face my dark side and many issues that I needed to work through. Luckily, I also knew it would be a change for the better and that it would be a lasting one.

And so, I began exploring the world of the Law of Attraction, Spirituality, Energy, Reiki and the Subconscious Mind.

Eventually I came to a simple conclusion: self-development in itself will not work unless you work on your energy and shift it to a place of authenticity, self-love and following your inner voice. And this is exactly what I teach through all my books. My mission is to explain the self-development concepts of personal success, focus, happiness, wellness, productivity and motivation, using the Law of Attraction and the re-alignment of yourself with your true core.

Please note that this doesn't mean we will be just visualizing and reciting some affirmations. It means that we will go much, much deeper, so that you can get rid of layers that may be preventing you from becoming the best version of yourself and living your purpose.

To unleash your true motivations, the first thing that needs to take place is healing. Healing of past traumas, mistakes and fears you may be facing. Healing is a normal process that consists of peaks and valleys. To be fully healed, you need to give yourself permission to face some truths that may feel uncomfortable at first. I am here to help you with that in a non-judgmental way.

Creating long-lasting motivation is not like taking a pill. It's a process. The good news is that this process has the power to truly transform your life, career and relationships. It can help you get back to your true self. You will be able to step into your courage and no longer fear other people's opinions and judgements.

As we go through the process I share in this book, I want you to imagine that I am gently holding your hand through each and every step. Even if today you're having a bad day, don't worry, you are totally allowed to. Just relax, enjoy the process and let it be without forcing anything.

The best things manifest themselves when you are not pushing, forcing and hustling. The best reality emerges when you are *allowing* while taking meaningful and purposeful action in alignment with your true motivation. This is what this book will help you discover. Your deep motivation.

How This Book Came About

After undergoing my own radical transformation in all areas of my life- health, career, finance and relationships, using deep LOA concepts, I made it my purpose to share and teach, using my books to share my message.

The idea for this book, which is a motivation/ Law of Attraction combo, was born after I noticed a pattern that prevents many people from living their best, authentic and happy life. And that pattern is "I lost my motivation, I lost my driving force, I don't feel like doing anything."

What very often happens is that people try to remedy this issue by trying harder. Or they turn to "gurus" who begin shaming them or calling them lazy. However, the root of the problem is very simple and it's not even a problem to be honest...it's a question of perception and knowing the correct order of things to focus on.

You see, most people pursue goals that are not even their own goals. They very often set goals in order to feel worthy in front of other people or to make other people happy. And since the goal is not really connected to their true vision, it feels like they always have to push and hustle to make something out of themselves. After some time, that "rat race" can turn into a burnout, both physical as well as emotional.

I am going to give you a sense of freedom now by telling you that it's okay to lose your motivation and you should not be ashamed of doing so. It's simply a sign that your subconscious mind is sending you. And that sign means that the goal you are pursuing may not be for you. It may also mean that the goal you are going after is for you, but you are sending out way too much importance and therefore creating a sense of resistance that pushes your results away, making you lose motivation in the process.

For example, a person on a date with someone they really, really like. They try so hard that the person they are on a date with feels lots of pressure and is not interested in another date.

Or, imagine a person with a pet, for example, a cat. If they start to stroke it too much, the cat will push them away.

Or, a person goes on a job interview and tries so hard that they come off as being too full of themselves, or too nervous.

Another sense of freedom I am going to give you now, in this introduction (it's still not the main meal), is that nobody is perfect.

There are many self-help gurus out there, gurus of all kinds, from business to spirituality. They all have a meticulously curated image on social media, they are always perfect, they are always doing the right thing and they never have a bad day.

You look them up online and you automatically start comparing yourself to what you see. This results in two possible scenarios:

1. You lose your motivation, thinking, "I will never be like them, so what's the point?"
2. You do the opposite, you take "massive action" and you try too hard while burning yourself out.

A friend of mine who wanted to be a famous influencer on social media, and grow all his social media platforms at the same time, burned himself out. He was comparing himself with big, famous gurus who have teams of people who help them create and post content, optimize their platforms and grow their following.

The problem? He was attempting to do that all by himself, while still working in a full-time job. Eventually he burned out and it took him a few months to recover. After going through the process I will be sharing in this book, he decided that to achieve big things, he had to start small and that he had to stop comparing himself to other people.

Finally, he realized that he didn't really care that much about fame or the number of followers he had. His personal goal was to have a job quitting income so that he could go full time with his passion while creating content and promoting products that help people.

He also realized he didn't need to have a big following but rather a following of people who really resonated with his message.

In alignment with that discovery, he simply focused on one social media platform and stopped comparing himself with big name gurus who very often spend 50 k a month on professional teams and paid advertisement to grow their social media platforms.

Does that mean he is not ambitious or is shooting too low? No. It means that he's going through a step-by-step process to grow a following at his own pace.

Another example: A person who is just getting started on a health and fitness journey may have a simple goal of losing some weight and cleaning up their diet. If they start comparing themselves with big name professional athletes, who, once again, have teams of doctors, nutritionists and high-performance coaches around them to monitor and measure what they do, eat etc. well...it will be very hard to compete with that, right?

A person who is simply looking for a side income, or wants to replace their job income with a small business that is more aligned with their passion, should not compare themselves with someone who is a multi-millionaire. Well, yes, they can use someone's success story as inspiration as for what is possible, and they can hold that vision. But...everything is a process that takes time. By trying to go too fast, you may end up burning yourself out and losing your motivation or even thinking you are not good enough.

Today, many of us want instant gratification and we overlook the importance of simple, step by step dedication.

It's time to change your relationship with the concept of motivation and accept a few truths:
1. Emotions that we may perceive as negative, such as not feeling motivated, are simply signs to help you get on the right track and re-align your actions, energy and thoughts using the Law of Attraction. (This is what the following chapters of this book teach.)
2. These emotions may also be telling you that you need to slow down.
3. You need to give yourself permission to stop thinking about what other people may think of you. That will allow you to set up goals that really excite you.

4. Real, holistic motivation is like a muscle that can be worked on. It's like going to the gym- you need to have a plan that is easy to follow, however that plan can't be about overworking and exhausting yourself. It must be sustainable. If you are new to it, you can't compare yourself to all those "gym rats" out there, whether it's a real gym, or an emotional / motivational gym.
5. You must be patient and believe in the process, but at the same time be impatient with the small, everyday actions you can take.

This is exactly what we will be discussing in this book while combing it with very practical Law of Attraction exercises.

Most readers who turn to my books have already been through a ton of entrepreneur as well as self-help materials and they have tried everything under the sun. And most of them, after going through my humble materials, discover that the goals and ventures they wanted to manifest were not even what they truly wanted.

They either wanted to impress someone or get some title or achievement to post on social media to feel worthy. I know, I know. Sounds a bit cruel. I was in that mindset for years, even before social media came along. I worked very hard, even when I was totally burned out, just because I wanted to achieve goals that were totally out of alignment with what I truly wanted to impress people who didn't even care about me.

All the meaningless and superficial achievement I was chasing was just to feel worthy and accepted by other people. I created my own mental prison and it took me years to get rid of it.

(My full story and the process I used to get back to alignment with self-love is something I talk about in depth in my book: Self-Love Handbook magnified with the Law of Attraction. I highly recommend that you read it if you're seeking deeper healing and connection with yourself to get back in alignment.)

Some readers are looking for motivation to transform their health and fitness. They have already tried all the diets out there only to end up confused and burned out. However, after going through the process I teach in this book, and by combining holistic motivation with the Law of Attraction, they could finally dive deep, listen to their body and create a healthy lifestyle they enjoy.

Some readers were able to use the process taught in this book to finally get involved in a creative or artistic activity they always wanted to pursue, like for example writing, music or art. By getting connected to your true desires and motivations, you also diminish the fear of rejection and criticism. You allow yourself to keep going even on a bad day. In fact, those bad days are just signs from the Universe to put us to a test and see if we are really passionate about what we do.

And don't worry if this doesn't make any sense now. After going through this book, you will know exactly what to do and how to do it to be unstoppable in your own unique way. (Some people around you will be under the impression that you've got some magical powers, trust me on that one- but the best part is that they will feel inspired by your actions.)

Let's be honest – motivation comes easily when things are going our way, we are getting results we have worked for and we are riding the wave of success. Then we feel like celebrating and taking more action to achieve even better results.

We feel excited about what we do, and motivation comes naturally.
The problem is, how do we stay motivated and consistent when things are a bit slow? How do we maintain the right mindset and keep going when life hasn't treated us well? What should we do when things get tough, the only thing we manifest is failure and we begin losing our passion?

Obstacles very often cause us to lose our motivation, and unfortunately, while there are many gurus who have speeches, seminars, books and other resources to help *you get motivated*, very few of those resources talk about *how to maintain* that motivation and what to do when things don't pick up as fast as we originally envisioned they would.

This is where I come in, to help you through this book. This is not yet another motivational book that you will read, feel good about for a few days but never feel inspired to take action or to create lasting transformation. This book is designed as a step-by-step transformational action guide to help you grow your motivational muscle using a holistic mix of the Law of Attraction, quantum physics, mindfulness, balanced self-care to stay nourished and energized as well as re-connecting with your subconscious mind on a deeper level. Most importantly it's about getting rid of the superficial layers and other people's negative energies and expectations that are holding you back.

The exercises taught in this book will also help you improve your personal productivity and focus. As a result, you will feel inspired to walk away from people, circumstances, events and even social media channels that might be draining your motivation.

Motivation can be compared to eating a healthy diet and living a healthy lifestyle. You need to commit to the whole package on a regular basis. It's hard to lose weight by only eating healthily occasionally, or by not doing any physical activity. At the same time, it's very hard to transform your health if you eat some healthy food here and there but never decide to eliminate foods that are making you sick and tired.

One thing to remember though- it's not about being perfect. You can live a healthy lifestyle and eat a healthy, clean food diet, yet every now and then indulge in pizza or a cake. Same with motivation. Once again, let me stress- some days will be less motivating and less "on track". Motivation is like a muscle, and it also needs some rest days. The problem is when there are too many of those rest days in a row and we start feeling guilty or feel like quitting what we were doing.

Most motivational books don't work because they offer information on a very superficial level. They never make you dive deep to help you realize what actually depletes you of energy and motivation so that you can get to the root of the problem and get rid of whatever is holding you back.

Taking action if very important, but most self-help books forget about taking an inspired, aligned and meaningful action. Action that helps you stay energized instead of burning you out. So, after consuming some more mainstream motivational content, you may start feeling bad about yourself thinking, "What's wrong with me? Why am I going so slowly? This guru really seems to be always getting it right. Why can't I be like them?"

Deep inside you may be even rebelling against another motivational quote or another "Just take massive action and hustle all day" cliché.

Well, the good news is this: if you can make a conscious decision that you really want to change your relationship with motivation and dive deep through this Law of Attraction for Motivation journey, this book will help you for years to come.

My biggest intention is to help you redesign your vision and goals (this is where LOA will be very handy) so that the motivation you create will not be short lived. It will be automatic, almost subconscious, as you start working through the different emotional layers that are holding you back from achieving your goals.

As humans, we have every capacity to live proactive, deliberate, self-actualized and fun lives. We can show our failures who is in charge, bag up our fears and turn them into this invisible force that keeps us going. We can become the screenwriters of our own lives and redesign what we don't like – or want to change.

But most importantly, you will change your perception and see everything that happened *to you* as something that happened *for you*. In other words, you will master the art of turning all kinds of circumstances into motivational fuel to help you be unstoppable.

Are you ready to take it a step further and ROCK ON in *your* life, career, fitness goals, and whatever other endeavors in your near (and far) future? I want you to achieve your goals, not someone else's goals, so that you can achieve true happiness and fulfilment in your life.

Part 4 – Law of Attraction for Motivation

Chapter 1
Reconnecting with Your Inner Guidance

The first step in the process is reconnecting with your inner guidance. And the best way to do so is to allow yourself to design your ideal day and reconnect yourself with that vision on a regular basis, so that your inner GPS can guide you, while keeping your motivation levels high.

Please do this exercise without any attachment or expectations.
Do it as a simple experiment.

The word *experiment* implies that there is no right or wrong. You cannot fail with an experiment, because all you get from it is data, right?

This is exactly what we want to do now.

It's time to dive deep and create your ideal day, while getting rid of all the layers, negative associations and all those annoying voices in your head as "but how can I do it?"

The exercises I will share with you can always be slightly changed over time. What I like to do is to give you different options so that you can pick and choose and focus on something that works best for you.

Tracking back my successes and failures, I can honestly tell you that, whenever I was successful, I would in some way do this kind of an exercise. Even before I knew about it and even before I got into the Law of Attraction, my mind was doing a very similar kind of an exercise. Then, of course, I felt very motivated and inspired to take action that was aligned with my vision.

At the same time, whenever I would experience long periods of feeling stuck, anxious or even depressed (yea, I am a positive person by nature, but I also have my ups and downs), it was because I lacked clarity and confidence in my action. Needless to say, that was draining my energy, productivity and motivation.

I would just take random actions without focus, self-awareness and vision. And again, it was when I was skipping the exercise I am just about to share with you. I would either get stuck in my mind thinking that it was no longer necessary or thinking that it was only for beginners or other similar excuses.

You may be thinking, but Elena, just show me how I can be motivated right here and right now and then I can go out there and change everything in my life.

But it usually goes the other way around and big changes start in your mind. Same with fitness, nobody can teach you how to be fit right here and right now. They can give you steps for you to work on your muscles, diet and also your mindset so that you have a blueprint you can use to transform yourself on a deeper level.

Motivation and self-image are like siblings. No big changes can be made without working on your subconscious mind. Your subconscious mind is a mechanism designed to keep you in what it thinks is your comfort zone. It has good intentions and it wants to protect you.

We are where we are because of our self-image. And as harsh as it may sound, our results equal our self-image and our motivation is a by-product of that.

Everyone creates something and some kind of a life and results. But whether it's the results they actually really wanted or not, is a different story. Most people just run on an autopilot, moving between careers they hate and self-imposed distractions to entertain themselves in between. Of course, some people are happy where they are. But you are here because you are into conscious living and you are looking for big changes and transformations in all areas of your life while creating a positive impact.

It's important to design your ideal day in your mind and write down all the details. Believe it or not, I used to be very sceptical about it. I would laugh at all of that rejecting it as some "woo-woo" and would even say, "Just show me how to stay motivated, be successful and make money and then I will be able to do whatever I want. Just give me the shortcut, give me the pill."

And so, I worked hard and hard and harder and harder and it all worked well for a while. But eventually I reached mental and emotional confusion. I got stuck on the same level. As a desperate way out, I began to compulsively look for strategies, and gurus. Of course, skills are important, but here's the thing...I lost clarity.

At some point I disconnected from myself and forgot about my why and my vision. All days were busy and disconnected. Friendships were rare and very superficial. Then, I realized that I had created a reality that was a prison, not freedom, because I was viewing money and success as end goals, not as tools.

So, I got back to doing the lifestyle design exercise to reconnect with my true motivation.

I know, I know. You may be thinking, "Oh, but Elena, I don't have clarity...not too sure what my ideal day looks like."

Well, don't worry. Even if you feel uncertain now, as long as you set up a small goal, a micro habit if you will, to sit down every day, and journal for even five minutes and just write down the details of your ideal day and try to feel them, live them and focus on the positive emotions you experience, you will be able to unblock and unstick yourself. It's not that you have to sit down and logically come up with the best version of your ideal day. Just start now, do it, and as you get more ideas, feel free to add them. It's really lots of fun.

Do you know what the most successful athletes do to stay motivated? Before the game or the event, they visualize the process and the successful outcome, they focus on their feelings and live it in their mind. They also do it after the game! Yes, whether the result was positive or negative, in their mind, they replay it as positive (if the game went well) to further anchor those feelings. If they game was not successful, they create their own replay where the result is successful. It's a technique based on the Law of Attraction, a technique that is free and effective.

So, no matter what happens, in their mind, at least two out of three games are successful. And if the real game is successful, they make it a triple success.

Coaches who specialize in high performance and training athletes, know the tricks of the subconscious mind. It's the invisible force that connects to our self-image and leads us towards some positive results.

Take a piece of paper and a pen, and if you are new to journaling, set up a timer to make sure you fully focus on this task and get in a flow. Make sure you avoid distractions and switch off your phone etc. I suggest you don't use your computer. Just a pen and paper.

Now, take a few deep breaths and allow yourself to think big.
Some people struggle to be able to create a step-by-step process for their ideal day. Like, it's hard for them to come up with events on a timeline. That's fine. I am also the same way. You can always journal random events from your ideal day.

Maybe the first thing that comes to your mind is a nice lunch out with your partner, enjoying the sunshine somewhere sunny and warm, ordering the food you love without checking the price tag.

Perhaps you want to go full time with your passion. Well, imagine yourself doing that for a living. Maybe you want to create an image of you, your camera and your amazing YouTube audience. You read comments you get from your tribe and feel happy. As you create that feeling, something else may come up in your mind. Think of it as a slide that you create. You can always arrange the slides in the order that you want.

For example, you imagine that someone calls you, offering you a speaking gig or wanting to hire you as a coach. You attract new business opportunities and meet new business partners.

From that slide, another slide may come to your mind...you wake up in a hotel, new location. You hear seagulls. You love traveling and speaking, getting paid to talk about what you are passionate about.

One of my slides is writing while overlooking the sea. Receiving emails from happy readers and being happy because of their transformations. Making a difference through my books and helping other people overcome obstacles and avoid my early mistakes. I can smell the ocean; the sound of the waves is calming.

Now, I live a one-hour drive from the ocean, so whenever I go to the beach, I try to merge myself with my vision while expressing my gratitude.

There's something else I do because I know that the subconscious mind loves this kind of "games". When writing at home, I listen to YouTube videos that contain the sound of the waves and the ocean.

Also, whenever I travel, I try to upgrade my room to a place where I can enjoy the sound of the waves and the beach. I imagine it's my own house.

You will have details coming up. Some may seem unrealistic, but don't think about *how*, just focus on the *why*. Feel worthy and deserving right here, right now.

Write everything down.

When do you wake up?

What does your bedroom look like?

Where do you live? City? Nature? Penthouse, villa, a cosy apartment?

Who do you live with?

Children? Spouse? Pets?

What is your morning routine? What do you love doing?

Maybe you have a personal trainer and nutritionist?

Do you wake up in a clean, organized space?
Do you hire someone who cleans your house?
What about your office? Where do you work?

When and where do you eat your lunch?

What do you do in the afternoon?

Part 4 – Law of Attraction for Motivation

What passions can you pursue?

What does it feel like?
When you do this exercise every day, even if you do it a disorganized, random "slide" way, you will eventually create an image and a movie that will fall into a step-by-step daily routine of your dream day.

What I also love about this exercise is that you can see the future you that is a stronger version of the current you. The new you has better habits and a better mindset. What you can start doing is to adopt your future habits right now. This is how you will bridge the new you with the current you and launch the new version of yourself. Eventually, what you see as your dream vision now will become your reality. Your subconscious mind will get comfortable with it and will push you like an invisible force to take action.

A friend of mine, who is an expert in sales and marketing, uses a similar exercise on a regular basis. Many people turn to him because they don't feel successful in sales, and they hope to learn some new techniques to help them get over it. But in most cases, it's not the new technique that needs work, but their motivation, confidence, self-image and mindset.

Here's a great exercise I learned from him, and you can add it to your motivation toolkit whenever dealing with a new stressful situation that requires you to leave your comfort zone. It can be a sales call, pitching someone or even getting interviewed.

Imagine exactly what you are wearing on the occasion you are preparing yourself for. Perhaps the occasion is a sales call, interview, athletic performance or talking to a stranger.

Are you wearing any jewellery? How do you feel? How do you feel while talking? Do not overcomplicate it in terms of what you will say, exactly word for word. That will make you nervous. It will feel like reciting something. Instead, focus on the feelings that may come to your mind as you are being interviewed, working out or talking to a stranger (depending on what situation you are imagining).

Keep that feeling inside you, by replaying the parts you especially enjoyed in your mind. Whenever you feel down, close your eyes and focus on people who make you feel good and appreciate you. In business, it can be people like your regular clients, or business partners you admire.

If your goal is to create a healthy, fit body, then imagine walking down the street and wearing your favourite clothes while getting compliments from other people who feel inspired by your transformation and also want to transform.

Create a slide of that feeling and re-use it whenever you feel like it. Whenever you feel down. Most people focus on the negative and on what they don't want. Ever since I started to focus on that simple trick while at the same time writing, "I attract amazing people to my private and professional life" in my journal, I gave myself permission to leave negative environments and made new friendships, on and offline, friendships that aligned better with the new, improved edition of myself that I wanted to launch.

Your action plan to get and stay motivated
It's very important that you do the exercises from this chapter every day, even if it's just for a few minutes every day. Most subconscious mind experts recommend doing them after waking up or before you go to bed, or both. You can accompany this with reading your goals (goals you really want, not someone else's goals and expectations).

Remember- we have feelings and emotions. We can be programmed like computers, and feelings and emotions do give us an advantage. By working with your feelings and emotions the right way, you get to improve your self-image by making your subconscious mind comfortable with the uncomfortable and the unknown. Once your subconscious mind starts to feel confident, you will feel confident and you'll perform confident actions.

It's very likely you will encounter negative voices in your head like "I can't do it" or, "I will never be able to..." Remember it's just a test. You can easily turn those questions around by asking, yourself:

-How can I do it?
-Who can help me?
-What is my next step?

Keep re-aligning yourself with your vision, by feeling and /or visualizing the random "slides" from your ideal day.

It can be:
"I am walking my dog on the beach and then we go back to my big beach house."
"I am on a plane traveling to a conference where I am a speaker. I feel so excited."
"I am in the gym, after a great workout, feeling so amazing. Other people ask me for tips and motivation. It feels so good that my efforts are finally manifesting as the healthy fit body I always wanted."

You can write these down, read them aloud, or even record yourself on your phone and listen to yourself. You can also close your eyes and visualize or meditate on the feeling you are experiencing, while giving yourself the gift of shifting yourself to your ideal day.

Part 4 – Law of Attraction for Motivation

You are now connecting yourself to your Invisible Motivational Force that will keep you going in your courageous attempts to manifest your dream life.

The next step will take it to the next level by combining the random pieces of your ideal day into a holistic vision board to help you stay motivated while transforming all areas of your life.

Chapter 2
Vision for Life and Vision Boards
The Mistakes to Avoid

If you have ever consumed any success, self-help, business, high performance of even classical LOA materials, you probably already know that in order to be successful with your goals, you need to know what you want.

It's not hard to make a vision board.

It's not hard to write down what you think you want.

And it's not hard to record what you want and turn your desires into affirmations and meditations.

All the above-mentioned techniques are amazing if you actually know what you want, and it comes from you, from your core.

The problem? Most people don't know what they really want, even if they intellectually think they do. Very often people get into spirituality and LOA because they are looking for something else out there. Maybe they got burned out in their corporate jobs or careers. Or maybe they spent years trying to achieve their goals and when they did, they ended up feeling miserable and unhappy.

So how do you become clear on what you want? How will you know whether what you want comes from yourself? First of all, you need to be very careful about what you put into your mind.

The #1 mistake that most people make with LOA is that instead of diving deeply into this step, they create their vision board really fast, without even checking if that vision truly comes from their hearts.

Then, they try hard to manifest. Another mistake. Trying too hard sends the following signal to the Universe: "I don't have it, it's not for me, I need to work harder because I don't have it."

Part 4 – Law of Attraction for Motivation

My number one recommendation when it comes to creating your vision is this: Take some time off. Allow yourself to be your only friend for a few days. Go to a town you have never been to. You need some time and space to think about what you really want. If you can't take a few days off, just allow yourself a few long walks after or before work. Go somewhere peaceful and quiet. Allow yourself to think. Write down all your goals for every area of life:

Health & Fitness
Energy & Vitality
Spirituality and Contribution
Work & Career
Finance & Money
Relationships & Love
Friendships
Passion & Hobby
Travel, Party and Fun

Go through all the above-mentioned areas of life, and start writing down everything that comes to your mind. Then, come back to that vision later. Read through it and question everything you put on paper. Do it in a mindful way, without judging yourself. Keep asking yourself:

"Is it good for me, will it make me happy? Is that what I really want?"

Finally, ask yourself, "Are all areas of my life in harmony?"
For example, a social life that involves lots of partying and drinking may interfere with your health and fitness goals. This will confuse you and the Universe. Needless to say, you will start losing your motivation and feeling like you're not making any progress.

One of my early mistakes with LOA was that out of fear, I created a dozen different vision boards that did not really connect to the same vision. Different vision boards with different houses and lifestyles.

I was thinking that any of them would be good for me. I guessed that by doing a shotgun approach I would at least be able to manifest something. Eventually something will materialize, right?

Wrong, wrong, wrong! A shotgun approach to manifesting will only make you burn out. A sniper approach works so much better! More on that later in this book.

Not surprisingly, during that time, I tried different business ventures. All of them failed. I invested a ton of money and never made any money. I could never commit to one idea.

Now, when it comes to creating your LOA abundance vision and manifesting the motivation level you want, the focus you need to adopt is the same kind of focus that the best high performers as well as spiritual leaders apply. It's better to have fewer goals but strong ones. You want goals that are really yours.

Take a few deep notes from your heart.

YOU, your motivation. Your feelings and your emotions.

You see, what you want is really a reflection of your feelings and emotions. Most people don't focus on their core but instead they just jump straight into creating a vision board. Using what I like to call a "rat race strategy".

Ok, lemmee see. The Joneses got a new car, so let me go on Pinterest and find something and put it on my vision board and manifest it.

There is nothing wrong with wanting to have a nice car, I also like nice things. The question is- do you really care about that car? Or do you want it because someone you look up to cares about it?

Maybe what you are really looking for is a sense of freedom and wealth? Knowing that you have enough to get a nice "toy" when you please? But at the same not being too attached to it?

A former client of mine had a vision board with a beach house on it. I asked her, "Why did you put it there? How do you feel about it?"
She said, "Well, I guess my parents would like it."
I asked, "What makes you think so?"
She said, "Because it's a house of someone who is successful and has a secure career. My parents would be proud of me if I had such a house."

Can you see where it's going? No wonder she struggled with motivation. The big beach house wasn't really her goal. She just wanted a peaceful life with a creative career she's passionate about and a cozy city apartment.

After a deep talk we realized that she didn't even care about a fancy beach house. Nor did she care about a job in sales. What she really cared about was establishing a stronger bond with her family and feeling accepted for who she is.

Keep asking yourself:
-Why?
-Why do I want it?
-How does it make me feel?

The second round of questions is:
-Does it make me feel light?

-Does it make me feel heavy?

In most cases, when you start off feeling heavy that vision is not your vision but someone else's. Other people may be quick at manifesting it, and maybe you thought you "could try too". Yes, you could, but is it right for you?

These are my recommendations for you to go through before you start creating your vision board:

-Allow yourself some time off and get connected to your true feelings and emotions. Meditate, walk in nature, take Epsom salt baths.

-Start off by asking yourself what would make you happy. Materialistic goals are fine if they are coming from you because you feel joy while being surrounded by the objects you want to manifest.

However, if the root of your goal comes from insecurity and not feeling worthy or trying to impress the Jones's then I recommend you redefine your vision. Otherwise you will quickly lose your motivation and may end up feeling burned out.

-After you have built those fundamentals in your imagination, set the intention to create a very simple and basic vision board, with just a few simple images that will not confuse your conscious and subconscious mind.

-Does it make you feel lighter or heavier? Of course, lighter should be the answer.

-As you go through this process, be sure to take care of your emotional state. Have an Epsom salt bath or get a massage if you have been having a stressful day. It's hard to align yourself with your vision if you're feeling stressed out and there is no point in creating a vision board just for the sake of doing it.

Okay, ready? Now that we have done the hard part, it's time for the fun part- making the vision board that is truly yours.

The images for your vision board can be cut out from magazines, or printed from online platforms. The only important thing to keep in mind is that the images must speak to you. Make sure they evoke a powerful feeling of joy, satisfaction and even a little fear (which is fine, because our best dreams can be scary!). That vision board will be with you for years, and the best part is that the You from the future is already looking at it with a sense of accomplishment thinking, "Wow, I can't believe it all is true now." Stay in that feeling for as long as possible. Take a few deep breaths, be mindful and enjoy this step.

Part 4 – Law of Attraction for Motivation

According to the Law of Attraction, in this moment, all the possibilities exist and what you want is already here. It's just a question of aligning yourself to your vision with your thoughts, feelings and actions.

Put several images of your perfect vision on a piece of poster board. Put this vision board in your plain view, in a place where you can see it regularly. I even framed my vision board and placed it next to my main bathroom mirror.

Wherever you place your vision board. Look at it often, revel in it, and ask yourself, "How am I going to make these visions come true?"

Once you have your vision board, look at each individual picture. Start with picture number one. Ask yourself, "What can I do today, this week and this month to get closer to my vision? What is the new, more empowered version of myself doing?"
Let's say it is a picture of your dream home.

Ask yourself why you need to have a home like that and when do you need to have it? Who will you share it with? What does it feel and smell like? What do you do for a living? How much time do you spend in your new home? Do you have any pets? Do you clean it yourself or do you hire help?

Keep asking yourself, "What does it feel like?"

That will help you stay excited about pursuing a new job or career that can help you manifest the amount of money you need to start living in your dream house.

Perhaps you think about some family planning and talk to your wife or husband about expanding your family to complete your vision.
Now, have a look at another picture. Maybe it's a picture of a healthy lifestyle, like a person who is really fit and working out. Ask yourself, "What does it feel like? What daily habits does this person have? What can I do today to get closer to my vision?"

Making your vision board opens up a world of possibilities to you and your dreams. It truly is a blank canvas to paint your own reality. You may even find dreams that you didn't know you have. I did! For example, a few years ago, I didn't know I would be a writer. As a teenager, someone who was an authority figure for me criticized my writing. Because of that I abstained from writing for nearly three decades. It was only after going through my own radical transformation with the Law of Attraction that I realized I wanted to become a writer.

On my vision board, I put a few words like:

Freedom

Creativity

Contribution

Self-Expression

Peace of Mind

After "meditating" with my vision board for a few months and constantly asking myself deep questions, I concluded that I could combine Freedom, Creativity, Contribution and Self-Expression as well as Peace of Mind by becoming a writer.

And you know what was incredibly crazy and amazing? I *loved* it. Suddenly, everyone cheered me on. When I started, I was feeling emotionally shaky from my previous fear of being rejected and laughed at.

The point of this story is this: sometimes you may not even know what your dreams and motivations are. That is why it's so important to allow yourself to find them, using mindful Law of Attraction exercises and creating your vision board and going through it every day. Vision boarding helps you envision what truly makes you happy and fulfilled and lets you play with it. It's like a puzzle game.

You can make your goals happen in the truest and best version you can. All the dreams are there, waiting for you. You just have to narrow down life's many options and decide what it is that you want to go after.

Aside from attraction, there is also action. Especially mindful, purposeful and inspired action. After all, you don't want to burn yourself out.

It's time to make a simple plan you enjoy. You want to focus on simple actions you get to repeat on a regular basis. Let's say that your goal is to create a healthy, fit body.

Your three big monthly goals could be:
-Sign up for the gym.
-Organize your schedule in such a way that you can work out three times a week.
-Research healthy meal prep and decide whether you will cook your meals or whether it makes sense for you to hire someone who can help you.

Your three big weekly goals could be:
- Work out on Monday, Wednesday and Friday.
- Pick up healthy meals and green juice on Tuesday and Thursday.
- Be in bed early and listen to guided meditations to fall asleep.

Daily goals:
1. Go to the gym.
2. Make a healthy green smoothie for today and tomorrow.
3. Stretch before going to sleep and practice gratitude.

No matter what, get specific with the details of what you need to happen. The Universe is fond of specifics– and once you put these details and desires out into the Universe and set a plan to go after these visions, watch the details and opportunities start to flow your way.

The final step to your vision board process is to, well, en*vision* what your dreams (and life) will be like once you have achieved them. In other words, what will your life look like once you have your ideal home or your super-healthy, fit body?

How will you walk and dress? Who will you hang out with? Use your senses to really, really imagine what your life will be like with your dreams come true. Smell the ocean, picture the look on your spouse's face when you tell them about the new goal you have achieved. Envision your own confidence level, as you will have created something incredible in your life such as achieving your fitness goals and inspiring those around you. You made it happen. So, how does that feel?

Envisioning these details is super important for your follow through and, as we said before, your deep motivation level.

Another note about vision boards: feel free to update them whenever you need. Our dreams and goals change as we go along.

Sometimes, we are meant to pursue something that in the end is not what we wanted, however, it gets us on the path to what we really want. Remember, you don't fail, you either succeed, or you learn.

To figure out the best career that will bring you joy and abundance, it may take a few different paths to try to see what you like. To find the passionate relationship you have always wanted to be in, it may require dating different people so that you can find out what exactly you are looking for.

Finally, to create a healthy eating plan you enjoy, it may take trying various diets or meal plans from different nutritionists so that eventually you create your own balanced diet plan that you like.

Part 4 – Law of Attraction for Motivation

The most important thing is not to stop. Keep learning. You are always getting closer and closer to your vision.

Also, show the Universe how committed you are by checking in with your vision board, preferably daily. As we said before, the best thing you can do is to put it in a prominent place where you can see it often.

Follow these steps and behold, your vision will start to play out in numerous ways you never could have imagined. Suddenly you will feel like you have the "third eye" or a higher sense of awareness because you can now see what has always been around, but you could not see before. That is what creating true motivation using the Law of Attraction will do for you.

I cannot wait for you to try this!

What if you still have no idea what to put on your vision board? Or what if you have so many ideas and you feel confused (and you don't want to confuse the Universe too, right) ?
Here are some suggestions:

In your mind, go back to when you were a kid. After all, we all still have a kid inside us *somewhere*. So, what did you like to do when you were younger? What made the time pass quickly over the weekend or the summer vacation from school? What got you excited about your day? Was it drawing, arts, sports, music?

Whatever it was, think about how you could bring more elements of those desired activities into your daily life. Could you sign up for music lessons as an adult? It all counts big time when it comes to making your vision board.

Another idea about how to figure out your dreams and visions is to imagine yourself at the end of your life. This one is a little harder, but definitely worth a try. Yes, at the end of your life, what would you like to have accomplished or seen played out in your lifetime that you would have liked to have been a part of? Use this exercise to influence what you want to put on your vision board.

Additionally, think about what you would have told your current self at the end of your life. For example, I can tend to be a bit of a worrier. *Am I doing it right, am I going to succeed?* I catch myself worrying about these things often.

In my older life, though, I imagine elderly-self telling my current self to *not worry*, but rather enjoy the ride a bit more. So then, I could incorporate elements of what it's like to enjoy life more into my vision and vision board.

This exercise will help you prioritize your vision-to-do list, as well. We only have so much time on this earth, much of it not to be taken for granted. So, what are the more important things – or things that are more important to *you* that you would like to achieve in the next few months, year, five years, etc.? And what can you let fall by the wayside?

I really hope you have an awesome time with your vision board. Give yourself permission to be a kid again for an evening and really imagine a new and improved life for yourself and/or your family. And enjoy!

Part 4 – Law of Attraction for Motivation

Chapter 3
The # 1 Motivation Killer and How to Mindfully Release It to Live Your Best Life

One of the biggest motivation killers is not the feeling of lack of motivation. It's a feeling of feeling guilty about not feeling motivated or mentally energized all the time.

That feeling also very often appears when you keep comparing yourself to other people and their (very often meticulously fabricated) success stories shown on social media. Don't get me wrong, even if the story is true, the way it is presented might be designed to make you feel inferior and not worthy.

Remember though, it's you and only you who is in control of your life, your actions and your motivation. You are the owner of your blank canvas. And with a blank canvas, you now have the capacity to welcome in the multitude of wonderful, positive, motivational, inspirational attributes of YOU that already exist and are waiting to be expressed.

The power of the Law of Attraction is triggered by love (including self-love). And here's the deal with self-love. Self-love is a little addictive – a drug in the best way possible. But what's amazing is that you *can never have* too much of it.

By loving yourself, you allow yourself to be the creator of the story of your life. You can start fresh and create the life that *you* want for yourself. *You.* Not your family, friends or some guru. *You.* Everyone is different and everyone has a different story. Everyone has their own strengths as well as weaknesses.

We are conditioned to celebrate strengths and wins and yea it's a great habit. Give yourself credit for your past accomplishments, no matter how small. But...it's also important to celebrate failure and learn from it. Change the meaning of *failing* to *learning*.

It always takes some time to see a bigger picture. Perhaps you didn't get a job you really wanted to get. You felt disappointed by that circumstance, however, after a few months you discovered a new, more exciting career opportunity and eventually came to the conclusion, "Wow. Thank God I didn't get that job back then. It's the best thing that ever happened to me!"

To stay motivated, you need to own and control your mind. Be like a filter. Think for yourself.

Give yourself some time to answer the following questions:

-What are the main things I want to happen in my life?

-What do I want out of life?
- What kind of story do I want to tell about myself, my life?

-What are the circumstances that I used to view as negative but now see as the best thing that ever happened to me?

-What is the feeling I get when I think about those circumstances? A relief? Joy? Abundance? Motivation?

-Was it really worth so much worry?

Now, take some time to have a look at what you consider negative circumstances that are happening to you now. The goal of this exercise is to imagine you are the New, More Empowered Version of You from the future and you are giving the Current You some tips and advice to stay patient.

To take it one step further, fill in the following sentence:

Right now, I am a bit worried about......

Yes, allow yourself to express what is worrying you.

Now, finish the following sentence:

But I know there is a reason for my worry because...

I know that all my effort, pain and suffering will eventually get some meaning....

Allow yourself to finish your own story. See everything as a movie where you are in full control of the characters and plot.

Assessing the above questions forces you to do some serious thinking about what is important to you, as well as your motivation.

If you don't know what you want to do in your life and you are still looking for your passion and purpose, don't let that stop you. Make it your motivation to find your purpose and have fun in the process.

The one thing you should avoid is saying, "Other people are motivated because they know what they want. I still don't know my purpose."

I have been there so many times, comparing myself to other people. I thought there was some time or even age limit where you were supposed to know your purpose and meaning. Just like I used to think that there was a time limit to where you were supposed to have a certain career and be making certain amount of money, live in a certain house and drive a certain car.

The question is- is it your motivation? If it's from other people, it will not last long.

Whenever you encounter a mental block or are feeling stuck or come up with negative self-talk such as: "I don't know how to do it", "I am not good enough", "I am not as good as…" remember that these are motivation killers. You have the power to get rid of them by using self-love. You can transform the negative self-talk into empowering questions, such as:

"Who can help me/ teach me how to …?"

"What can I do right here, right now to get better at…?"

"What can I do to move forward?"

"How can I attract a great mentor into my life?"

Your mind is like a search engine. Be sure to ask good, empowering questions. This step works very well when applied after the first two steps in the book (designing your ideal day and creating your ultimate vision board).

Right now, you are working with long-term intrinsic motivation, which is the most authentic kind of motivation you can align yourself to.

Part 4 – Law of Attraction for Motivation

Intrinsic vs Extrinsic Motivation

So, what is the difference between intrinsic and extrinsic motivation? And why is intrinsic motivation preferred for long-term success?

Let's have a look:

Intrinsic motivation - deep, lasting motivation connected to your authentic vision and your core. It is the mother of all motivation and should be paid special attention to.

Intrinsic motivation focuses on:
- What you believe in
- What you love /hate
- What makes you connect with other people

Intrinsic motivation is the root of sustained desire, which, as we all know, is incredibly important to pay attention to when getting stuff done.

Now, let's have a look at *extrinsic motivation*.

You know, it's when you want something so that you can show your achievements on social media. It may keep you going for a while, until you burn out, or you achieve your goals but will feel depleted of fulfillment.

Extrinsic motivation focuses on satisfaction happening more on the exterior, or surface level:
- Appearances
- Money
- Praise from others

Extrinsic motivation surely works but it can help you stay motivated only for a short period of time.

Multiple studies have shown that it is intrinsic motivation, sustained desire, that really gets you to your goals.

Example: Going to the gym

If you are *intrinsically motivated*, you work out because it feels good to go to the gym, it elevates your mood, and you feel healthy. You know you are investing in your wellbeing for years to come.

If you work with *extrinsic motivations* you want to look hot and shredded, or toned, preferably as fast as possible.

Don't get me wrong, both scenarios can be motivating, but, from my personal experience, the difference is that intrinsic motivation sets you up for long-term success.

Back to the above-mentioned gym example:

If your only motivation is looking hot, you may be tempted to stop going to the gym as soon as you hit your goal. Some people may even feel tempted to experiment with weight loss pills and some supplements (legal or illegal) that are not always healthy, just to keep their shredded look.

However, if you focus on your core and your intrinsic motivation of going to the gym such as:

-feeling good
-getting rid of stress in a healthy way
-setting up a good, healthy example to other people
-using fitness to build up your discipline and mindset
-staying fit to focus on vitality and longevity and optimize your health

You will not be that likely to quit because fitness will be a part of you, it will be your lifestyle.

Another example: starting a business.
If a person is only driven by extrinsic motivation and some kind of an entrepreneur status to show on social media, they may burn out after reaching a certain financial milestone. Some individuals who are driven entirely by money and want to make it as fast as possible, may even turn to illegal or unethical activities, just to make their money quickly and they may lose their business.

However, if a person has a deep *why* behind their actions and can access their internal motivations such as:
-create products and services that really help people
-set a good example to other entrepreneurs
-grow their business to be able to offer jobs in their local community
-be a true expert in their field and grow their knowledge while helping other people

Then, they will keep going and going uphill even if they encounter some obstacles on their journey.

All world-famous bestselling authors have written dozens if not hundreds of manuscripts before their career took off. They kept going because they were truly passionate about writing and creating their characters while providing entertainment and escapism for their readers. That was their goal and motivation. Had their only motivation been to become an instant bestseller, they would have quit after a few rejected manuscripts.

So now that you have a blank canvas and are aware of some of your intrinsic and extrinsic motivations, let's take those and apply them to our metaphor of painting a life picture filled with deliberate self-love and care.

You now know what motivates you, both on the inside and out. Let's take those motivations, knead them a bit, and lay them out for the base of your story – one immersed in self-love and desire…

Remember it's okay to use a bit of extrinsic motivation and a bit of ego here and there. Just do not allow it to be your only source of motivation. Yes, it will feel nice to lose weight, get toned, and reward yourself by buying some new clothes and posting a selfie on social media. If that helps you get started- do it. If it helps you keep going by documenting your journey and you enjoy sharing what you do with other people and you feel it gives you extra motivation- do it. Why not?

Remember though- the best motivation is your intrinsic one.

The following questions and exercises will help you access your intrinsic motivations for all areas of your life.

Be sure to give yourself some time and space to go through the following set of questions several times. Each time do it in the context of a different area of your life such as
-Health & Fitness
-Career & Work
-Family & Friends
-Love & Relationships
-Money & Finance etc.

Questions:
-How do I see myself in the next five years?
-What does the New, More Empowered Version of me do?
-What do I want to change in the world?
-What makes me happy?
-What annoys me?
-What do I want to be remembered for?
-How do I want to inspire other people?
-What do I want to be known for?

Part 4 – Law of Attraction for Motivation

The Self-Love for Motivation

I am sure you are probably wondering, "What is the connection between the Law of Attraction, motivation and self-love?"
Well, here's a traditional self-development "formula":

Motivation -> action - > results - > self-worth and self-love stemming from achievement
You somehow get motivated, you take action, and get results.
Then you start feeling good about yourself.

It looks logical and innocent, but...nobody talks about possible consequences.

Action -> results - > lack of results - >failure -> shame -> feeling worthless -> losing motivation

It basically means that if you take action from a place of lack, even though you may create some results, they will not last long. They will turn to what you perceive as failure which leads to shame, guilt and eventually a loss of motivation.

Here's my preferred formula, please note it leaves lots of space for different variations. I always say there is no fixed blueprint. I like flexible blueprints that can be adjusted depending on a person's needs and preferences:

Self-love -> energy of abundance and fulfillment –> full alignment –> fusing yourself with your goals –> meaningful action aligned with intrinsic motivation- >repeat and enjoy!

The only thing you can actually afford to chase is self-love. You don't need other people's permission or approval and you have the right to be yourself.

I am now going to get to the "nitty gritty" on what needs to happen for you to love yourself fully and what tools you can use to access joy, inner-peace, and lasting dedication to your dreams.

Why? Several reasons, most importantly *why not*? Also, self-love – the practice of caring for and about yourself – is the basis not only of your doing well, but once you've satisfied your own needs in terms of care, you will be in a much more giving place to care about others.

We come from a mindset that selflessness is best. "Think of others before you think of yourself", we say. Yes...but also no – at least not in my humble opinion.

Yes, I think about you, my reader. Because of that I want to write good books, hire good editors and narrators. I make sure the team helps me spread my message and that they are also passionate about it. But to do that, I need to put myself first. I need to take care of my body and mind. I need to eat healthily, be in bed early and wake up early so that I can write when my productivity is at its peak, and before I have to work on other projects.

When I commit to writing, I make sure I stay hydrated, get enough sleep and switch off all my devices and email. I answer emails from my readers only after I am done writing. Otherwise, I would not be able to help anyone.

Of course, there are some circumstances in which we need to think of others before ourselves, but the vast majority of giving, thorough, honest and genuine giving comes from a place of feeling satisfied and full ourselves.

Here are a few tips on how to use self-love to stay motivated:

-Forgive Yourself (Stop Dwelling on Failures)

We already discussed this in brief, but let's take it a little further. You can change the thoughts and words in your head into empowering questions that will stimulate your subconscious mind.

Negative self-talk and self-guilt such as, "Why do I always fail?", "I will never be successful at this", become
"Who can help me with this?" and "What can I do to learn how to do this?"

Eventually, you will start turning those small empowering questions into small consistent actions, such as:

-using two hours every evening to work on a new business, or learning a new skill. Perhaps you will start waking up one hour earlier to write that book you have always wanted to write or work out to feel more energized throughout the day. As you get on what feels like the right track for you, start affirming what you do by using affirmations such as:

-I love waking up early. I am a morning person
-I love working on my new business venture and I am really passionate about it

Practice those small actions to stay in motion. Motion leads to motivation, remember what I said about being patient and impatient at the same time? Be patient about the long-term results, they do take time. But...be impatient and start taking those small, aligned actions to manifest what you want.

What you want to avoid are mindless affirmations, taken from a place of lack and scarcity. You want to feel totally fused with your goals, not separated from them. Separation will eventually result in a lack of motivation and we don't want that to happen.

These shifts are really, really cool to experience, especially as they start to happen.

In order to move past mental blocks, you need to thoroughly and unconditionally forgive yourself. One of the reasons you can't get started may be that you are scared. Something went wrong in the past and your natural reaction is fear. It took me a while to work through it and really believe it. Now I feel it. I totally accept the fact that every project is a process that involves making mistakes. Perfection does not exist but there is an art of balancing.

Guilt is an absolutely wasted emotion. Sitting around and feeling guilty does nothing but add toxic elements to your existence (not to mention your energy) and is beyond detrimental to your recovery and life improvement journey. Yes, allow yourself to feel guilty. Just make sure that you set a timer and ask yourself- how long do I want to feel down for? Feel bad for a few minutes, but then ditch that guilt. Have a short-term memory about whatever it is you're feeling guilty about.

Take Some You-Time

I remember teaching this process to an entrepreneur friend of mine. The guy was a big fan of a non-stop hustle and he kept going until he burned out.

It was a very hard task to teach him the process of self-care and self-love. He just had this idea he neeed to be productive. Once he released that guilt though, he saw his business ventures in a new light and changed his relationship with motivation.

Once you have released your guilt, it is time to take the time for YOU that you need. This may sound unrealistic, depending on your circumstances, but taking the time to dream and let what you love about life soak in, is absolutely necessary for welcoming improvements into your life.

Now, I realize that most of us are busy. Time is scarce. We have obligations, families, events, social lives, work commitments, etc. Who has the time to sit around and dream, you may ask! Well... you do! It just takes a tiny bit of astuteness, intuition and a little efficiently appropriated time.

YOU time is a huge part of writing your self-love-filled life story. (And again, even if you can't take that time in large quantities, make what you can do count. And count big.) If we don't take the time for ourselves, we will run on empty, sputter, and eventually run out of gas. This empty frenetic energy is what makes people so unmotivated.

The Art of Saying *No*

This one can get pretty hard. Especially if your goal is to be a kind, loving person who never says *no*. But here's the gist: do not overcommit. Say *no* to things that do not align with your vision. You can still do it from a place of kindness. If you want to be in charge of your life, you need to set boundaries. As you keep pursuing your goals, people who are your true friends will be inspired by what you do and will want to do the same.

Saying *no* to things that aren't your responsibility is actually quite empowering! Most people will feel inspired by the fact that you have goals and an agenda to follow and that you are working on something big.

Trust the Process and Love Every Minute of it.

Ah, patience. Be patient, my friend. Challenges are just hidden opportunities. Your awareness in this present moment is much higher than it was, for example, five years ago. When you look back at something that happened to you several years ago, something you used to look at as a failure, your current state of awareness may see it as a blessing.

Use this mechanism to ease temporary pain or disappointments that, let's face it, are inevitable. In five or ten years' time, your sense of awareness and perception will be higher than it is now, and what you now see as struggle will seem like a blessing to you.

Chapter 4
The Mental and Emotional Peeling to Welcome the New and Get Rid of the Old

Improving your relationship with yourself is proportional to improving your motivation. Most people don't really struggle with motivation, they struggle with their self-image.

Success is not about achieving what other people expect you to do and it's not about fitting in. Success is about having the courage to be yourself.

Learning (or re-learning) how to love yourself.

The Law of Attraction magnifies what you constantly focus on. So, constant negative self-talk and torturing yourself with:

-*I am not motivated*

-*I am not good enough*

-*I don't know how*
will only amplify the negativity in your life while destroying your motivation.

We must first, as the saying goes, go "out with the old". In other words, let's figure out – and then ditch – our pervasive and unhelpful self-talk habits. Think of it as an emotional and mental peeling. You have the power to get rid of the layers that are holding you back from living your true potential.

It's time to turn negative into positive and align your energy, actions and thoughts with your vision.

The first step here is to notice how you talk to yourself.
Notice -- *What am I saying to myself?* Simply notice.

Note: Do not make judgments or analyze this self-talk – yet. For some reason, we love to beat ourselves up about minor and/or insignificant details such as saying something stupid in a meeting, or not saying what we really wanted to say.

Throughout the next day or two, make a small list with two or three negative things you say to yourself daily. Read it often – and, again, *without judgment*. Simply say:

"I say _____ to myself often" – and leave it at that.
Transform it into something positive.

The absolute best way to combat negativity in your mind – to get rid of it using our mental and emotional peeling technique– is to reverse the aforementioned negative self-talk with positive affirmations coming from a place of wholeness and abundance.

Now, what you want to do here is take your little list of negative self-talk and next to each negative statement, write a positive affirmation. (An affirmation is a statement expressed in the positive voice, right?)

Let's do an example. Say you constantly tell yourself some negative lines, such as:

"No one will ever hire me because I'm not as smart as other candidates."

First of all, this is not a true statement. It's just a statement but, if you keep repeating it over and over again, it may become your belief, to be precise-your limiting belief.

Now, let's change it.

- "No one will hire me because I'm not as smart as other candidates" will now become:
- "I am smart and bright, and there are thousands of people who would love to hire me very soon."

Let's take it even further:
"Because I am so smart and dedicated, I am passionate about learning. I love taking professional courses and increasing my qualifications."

Now, if you decide to enroll in a professional course, coming from this Passion Mindset ("I love it, I study because I am passionate about learning" etc.), you are bound to be successful and fulfilled and your motivation will be long-term.

However, if you pursue education from a place of feeling unworthy and not being good enough, chances are you will translate the same pattern into a new environment, whether it's a work place, gym, or a professional course you want to take.

But what if it's not true, you might be thinking. *I'm not smart or bright or about to be hired...*

The thing about affirmations is that you write them NO MATTER WHAT YOU THINK. It's a tough pill to swallow, but your perception may be off anyway. Trust that there is a world out there in which thousands of people would love to hire you very soon.

Another example: "I can't go to the gym because I'm out of shape and I will look so stupid."

So, let's rewrite this story into something more empowering:
"I love working on my body and aligning myself with the new, healthy version of myself", or "my body loves the gym and so does my mind!"

Again, even if you doubt these affirmations (or this process) with every fiber in your body, continue to write them. Do it anyway.
Brainwash yourself (in a good way of course).

When it comes to being the hero of your own life and/or the author of your own story, affirmations are worth spending time on.

There is no right or wrong. The only right way of doing your affirmations is what makes you feel good in a given moment.

Put some passion into these, even if it's hard or you don't want to, and write these awesome, positive statements down as frequently as possible – in a notebook, on a napkin. Just do them and do them *often*.

Releasing Pressure and Judgment to Feel Free and Naturally Motivated

Let's face it...we have all been guilty of judging others.
For me personally, I was as strict on myself as I was on other people. I was confusing high standards and true ambition with high pressure. Unnecessarily high pressure.

A former mentor of mine whom I deeply trusted back then had taught me to be like this and since I had no clue about "owning and controlling my mind" I had made the mistake of blindly following through. That led me on a path of self-destruction as well as criticizing others. I would spend at least a few hours a day thinking or saying negative things about myself and other people. Caught up in unnecessary gossip, I was hurting others and myself.

Since I was in a non-stop judgment and criticism mindset, I was constantly afraid that others would judge me too, and needless to say, my negative energy was coming back to me all the time. I felt drained and could not find the motivation to purse my true goals, goals I was passionate about.

Finally, I realized I was wasting my time and energy that could be spent on something more positive and empowering, such as doing inner work, meditating or taking care of my body. I decided to go on a "judgement detox" and it worked really well.
At first, I vowed to myself that I would stop judging myself about feeling judgmental. Instead, I decided to simply become aware of my feelings and thoughts. I decided to catch onto the negative patterns.

Whenever I felt like criticizing someone, or I had a gossip friend of mine criticize someone else, I made a conscious effort to turn it into a positive statement by finding something good to say about a person, situation and myself. It all began by rearranging my wording and creating a new, empowering habit. That one simple step led me to increased energy and motivation.

At the time of my transformation, I was running a small business where I was managing a team of several employees. When I changed from a strict and judgmental high-pressure mindset to an understanding and positive mindset I was able to communicate much better with the team I was managing and increase their motivation too. Whenever I had to give someone feedback, I made a conscious decision to first remind them about their true potential and what they did well instead of being judgmental about what they do. I could give them honest feedback in a way that was motivating and empowering.

That change however, started with myself and how I talked with myself. To motivate others, you must first understand your own motivation. What is happening to you and around you is a reflection of your inner world. And you can shift your inner world to any place you like.

Remember…it all starts with self-love and using it to erase self-judgment. You take action because it feels good and because you enjoy it. You don't need to use pressure (on yourself or others) to achieve your goals and to be happy.

A positive self-image is the gateway to some awesome self-love coming your way. It also helps you attract people who are on the same vibration. So, pay attention to where you can throw in some positive self-talk to describe your efforts. It may seem weird at first, and like it's not helping you. But over time, you will learn that less value judgment in the short term equals incredible self-motivation in the longer term.

You are enough, and your efforts are fabulous. You are also a beacon of light, so keep going forward and acting as such. Adjusting your wording will help you write or re-write this aspect of your newly changed, more self-actualized story. Deciding to ditch the value judgments gives you longevity in your thinking, flexibility in your perception, and creativity to expand the lenses through which you see the world.

Chapter 5
How to Deal with Adversity and Keep Taking Inspired Action

To create a positive, lasting change and unleash your deep motivation, you must also accept the negative. Have no fear though- we will have a look at the negative in a very empowering way to make you stronger and to make sure your motivation muscle is so powerful that nobody and nothing can stop you.

One truth to accept is that as you change and grow and become even more transformed in this process, you might come up against a few challenging situations.

How to Deal with People who Question Your Journey

When we decide to transform, if others, specifically friends and family, remain where they are, they may not exactly understand the changes we are working on to create our best lives. In some cases, they may even try to slow us down or stop us from moving forward. Unfortunately, sometimes people get so used to our being the way we have always been, even if that way is a bit "blocked". As we liberate our own minds and spirits, it seems a bit scary for other people. As we evolve and create exciting visions while taking action to align with what we want, it feels like we no longer fit into the mold that our closest ones are so used to seeing us in.

In most cases, our family and friends still love and care for us, so we need to be patient with their reactions. It's not that they want to criticize us, it's just they may fear we are "getting too big" or "acting weird". Maybe they don't want us to get hurt. Again, just understand where they are coming from. Be grateful that other people care about you but remember that your motivations are different than theirs. It's okay to be different and to work on something that other people may not understand.

Also remember that as you keep going and getting closer to your vision by taking meaningful action and manifesting the reality you want, those who truly care about you and wish you well will be inspired by your transformation.

In fact, one of my motivations I still use to do my daily writing sessions and my daily workouts is:

"I do it to inspire and motivate those around me."

But it wasn't always like that. When I first got started on my transformational journey, most of my friends and family thought I had lost it. Some would even make jokes about me and my work. However, I decided to be patient, listen to my inner voice and just ignore certain remarks. By reacting to them, I knew I would attract more of that negative energy and it would have a negative impact on my motivation. What you focus on, you attract more of.

Had I listened to what other people were telling me, I would have never transformed my health and I would have never gotten into writing. After years of feeling disconnected from myself, I began asking myself what was happening and why I could never follow through on my real dreams and ambitions.

By using the process, I described in the earlier chapters, I quickly realized that I had way too many negative voices in my head and these were becoming my excuses. I quickly identified all those negative voices as well as the limiting beliefs that were pretty much coming from other people, including my friends and family, and were installed on my hard drive after so many years of feeling disconnected from my vision and goals.

But here's the thing: you cannot just remove a limiting belief and hope for the best. You need to replace the limiting belief with an empowering belief.

For example, the beliefs I got from my family:
- "If you work out you won't have time for your family."
- "Eating healthily is only for rich people."
- "Eating healthily doesn't taste good anyway, come on, you gotta have something good in your life. Life is already hard enough."

I began replacing these with self-love and empowerment, one by one. For example, instead of, "If you are always working out, you won't have time for the family", I said, "You can both work out and hang out with family and friends."

I began organizing hiking trips that were fun. I would get some of my friends and family members and we would just walk in nature, burn calories and have fun. We could still catch up, but instead of going to a bar, we would get some fresh air, admire nature or even join a yoga workshop. Then, eventually, we felt inspired to combine our hikes with eating healthy food.

Aside from that, I realized that health is the most valuable asset we have. I can still remember what it felt like when I could not get up and felt absolutely powerless. The doctors just prescribed antidepressants, but the truth is that my body lacked a healthy, clean diet and exercise.

Now, I have never been a gym person. So, I decided to focus on other activities, mostly in nature, like hiking, for example. I also joined yoga and Pilates classes. I gradually added more positive changes. I kept track of my progress. I still allowed myself to get off track every now and then. That is absolutely fine. You don't want to be too strict on yourself. It's better to focus on your long-term vision.

Eventually, I really started enjoying my hikes. Getting outdoors in the fresh air felt amazing. I loved my hikes so much that I decided to take them to another level, and I began jogging. Another change and shift added gradually. Had I vowed to jog every day at the beginning of my journey, I wouldn't have had any success with it. I would have worked on willpower alone. And that can only last so long.

A friend of mine, who was going through the same process, decided to transform his health and fitness as well. Aside from that, he became very inspired by what I was doing with my writing. His challenge was time, because he had a full-time job and a family to support. But he managed to do it anyway. He started small. He started waking up ten to fifteen minutes earlier and doing some simple exercises that required no equipment. Just watching YouTube videos and following online fitness courses and DVDs.

He made a small commitment that only took fifteen minutes a day, every day, first thing in the morning, before things became too hectic.

His old limiting belief had been that if you had a full-time job and a family to support, and you wanted to be a good dad, you had to give up on your passions because continuing with them would be egoistical. He had heard this from his dad, his uncle, and his grandpa. But his new, empowering belief, fueled by self-love, was this:

"As a good dad, I need to take care of my health and fitness and set a good example to my family. This also allows me to be more productive at work and increases my chances of getting a promotion."

So, he kept going. Eventually, he started waking up even earlier and added more exercises to do in the morning because it felt so good. His wife also became inspired to do fitness training.
Then he decided to add another habit. While at work, he had a one-hour lunch break. He didn't need a full hour to eat anyway. He could enjoy his lunch within twenty minutes, and then instead of browsing through his phone, he decided to focus on writing. He soon realized that half an hour a day can be easily turned into a thousand words. That's thirty thousand words a month which can be a short novella or a smaller size nonfiction book.

Think beyond yourself, your mission, your purpose. Beyond the work you are meant to be doing. Who did you allow to enter your mind and why? Perhaps you fear it will be hard or that it will take too long, or that you will get laughed at. You can help other people by becoming the best version of yourself starting right here and now. You don't need to wait for the perfect moment. Be yourself and shine your light. Also, give yourself permission to move at your own pace. Remember, you don't fail - you succeed, or you learn.

Careful with Toxic People Though

As you make changes and self-improvements on your journey, watch out for the person in your life who suddenly becomes very needy for your time and attention. Perhaps they were always needy, and you didn't realize it, or perhaps they are subconsciously noticing your changes and becoming a little scared.

Either way, assess to what degree these people still fit into your life. You may need to distance yourself from them for a while, and that is fine. You need to protect your mind, energy and vision. Do what you need to do for *you*.

It's up to you to be in charge of whether you can afford to have any "toxic" personalities in your life. Decide in what capacity you can handle them *without* them interfering with your journey and progress.

How to Deal with Self-Sabotage

Another thing you need to be mentally and emotionally prepared for is self-sabotage.

When you are motivated to make some amazing changes in your life, and your vision and purpose are being actualized, your old self may decide to make a comeback to get you back to the old reality. It can happen if you are not careful.

It's called self-sabotage.

Self-sabotage comes from your mind's scared place that subconsciously tells you that staying motivated to manifest your own greatness is not something you should pursue, so you try to stop yourself, whether on purpose or not.

Here's a simple example from my life. For a very long time, whenever things would start to go well in my life, I would get very sick. A cold, the flu, some random allergy or food poisoning. But no matter how I tried to change it, every time I manifested something great, I had to "get back to earth" and it felt like a vicious cycle of waking up from a wonderful dream. That thing became a pattern.

I would end up on these doctors' visits, one after the other, thinking something was really wrong, and they would tell me it was a virus, or some digestive issue, or that I just needed some rest and more sleep. And they were right. My self-imposed sabotage would always lead me to staying up late, going out and drinking where I should have rested. These negative patterns were eventually leading me to sickness. I was creating my own sickness, by taking self-sabotaging actions that were out of alignment with my new self and wanted to bring the old me back. The old me that would play it safe.

The point here is that I'd learned this pattern of sabotage early in my life – for whatever reason – and that it was preventing me to create long-lasting changes in my life.

I had to let go. So, I focused on journaling and affirmations to gently center my awareness on the root of the problem by aligning myself with a better self-care. I began paying more attention to my impulsive actions like having that one more glass of wine when I should have had a soft drink instead, or ordering some junk food when I should have gone for a salad. It may seem like not a big deal but all those small, self-sabotaging actions combined, would make me get sick on a regular basis, especially when I was close to manifesting a big success. It's like this old self desperately trying to put the new self back behind the curtain.

Back then, I knew I had to regain my power and re-work my negative and self-sabotaging actions so I changed my affirmations to include statements about a healthy body and mind and how I loved myself. It took work, lots of work but I no longer would get down the road of manifesting abundance and have to back up after a few weeks just to take care of some annoying ailment.

Don't be afraid to be on the lookout for self-sabotage. You're your own self-awareness detective. Don't judge what is happening. Simply become aware so that you can start taking small actions to turn negative into positive.

Especially as you get closer and closer to achieving some of the items on your vision board, keep a keen eye on your own efforts to subconsciously slow down your progress. Whatever you do, don't give into it. Additionally, we have other people's sabotage efforts to deal with. Remember those toxic friends? Yes, make sure they are not sabotaging you, either. They may even do it without realizing it.

Your Awareness is Your Power

Be mindfully aware of when you get closer to your dream reality. Or even when you get close to a milestone on your journey toward them. A friend might need help with moving to a new house, or a family member may need you for something else, when it's your last opportunity of the day to work on yourself and your vision.

I'm not saying get rid of all responsibility here; but I am saying be aware that this will happen and be very mindful about where you want to spend your time, energy, and efforts. Keep your eyes on your vision – because you absolutely deserve to. One thing I am a huge fan of are mindful morning rituals, and it's something we will be discussing in the next chapter. The best thing you can do for yourself is to do all your important Law of Attraction-Motivational work early in the morning, so that when life gets hectic, you feel grounded and aligned. It feels good to know you start your day by taking care of your vision and it will also allow you to help others to the best of your ability.

Part 4 – Law of Attraction for Motivation

Chapter 7
The Best LOA Tools to Stay Motivated

Mindful morning rituals are incredibly important for aligning yourself with your vision and staying motivated throughout the day. Remember- motivation is a muscle and it deserves to be worked on.

If you don't have a Mindful Morning Ritual yet, now is the time to change that. Sleeping past your alarm, skipping your morning smoothie, meditation or self-care will prevent you from creating sustainable energy to help you keep going.

Imagine, that you have an 8:00 a.m. work meeting. You set your alarm for 5:30 a.m. with intent on hitting the gym, cooking a light breakfast, taking a shower and driving to work. But unfortunately, you hit snooze, hit snooze again, then again. Before you know it, it's 7:00 a.m. and you've missed your time to work out, so you jump out of bed, hit the shower, skip breakfast and rush to get to work.

You are a little groggy still, flustered, and feeling guilty about not working out. You haven't taken the proper time for yourself to set up an amazing day. And your energy around your workplace reflects it.

Eventually, that negative energy actually attracts more negativity into your day, and you begin wondering why you are losing your motivation.

Setting yourself up for success first thing in the morning is the goal here. Running on "doing just what you need to" is low frequency and stepping away from your vision.

Now, before you go to bed, imagine a morning where you wake up on the first buzz of your alarm. You tell yourself that today is going to be an amazing day and that little miracles will take place. You make your bed, brush your teeth, mediate and work out, shower, make a healthy smoothie for breakfast and allow yourself plenty of time to start your day the right way.

The Universe works in mysterious and energy-related ways. So, you might as well set yourself up for the latter.

Mindful Exercises to Raise Your Vibration First Thing in the Morning

Experiment with these exercises. See how they affect you.
Don't force yourself to do activities you don't like. Stick to your preferred form of morning ritual.

Part 4 – *Law of Attraction for Motivation*

The Power of Mindful Journaling

Journaling is a tool that can help you get rid of negative emotions such as anger, resentment, and guilt. At the same time, it can help you celebrate your small successes and bring your dreams even closer into your reality. Have a blank journal to write in, right beside your bed. When you wake up, grab it and start writing whatever feels good.

It can be what you are grateful for (give priority to one specific area of life that needs most of your attention, while also being grateful for things, people and circumstances related to other areas of your life as that will bring balance).

For example, if your number one thing you are trying to transform is your career and finances and you want to manifest more abundance, while staying motivated to pursue your deep ambitions, start off by writing what you are already grateful for when it comes to your professional life. What are your achievements? You can also be grateful for something you haven't achieved yet, in fact, it's very powerful.

Then, be sure to quickly scan other areas of your life and be grateful for your health, relationships and family. Balance is very important, and you don't want to get too caught up in only one area of your life.

Some days you may be too busy to write in your journal. And so, what you can do instead, as you drink your morning coffee, is quickly read through what you have written so far. In fact, it's a very powerful, vibration-raising activity that will help you stay aligned with your vision while increasing your *why* and your motivation.

What else can you write about? ANYTHING. EVERYTHING.
You can write down your goals in a present tense and feel grateful for them. You can write down a simple action plan for today, to make sure you stay mindfully focused on those small, consistent actions.

At the same time, what journaling allows us to do is to empty our brains of toxic, negative thoughts. We can organize our thoughts and come up with new ideas.

Many of my book ideas come from something I wrote in my journal years ago. When I look back, I see certain patterns and thoughts I can turn into processes I get to teach through my books.

Mindful journaling unleashes that feeling of being proactive and filled with joy and positive energy. That is pure motivation, not only for you but also for those around you. Trust me on that one. The good energy you are spreading will come back to you.

How to Use Affirmations to Stay Motivated

Have a look at your vision board. What are the things you want to have more of in your life?

Include them in your affirmations and combine them with a feeling of gratitude. For example, if you want more abundance in your life, an affirmation such as, "I am well-compensated for my efforts at work, I attract abundance in all areas of my life, I attract amazing opportunities to my business and life" is something you want to focus on. Be sure to use your affirmations in a mindful way. Feel them, don't just recite them. Also, create them in a way that feels right and powerful for you in a given moment.

At first, it may seem to you that the affirmations don't work or don't do anything. You need to trust the process and be patient. You will realize the power of your efforts when you catch your inner voice guiding you in the right direction.

For example, you feel like skipping your workout or a heathy meal. Then, all of a sudden, the affirmation you've been repeating for so many months comes in to save you, in a very subconscious manner. It tells you:

"Come on! That is not who you are, you love working out, you love fitness, you love going to the gym, you deserve a healthy fit body."

This happens only because several months earlier, you mindfully created an affirmation that said, "I deserve a healthy, fit body and I just love going to the gym."

Or perhaps you are on a call with a client. Your old self feels like undercharging for your services. But, then, you receive the guidance from the new, more empowered version of you that tells you:

"Wait, that's not who you are! You deserve to charge more. People will appreciate your services and will want more of them."

This happens because you mindfully came up with a powerful affirmation that said, "I attract amazing clients who value my work and are happy to pay higher prices. I deserve a business I love, and I deserve abundance through the work I do."

Again, choose an affirmation that speaks to you in a positive way, or even an affirmation to which you have a negative or uncomfortable reaction. It's okay, because sometimes a strong negative reaction towards an affirmation or area of weakness means we need to really work on that specific area. The best emotional and long-lasting motivational growth happens here.

Write the affirmation over and over again. You can also record it and listen to it while you are doing some things around the house. At first, it will feel weird, even a bit uncomfortable to listen to yourself (unless, of course, your profession is around acting, singing or being a voice artist). But, any feeling of discomfort is temporary and will soon offer you unexpected empowerment exactly when you need it.

Meditation to Stay Motivated?

This one is my favorite and you can easily do it, even if you are new to meditation. All you need to get started is the willingness to give your mind some space to let go of distractions.

Think: five minutes of quiet time, when you can be free and just focus on you.

Before you begin your meditation, start with an intention. For example:

"I am relaxed."
"I am focused."
"I am productive."
"I enjoy my dream house."

You can also focus on your ultimate vision, and in your mind, go through various pictures from your vision board. Then, with your intention in mind, simply sit somewhere in your room or outside in nature, it's totally up to you.

Sit cross-legged or in a way that feels good. Breathe slowly and deliberately, but don't force anything, just let it come. Focus on your breath. Breathe in and out, in and out. Picture the air going into your lungs, resting there for a second and then moving out.

When any stressful thoughts creep in, relax, accept them and go back to focusing on your breath. Meditation is a fantastic and very often under-valued tool to work on your motivation muscle. You see, meditation is about gently overcoming distractions by accepting them and bringing the focus back to your main thing, which, in the case of meditation is your breath.

Just like in life, there will be distractions, toxic people and circumstances to put you to test, but you will be prepared to accept them. You won't feel guilty about them and you will just go back to doing your main thing- getting closer to manifesting your vision.

So, meditate and don't worry if your mind wanders, it's normal. Keep breathing in and out. Like a steady heartbeat. Take at least five minutes a day to mediate and always be sure to start off with one clean intention.

I know what you're thinking…Meditation for motivation? Really?

After all, doesn't meditation have to do with just resting and being content? And if motivation is anything, it's the drive to achieve or gain something, right?

But meditation is about more than contentment and peace of mind. Meditation is about clarity and living in an honest, straightforward relation to your world. Meditation does not just make a permanent dent on your cushion. It also makes a deep impact on the way you live your life and how you get and stay motivated. Besides, things go better when you are at peace with yourself.

I know it can be challenging to find some self-care time for yourself. But something is better than nothing. Two minutes a day, every day will eventually compound. Just like with any goal in life- it doesn't have to be all or nothing. Focus on the baby steps and enjoy the process.

Even if you meditate a few minutes before you go to bed, that works too and you can set an intention to rest well, reconnect with your vision and even allow your subconscious mind to give you answers to your questions while you sleep. By allowing yourself to close your eyes and meditate before you go to sleep, not only will you sleep better but you will also wake up more energized and happier the next day.

Also, give yourself some space to experiment to see what works for you: Each and every one of these rituals is, well.... a *ritual*. You can't run a marathon without training, just like you can't change your life or do a 180 on one aspect of your life overnight. It's one small baby step at a time. Over time, the transformation will come.

Throughout my ongoing journey of holistic self-help and spirituality, the lesson of ditching perfection for progress has been the hardest one to learn. When I first got started on mindful morning rituals, I would do one day of the practices from this chapter, not see a ton of change right away and give up, feeling like a loser. Nope, nope. Doesn't work that way.

The trick is always, "slow and steady wins the race". Start off with just a mini five minute mindful morning ritual you can commit to.

See how you feel. For example, you can start off with journaling, then add in the affirmations, then the meditation. Or start off with whatever practice you feel attracted to now. Listen to your body and mind, they have all the answers. Follow your instincts. You can even keep switching between your favorite practices, so that you don't get bored. The essence of doing all this is basically to grow your motivation muscle by aligning yourself with your core and your ultimate vision on a daily basis. It's about following up with a simple, daily action plan that feels good and natural for you.

Pretty soon, you'll have an awesome morning routine that will keep you in the moment, present, and ready to take on life's challenges at their core. At your core. Because your core is strong and ready for the tasks at hand.

Conclusion

Be yourself. Embrace your uniqueness. Be the best you that you can be. Do *not*, for any reason, settle for less.

We can elevate our frequency and push ourselves to be even better simply by working on our beliefs and inner game.

When things don't go your way, allow yourself to take a step back. Revise your vision, drive and motivation. Go through the exercises from this book several times. Are you still going in the direction you truly desire? Continue to stay the course, even though occasionally it may need to be revised.

Reality will win out if you let it, so think big. Think vast. Think tall and wide and deep and thoroughly. Know that you have the power to change someone's life and, most specifically, your own.

Understand the value in that. And then go out and spread the love. Love conquers fear. Love unleashes your power and unstoppable motivation.

We get one life. One. Get serious about changing it for the better. Because you truly can, you deserve to, and the world is a much better place because of your transformation that inspires those around you.

Motivation and happiness can be found through many avenues and for all of them the journey itself is usually the joy. The destination is what we want to achieve, but it is in getting there that we constantly find out more about ourselves and our own uniqueness.

It's the process that makes us stronger and grows our motivation muscle while helping us transform on a deeper level. And this is the most fascinating of all. Who you become in the process of learning about your vision, ambitions, and motivations.

Part 4 – Law of Attraction for Motivation

Part 5 – Book 5

Law of Attraction for Amazing Relationships

How to Drastically Improve Your Love Life and Find Ever-Lasting Happiness with the Law of Attraction!

Introduction

Having written numerous books on the Law of Attraction, I have always tried to find a way to explain this topic in a way that was relatable to everyone. When it was suggested that I write about relationships, I knew that I had received my answer.

Any challenge that we have with relationships is due to our lack of understanding of how the Law of Attraction works, that we attracted the people who are in our life, for better or for worse. Unknowingly, most of us try to deal with relationship issues without ever addressing the main source, ourselves.

To deal with relationship issues, we often turn to our friends or experts. Many of us read self-help books, see a counselor, or turn to some spiritual teaching like astrology. Yes, I said "spiritual teaching"! You may be saying to yourself "Wait a minute! Isn't the Law of Attraction a spiritual teaching?" My hope is that, by the time that you finish this book, you will understand what I mean by this statement. While talking to a friend, reading a self-help book, seeing a mental health professional, or turning to a spiritual teaching can be helpful, it is rare that any of these sources can direct us to the root cause of our challenges.

Because we so often restrict our search to the surface level, the frustrations that we experience in our relationships usually live on, despite our best intentions.

It is my hope that the content in this book will trigger the intrinsic knowing that exists within all of us and cause you to remember an essential truth, that you are the creator of all of your experiences. It is only in our amnesia of this truth that we experience frustration or suffering in our lives, which is the purpose of our relationships.

Our relationships are our mirror to our inner selves; they provide us with a glimpse of ourselves that we may otherwise miss.

From the perspective of higher awareness, there is no such thing as a relationship problem. What we call "relationship problems" are really the gifts of the universe that allow us to take a deeper look at ourselves.

Throughout the book, I have used a variety of terms for consciousness, including the greater consciousness, the greater consciousness system, the higher self, or the true self. I have done this just to avoid repetition and to provide variety.

All of these terms refer to the same thing, which is pure consciousness, that which exists beyond our conceptual understanding. If you are ready to take a deep look, I welcome you.

Chapter 1: Thoughts, Beliefs, and Reality

We will start off this chapter with an exercise. Sit down, make yourself comfortable, and close your eyes.

1. I want you to imagine a full moon. Make this image as real as possible.
   Note: Everyone visualizes differently. The visualizations of some people are vivid, while those of others may be blurry or murky. Just visualize the way that is natural for your and trust yourself.
2. Now, I want you to visualize a red sports car, making it as real as possible.
3. Finally, I want you to visualize a red rose.
4. Now open your eyes.

Did you learn anything from this exercise? If you are unable to answer this question, do not let it bother you. Most people would have difficulty answering it. So, just in case, let me help you by guiding you to the answer.

First of all, you imagined a full moon, a red sports car, and a red rose. Most likely, you did not confuse any of these images with who you are. You did not think that you were the full moon, the red sports car, or the red rose. Why didn't you? There are two reasons for this. The first reason was that you were the observer of these images. Second, these images lacked significant meaning for you. You are not your thoughts! You are the observer of thoughts.

The challenge that we face is that we often forget that we are not our thoughts. It was easy for you to understand this when doing this exercise, but what about the times when you are experiencing thoughts of anger, frustration, concern, jealousy, or fear?

During these times, it is very easy to get caught-up in our thoughts. If we have thoughts of anger, we become anger. If we have thoughts of insecurity, we become insecurity, and so on. All these thoughts are no different than the thoughts of the full moon, the red sports car, or the red rose. Regardless of the thought that you have, you are not it.

The ancient Greek philosopher Plato put forth a theory which he termed the "Allegory of the Cave." This allegory was intended to cause the listener of his teaching to question the accuracy of their perceptions and thinking and look toward a more reliable truth. In his analogy, he proposed a scenario where he asked his student to imagine a cave which is inhabited by people. These people were born in the cave and had never experienced the world outside of it. In fact, they are not even aware of its existence. The people in the cave are chained in a manner that the only direction they can look toward is the back of the cave. They are unable to view the mouth of the cave.

Part 5 – Law of Attraction for Amazing Relationships

Unbeknownst to the people in the cave, there is a fire that continually burns near the mouth of the cave. Anytime a person or animal passes between the fire and the mouth of the cave; their shadows are cast against the back of the cave. The people of the cave believe that the projected shadows are real, that they are actual beings that also inhabit the cave.

One day, one of the cave people managed to break out of his chains and ventured out of the cave. He was bewildered by the new world that he saw, believing that it was some illusion.
As he became more familiar with this new world, he began to realize that this new world was not an illusion, that it was the shadows on the cave's wall that were illusionary.

This denizen of the cave who broke out of his chains and ventured into the outside had expanded his level of awareness. It took a totally different experience for him to gain the understanding that he had believed in the illusions of the shadows for all of his life.

The chains that bounded this person are also part of the metaphor in that they represent our experience of life when we trust our misperceptions. It is only when we have the courage to venture out of the cave that we experience a greater truth, which requires us to break the chains that are holding us. What are these chains that are binding us? Essentially, it is our fear and our conditioning.

The analogy of the cave is a great metaphor for understanding how we are affected by our thoughts and perceptions. An understanding of the illusionary quality our thoughts and perceptions are essential if we are to understand the Law of Attraction and how it impacts our relationships. But before we go any further, let us consider another analogy for challenging our notions of reality, which everyone can relate to.

Most of us believe that our everyday experience of life is ultimate reality, that how we experience ourselves and the world around us is reality. Consider this: When you have a dream, doesn't it become your reality while you are experiencing it? What about when you have a nightmare? Can anyone who has ever had a nightmare deny that the experience was real for them? Some nightmares are so vivid that even when we wake-up we experience moments of disorientation and confusion.

When we have a dream, we are projecting our thoughts, which we experience as our dream self and its dream world. I used to have reoccurring dreams where I could fly to get from place to place. With each place I flew to, I engaged with other dream characters and dream environments. In one dream, I descended onto a busy market place in some third world country. I experienced a vibrant and bustling market place where other dream characters were going about their business. Further, my experience of myself was very real. I had thoughts, experienced feelings, and emotions, and I took action in this dream world.

Part 5 – Law of Attraction for Amazing Relationships

All of these experiences were a projection of my consciousness. When I woke up the next morning, I realized it was just a dream and experienced the reality of my waking world. But who can say that our waking world is not just another dream?

Who can say that our experience of daily life is just another projection of some greater truth? Some of you may make the argument that our waking life is real because we live it every day; we are working, taking care of our families, and making important decisions. But don't these things occur in our dreams as well?

I present to you these scenarios for one reason, which is this: How we experience our relationships, and anything else in life, is based on how we interpret the information that is contained in your experience. How you interpret the information of your experiences is based on our beliefs, the same beliefs that led the cave denizens to believe that the shadows were actual beings or for me to believe that I was flying in a third world marketplace. My question to you is what beliefs do you hold to that are hindering or empowering your relationships?

When you have an issue in your relationship, what thoughts or beliefs do you normally experience? Do you frequently experience thoughts like:
- "I cannot believe he did that!"
- *"She is always nagging or criticizing me."*
- "Does he love me?"
- *"Why did he say that?"*
- "She does not believe me."
- *"I can't trust him."*
- "He never tells me what is going on."
- *"I wish he would be closer to me."*
- "Men, they are all alike."
- *"Women, they are all like."*
- "I do not think he loves me."

Regardless of the thought, you have about your relationship, if you regularly give it your attention, you strengthen that thought. There is a metaphor that I once heard that I really like regarding a table. Imagine that thought is like the legs of a table. If you have a particular thought about your relationship, which occasionally arises in your awareness, it is like a table top with only a single leg attached to it.

A table top with a single leg is not stable and can easily collapse. Now imagine that you experience something in your relationship that reinforces that thought, now is as though you have two table legs supporting the table top.

Part 5 – Law of Attraction for Amazing Relationships

For example, you occasionally wonder if your boyfriend or girlfriend is taking you for granted; however, you do not take that thought seriously. Then one day, he or she seems to blow you off when you are obviously having a bad day. Your original thought has a new reference point that strengthens or confirms your original thought.

Now let us say several other incidents occur where you feel like you are being taken for granted. These additional incidents are like the third and fourth table leg. Now the table top stands steady; it is firmly established. The table top in this metaphor is what we refer to as a belief. A belief is a thought which you have a sense of certainty about as being true.

Now let us shift from metaphor to how your thoughts actually work. To begin with, your thoughts are nothing but bits of information, which you attract to you. What causes thoughts to be attracted to you is the attention that you give them. I use the words "are attracted to you" for a specific reason. Though it may be difficult to believe, particularly in the early stages of this book, you do not have thoughts! Your brain does not create thoughts!

You can think of thoughts as a signal from a cell phone tower. In this metaphor, you are the cell phone. Just as signals from the cell phone towers are received by the cell phone, the bits of information that you receive, known as thoughts, is received by you.

You may be wondering where the thoughts that you receive come from. The answer to that question will be discussed later on in this book. For now, know that you do not create your thoughts; you are the one that attracts them through your attention.

Your thoughts are powerless in that they lack any inherent power of their own. The only power that our thoughts have is the power that we give them through our attention.

So let us return to the previous example that you believe that the person you are having a relationship with is taking you for granted.

That belief started off with a thought, which you were entertaining. Because you gave this thought your attention, it energized it, giving it some power. Because it became energized, that thought attracted other thoughts that were of similar quality. Your original thought "I think my partner is taking me for granted" attracted other thought of the same energetic level, such as "He or she did not bother to inquire how I was feeling."

Because you gave that thought your attention, it attracted the next thought, perhaps "He did not ask if he could do anything to make me feel better." In this manner, our thoughts are like a magnet that attracts iron filings. Just as iron filings accumulate around the magnet, the original thought that you continually gave your attention to attract an army of other thoughts of like quality.

Part 5 – Law of Attraction for Amazing Relationships

Now let us use another scenario, using the same theme as the last one. In this scenario, you are feeling down and there is someone, who you have absolutely no interest in, who totally ignores you. The fact that this person is ignoring you does not disturb you a bit. In fact, you are glad he or she is not trying to interact with you because you have no desire to talk to this person. Your attention is no longer attracting the thought " He is taking me for granted." Because you do not give this thought your attention, it fails to carry any potency in our conscious awareness. Why is this information important to understand? Well, there are a number of reasons, which we will discuss later in this book. For now, let us focus on the power that beliefs have on our lives.

You can think of beliefs as colored tinted sunglasses. If you wear sunglasses that are tinted yellow, then everything that you experience will appear to be yellow in color. If you wear red tinted sunglasses, everything will appear to be red. Just as tinted sunglasses color the world that we see, our beliefs color our experience of life, especially our relationships.

Whatever belief you have about your relationship, it will color every aspect of your relationship. Your beliefs determine what you focus on in your relationship; they will determine how you feel about your relationship; they will determine the decisions that you make about your relationship, and they will determine the kind of actions that you will take regarding your relationship.

The question is what happens if your beliefs are not accurate? Once you believe something with conviction, it is extremely difficult to see any other perspective, even when your perspective does not accurately reflect how the other person feels.

When you proclaim that you know what another person is thinking or feeling, and they tell you otherwise, you will conclude that they are not honest with you, when in fact they may be very sincere.

Does this mean that you should never trust your beliefs and believe whatever they say? No, of course not! We will explore this further later on. For now, realize that each one of us creates our own unique perspective on our experience in life.

The perspective that each one of us has is determined by the beliefs that we hold, and the beliefs that we hold are based on the thoughts that we attract, which brings us to the Law of Attraction. The thoughts that you attract is just one example of the Law of Attraction in action.

Each person is giving their attention to a particular thought, which is attracting other thoughts. It is through the attraction of thoughts that each one of us creates our own unique perspective.

Is because of this simple fact that relationships always have and will always be complicated; they are complicated because no two persons in the history of this planet will ever share the exact same perspective. What may seem to be a cruel joke on the part of the universe is actually a gift.
We will discuss this soon in another chapter. For now, we need to talk about emotions, which is the subject of the next chapter.

Chapter 2: The Link between Thoughts and Emotions

In the previous chapter, it was explained that our thoughts are bits of information that we attract through our attention. Our emotions are a mirror to our thought, or we could say that our emotions are a message to us indicating the kinds of thoughts that we are experiencing. We may not always know the thoughts that we are experiencing, especially if they are subconscious; however, our emotions will inform us to the kind of thoughts that we are experiencing, regardless if we are aware of our thoughts or not. If you are experiencing the emotion of anger, it is because you are having thoughts of anger.

It is important that we further explore the statement that I made regarding "thoughts of anger." Let me begin by saying that there are no angry thoughts, nor are there happy thoughts or thoughts that depict any other kind of emotion.

Thoughts are just bits of information that we process, just as information is processed by a computer. The information in your computer is not bad or good, happy or sad, frustrated or relaxed; it is just information. Similarly, your thoughts are just information. We create "happy thoughts" or "sad" thoughts by projecting meaning on to our thoughts. To better understand this, let us look back in history to a famous experiment.

Ivan Pavlov was a Russian scientist who conducted an experiment to demonstrate conditioning. Pavlov would show a piece of meat to a dog, which caused the dog to salivate. The dog had become conditioned to associate meat with food as part of its evolution in becoming a predator. Pavlov would then ring a bell at the same time that he presented meat to the dog. He would do this repeatedly, present the meat while ringing the bell. With time, Pavlov only had to ring the bell and the dog would salivate.

Originally, the bell would not elicit any response from the dog. It was after repeatedly pairing the bell with the meat that the bell took on a new meaning for the dog. In the same way, your thoughts are like the bell before it was linked to the meat. After repeated experience, you had learned to associate meaning to your thoughts.

Simply stated, nothing in this world has inherent meaning to it. Rather, it is you that creates the meaning of your thoughts; thus, your experience. Since your emotions are a mirror of your thoughts, you also create the meaning that you experience through your emotions.

Returning to our original scenario of "my partner takes me for granted," the person who had this thought was projecting it on her partner. She created the meaning and then projected it on him; just as when I projected my thoughts and created an alternate reality where I was flying to a third world market place while dreaming.

Chapter 3: Who Are You?

The question of who you are is the most important question that you will ever ask. No question can ever be more meaningful than this one. I do not care if someone is a great scientist, a great philosopher, or a world leader. Without understanding who we are, we are no better than the people of the Allegory of the Cave. Just as the shadows were the reality of the people in the cave, we take our experiences to be reality. Before we can understand our perceived reality, we need to understand the perceiver.

Unless we do this, we are like the shadow gazers in the cave or the one who wears yellow tinted sunglasses and believes the world is yellow. The quality of your relationships will reach new heights when you first learn to understand yourself.

Who is the one that is aware of this book that you are reading? Who is the one who could conjure up images of a full moon, a red sports car, or a red rose? Who is the one that was aware that you were neither of these things? Who is the one that is aware of thought, perception, or sensation? Who are the one that is aware of the dream world and the awakening from it? The most obvious answer to these questions would be "I am," or "Me." Yet, you are aware of this as well. Who is aware of "I am" or "Me"? The words "I am" or "Me" are just thoughts or concepts; yet, there is awareness of them.

I have had out of body experiences before. I was aware of being out of body, and I knew when I returned to my body. Who was the one that was aware of these things? When you go into deep sleep, beyond any dream, you have entered a realm that is devoid of all thought.

Because there is no thought, there is no sense of experience. Since there is no experience, there is no memory of deep sleep. Yet, you know that you had experienced it. Who is the one that is aware of deep sleep? If you continue to respond to these questions with answers like "I am," "Me," "my mind," or "I don't know," who is the one that is aware of these answers?

The answer to all of these questions cannot be found by thinking about it. Any answer that you could give is recognized or known by you. Who are you? How can you be anything that you are aware of?

There is the one that is aware and there is the object of awareness. Any answer that you can give is an object in your awareness; otherwise, you would not be aware of it! Rather than just reading about it, I want you to start experiencing for yourself what I am talking about.
1. Sit down, make yourself comfortable, and close your eyes.
2. Breathing normally, place your attention on your breath. Your only job is to be aware of the sensations that you experience as your breath travels in and out of your body during inhalation and exhalation.

3. At some point, you will get distracted by your thoughts. Do not try to control or stop your thoughts. It will not work! Rather than trying to do battle with your thoughts, offer them your complete acceptance.
4. As soon as you acknowledge your thoughts, return your attention back to your breath. No matter how many times you get distracted by your thought, just return your attention back to your breath.
5. Do not judge anything that you experience. Do not try to control or resist any of your experiences. Do not try to use your imagination or try to make things happen. Just observe your experiences through your awareness of it. To be aware of anything is to know of its existence.
6. The more you catch yourself getting distracted by your thoughts, the better you will become in recognizing that you have become distracted without getting caught up in them. The more you practice this exercise, the calmer your mind will become.

When you start experiencing a calmer mind, take your experience as step further by doing the next exercise.

Part 2
1. Sit down, make yourself comfortable, and close your eyes.
2. Breathing normally, place your attention on your breath. Your only job is to be aware of the sensations that you experience as your breath travels in and out of your body during inhalation and exhalation.
3. If you get distracted by your thoughts, just return your attention back to your breath. As your mind becomes calmer, remove your focus from your breath and allow yourself just to relax. Do not try to focus on anything. Just remain aware of anything that you experience.
4. Be aware of any sensations that you experience.
5. Be aware of the coming and going of thought.
6. Be aware of any perceptions or images that may appear.
7. Be aware of the sounds that you hear in your surroundings.
8. Be aware of all that you experience.
9. Do not try to identify, analyze, or get curious about anything that you experience. Do not engage in any thinking. Just observe.
10. There can be no experience without the awareness of it. Can you find that which is aware of all that you experience?

Chapter 4: The Law of Attraction Works through You!

In the last exercise, were you able to identify that which is aware of all of your experiences? If you were not able to, know that you are on the right track.

That which is aware of all of your experiences is your most essential nature. Who you are is beyond any thought that you could ever conceive. Who you are is beyond anything that you could ever experience. Who you are is awareness itself!

The advance of the sciences, such as quantum physics, has demonstrated that the world of form is just an illusion. The world of form is like the shadows in the allegory of the cave.

It has been discovered that the atom, once formerly believed to be a solid structure, is now known to be formless. In other words, the building blocks of all physical form are nonphysical! You are no different. Though you may believe that you are physical being, this belief is only a half truth. You are a multi-dimensional being in that you are both physical and a non-physical at the same time.

In your physical dimension, you experience yourself as being a unique and separate individual who lives amid a physical world with other physical beings. In your nonphysical dimension, you do not exist as an individual being as your most essential is that of oneness. Popular expressions such as "God is love" or "Everything is One" refers to your nonphysical dimension. Everything that exists in the physical realm merges into the non-physical. Conversely, the non-physical realm is the source of the physical realm. At the non-physical level, there is no individualization or separation, at this level, there is no sense of relationship.

For a relationship to exist, there must be a sense of separation. You experience yourself having a relationship with other people because you experience yourself as being separate from them. How can there be a relationship when there is no sense of separation? Without a sense of separation, there is no "you and me" or "us and them," there is only energy and information. The basis of the entire universe is energy and information; everything that appears to be physical is simply a temporary manifestation of this energy and information. That which we refer to as love, especially the higher forms of love (as opposed to conditional love), is referring to this energy and information. It is referred to as love because it is totally inclusive, all encompassing, and whole. If you were able to successfully do the last meditation, you were fully aware of all of your thoughts, sensations, and perceptions. Not only were you fully aware of them, but you also offered complete acceptance of their existence. These are the qualities of inclusiveness and all encompassing. Your experience was inclusive because you did not judge any of your experiences. Your experience was all encompassing because you were aware of all of your experiences. If you experienced a sense of wholeness, it was because you were not experiencing any scarcity, needing, or desire. Your experience was enough for you to feel complete.

Part 5 – Law of Attraction for Amazing Relationships

The non-physical aspect of you is consciousness, and it is the purpose of consciousness is to expand. Expansion can only come about through the encountering of experience.
Since the nature of your highest aspect is oneness, consciousness differentiates itself by manifesting into physical form. By taking on a physical form, a sense of separateness appears, and a sense of separateness creates experience. It is through the act of experiencing that information is gained. The gaining of information is what leads to the expansion of consciousness.

Every experience that you have leads to the gaining of new information and that new information leads to the expansion of consciousness, not only in your physical form, but in the larger consciousness system.

The quality of information that you provide the consciousness system determines if whether you are evolving into love (the larger consciousness system) or if you are becoming further removed from it and staying identified with your physical form, which leads to suffering. We suffer because we identify with our physical form, which is the result of the ego. Since we identify with our minds and bodies, we experience a lack of wholeness, that something is missing from our lives. We seek out relationships in our attempts to regain that sense of wholeness.

Because most of us have identified with our minds and bodies, we have forgotten our connection to the larger consciousness system, which is our essential self. With that forgetfulness, we have lost our sense of connection with the rest of the universe.

There is nothing special about the Law of Attraction, and it is operating in our lives at every moment. The basis of the universe is energy and that energy contains the potential to manifest itself in infinite ways.

Your manifested form, your physical body, is made of energy, the same energy that belongs to the larger consciousness system. You are no more separate from the larger consciousness than a drop of ocean water is from the ocean itself.

However, as a manifested form, you have qualities about you that the larger consciousness does not have. The larger consciousness is pure, without any form distinction or differentiation; it is oneness. In your manifested form, that pure consciousness becomes conditioned by the thoughts and beliefs that we adopt.

Just as Pavlov's dog became conditioned to salivate at the sound of a bell, we have become conditioned to believe that we are our minds and bodies. The conditioned consciousness takes on different qualities and those different qualities of consciousness attract other forms of energy that are of a like kind. Let's examine this more closely using examples that we can easily identify with: Alice grew up in an environment, where she was deprived of attention and warmth. Alice's essential being is that of pure consciousness. Alice's physical being is a localized expression of her higher self. Additionally, Alice, like most of us, identifies with her physical form; she believes that she is her thoughts and physical body.

Because she did not receive attention and warmth as a child, she developed beliefs about herself like: "Expressing warmth and vulnerability is scary" and " I am not lovable." These beliefs condition her consciousness in a way that her life's energy will attract those things into her life whose' energy is of like quality. When it comes to relationships, she will attract those partners who also resist expressing warmth and vulnerability, which will reinforce her beliefs that she is unlovable. Should a partner express warmth and vulnerability, it will create discomfort within her because she does not know how to act.

Energy cannot be created or destroyed; the only thing that it can do is to take on a different form. Let us imagine that year's pass and the energy that Alice repressed (by fearing warmth or vulnerability) finally takes its toll. Alice experiences some major life changes, and she is unable to handle those changes emotionally.

She has hit bottom; her pain is so great that she gets professional help. She gradually learns to stop repressing her feelings and gains the courage to express them. All those years of resisting the experiencing of her emotions and feelings have reached their breaking point.

By allowing herself to express and experience them, her life's energy takes on new quality, one that will attract into her life those relationships and conditions that are consistent with her higher level of energy.

In Chapter 1, we discussed the nature of thoughts, emotions; however, we did not discuss feelings. Now it's the perfect time to do so. Your feelings are your direct connection to the greater consciousness. When you are experiencing feelings of frustration, fear, anxiety, or concern, you are out of alignment with your higher self. When you are experiencing feelings of well-being, joy, love, or appreciation, you are aligned with your higher self or greater consciousness.

One of the most valuable things that you can do to effectively attract that which you desire, including the relationships that you want, is to develop greater awareness of your thoughts, emotions, and feelings for they are an indicator of what you are attracting into your life.
As stated earlier, you are always attracting things into your life, whether you believe in the Law of Attraction or not. It is like gravity. Whether you believe in gravity or not, gravity affects you. The only difference between someone who consciously applies the Law of Attraction and someone who does not is the quality of their experience.

The first person will attract into their life a broad range of beneficial experiences that support them in their growth as an evolved human, while those who are not conscious of the Law of Attraction will judge themselves or their experience as a reflection of their self-worth, as well as being out of their control.

While the first person understands that they are responsible for what they attract, the latter will blame their misfortune on others, bad luck, or themselves. When we blame ourselves, we believe that we are not worthy, which lowers our vibration.

In writing that the first person understands that they are responsible for what they attract, I do not mean this in a way that implies morality or guilt. Rather, they take responsibility in that they are aware of the vibrational level of their life and change it as needed so that they are attracting that which they intend.

Part 5 – Law of Attraction for Amazing Relationships

Chapter 5: The Vibrational Level of Your Life

I will be using terms like vibrational level or frequency often in this book, so now is the time to clarify what I mean by these terms.

There is nothing abstract or mysterious about these terms; we experience them on a moment by moment basis. As mentioned earlier, everything in existence is comprised of energy, so your vibrational level or frequency is the quality of your energy.

You experience this energy through your thoughts, emotions, and feelings. To be aware of your vibrational level or frequency is to be aware of your thoughts, emotions, and feelings. The quality of these three phenomena reflects the quality of your experience of life, including your relationships. This becomes very obvious when you look at the quality of your relationships or in the relationships of those who you know. The following are just a few hypothetical examples of how the quality of life's energy attracts those of like kind:

- A woman, who feels insecure and significant, enters a relationship with a man who becomes abusive toward her. Her low vibrational energy makes her an easy target for him, while his low vibrational energy causes him to control her so that he can feel a sense of power.
- *A woman, who wants to feel complete, feels that being married to a rich and successful husband will make her happy. She meets such a man and gets married to him. What she does not realize is that he also wants to feel complete. In order to feel complete, he is super focused on achieving, in order to feel better about himself. Since he has little time for her, she remains feeling incomplete.*
- A very attractive woman has a best friend who is very plain looking. The attractive woman is tired of the attention she gets from men, making her feel uncomfortable. Further, she finds that other women become jealous of her because of her look. Her plain friend wants to remain inconspicuous because he does not feel desirable.

A man, who has had limited experience with women in the past, desperately wants a girlfriend. He meets a woman who has recently broken up with her boyfriend. She wants to be in a relationship because she does not like being alone and seeks her security by being in a relationship.

Both of these people enter the relationship with an energy that is low in vibration as it is based on fear and need. At first, they cannot get enough of each other and the relationship seems perfect, that is until their needs for being in a relationship is met. When this need is met, they realize how neither one of them are getting their needs met. Their needs for being in a relationship was met, but their relationship needs were not.

The point is simple; there are no accidents in this life. Every person that enters your life is there for a reason. In the next chapter, we will explore why every person that enters your life is a gift to you from the universe.

There is a term that is commonly used in the spiritual community, which I want to challenge, that term is the "twin flame." This term refers to the belief that there is one person in this life that is your perfect match. It is my argument that the whole idea of a "twin flame" is just a romantic notion. From the perspective of the Law of Attraction, every person that you meet is your perfect match, though that may seem otherwise.

Remember, at the level of the greater consciousness there is only oneness; It is in our physical manifestation that we experience separation, which creates a sense of relationship between you and others. It is in your relationships, be they casual or intimate, that lead to the expansion of consciousness, both at the individual and cosmic level.

It is only through you interacting with others that the expansion of the universe can occur.

Your perfect mirror

Earlier, I offered you a metaphor of your relationship to the greater consciousness, which was a drop of seawater in the ocean. While it may seem insignificant, a drop of sea water has the same composition as the ocean itself.

When the greater consciousness differentiated itself, leading to your physical manifestation, you became a localized aspect of the greater consciousness. As the drop is to the ocean, you are to the greater consciousness.

The greater consciousness differentiated itself so that it could experience contrast through experience. You have probably heard adages such as "You cannot know the light unless you first know the dark," or "You cannot know peace unless you first experience war."

These adages are referring to contrast. It is only through contrast that the higher self can experience itself, which leads to its expansion. The greater consciousness system is unable to experience contrast because it's nature is oneness, which is why it appears in manifested forms, as with you and I.

Experience occurs when there is contrast, and experience leads to the creation of information. Imagine a small child who has never seen a stove. The child touches the stove and burns itself. The child has just experienced contrast: The absence of pain and the existence of pain. This contrast creates experience. Further, the child gains information, which is that stoves are hot. You are the interface that makes it possible for your higher self to learn about its own existence!
When the larger consciousness gains its formation from your experience, it creates experiences that are consistent with the information that it has received.

What is the information that consciousness receives that determines the experiences that it creates for you? The answer to that question is your vibrational energy, which you experience as your thoughts, emotions, and feelings.

We have already discussed the basics of thoughts, emotions, and feelings. In the next chapter, we will discuss their vibrational quality and how they affect your ability to attract that which you want in your life.

Part 5 – Law of Attraction for Amazing Relationships

Chapter 6: About your Vibe

In this chapter, we will discuss how thoughts and emotions contribute to your vibrational level.

Thoughts

It is a popular misconception that we attract into our life that which we think of, that our thoughts are what creates our manifestations. While our thoughts are definitely a component of the manifestation process, what is even more powerful is our emotions and feelings. If you are looking to find inner peace, a sense of well-being, or to become a conscious manifester, the less that you depend on your thoughts, the better you will be.

Depending on our thoughts to manifest is unreliable because our thoughts are unreliable. Our minds are all about self-preservation, the preservation of our ego. Let me share with you an example of this from my own experience when I was just starting off learning about the Law of Attraction.

I meditated to develop a quiet mind and then made the intention that I wanted to know what book or magazine cover I would encounter when I went to the library that day. I received an image of the cover that I would see, after which I quickly forgot about it. When I got to the library, I walked around the book aisles just to browse (I had forgotten about my intention). As I browsed, I came across a magazine that the same cover that I had experienced in my meditation. It was a cover that I had never seen before, other than in my meditation.

I was so excited that I had successfully manifested intentionally! I then decided to test my abilities out again. I went into my meditation and made an intention that I wanted to see a certain object when I was out and about. At first, I did not think about the object but then my mind got actively involved. I was actively looking for the object, which later led me to start doubting myself. Needless to say, I never encountered the object.

There is a term in spirituality known as detachment, the ability to not cling on to anything, including our thoughts. Detachment was a characteristic of my first manifesting experience; it definitely was not in my second experience.

The challenge to developing detachment is that it takes practice and patience as it is very easy to engage with the mind when you are trying to practice detachment.
The second challenge of relying on thoughts for manifesting is that there may be thoughts that we are not aware of. Subconscious thoughts, more accurately known as subconscious beliefs, can easily act as a counter force against any conscious thoughts that you may have.

Emotions

Your emotions are a more dependable and a more effective point of focus than your thoughts alone. First of all, your emotions are a reflection of your beliefs. The second advantage is that by focusing on your emotions, you remove your focus from your thoughts. The advantage of this is that you remove yourself from the influence of the ego. The following is a list of emotions that are ranked according to their vibrational level.

1. Apathy
2. Shame
3. Guilt
4. Grief
5. Fear
6. Anger
7. Acceptance
8. Joy
9. Gratitude
10. Appreciation
11. Love/Compassion
12. Enlightenment

Apathy: Apathy is ranked the lowest of the emotions on the list because all emotional connection is cut off when we are experiencing apathy. Apathy is a condition where emotions are suppressed. Since emotions are energy, apathy is the suppression of energy.

Shame: The emotion of shame is the second lowest emotion as it involves negatively focusing on yourself. Since you are energizing the low-frequency thoughts that you have of yourself, you are attracting other thoughts of the same frequency.

Earlier in this book, I had you imagine a full moon a red sports car, and a red rose. You were to focus on these images; yet, you did not identify with these images, at no time did you believe that you were these images. These images were a form of thought. Unlike these thoughts, you experience other thoughts which you do identify with. If you ever found yourself caught up in anger, jealousy, or frustration, you had identified with a thought. The emotion of shame takes self-identification to an all time low.

Guilt: Guilt is the next lowest emotion because guilt, like shame, a degree of identification with the ego. The emotion of guilt is intended to be a message to you that you need to change your beliefs about your relationship toward other people. If you change your beliefs for more empowering ones, then guilt has performed its function. If you dwell on how inadequate you are as a human being, you have thrown yourself to the mercy of your mind. Where shame is based on self-worth, guilt is more based on behavior.

Grief: Grief is the emotion of loss and the sense of loss is based on a sense of separation. From the point of higher levels of consciousness, it is impossible to experience grief because the sense of separation does not exist.

Fear: While grief is the emotion of loss, fear is the anticipation of loss. One of the biggest challenges in a relationship is based on fear, the fear of losing an aspect of ourselves and the fear of losing the other person.

Anger: Anger is a reaction to fear, and it has a higher frequency than fear. We experience anger because we feel something that we have identified with is being threatened. If you did not feel identified with that which is being threatened, you would not be angry. You would most likely not feel angry if someone rear ended another driver; you are more likely to experience anger if the car that was rear ended is yours.

Satisfaction: The emotion of satisfaction is a higher vibration than anger because it involves less identification. Both anger and fear are experienced as result of identifying with something outside ourselves. The emotion of satisfaction is an indicator that the emotion of fear is temporarily absent. While a higher frequency than anger, the emotion of satisfaction will be fleeting as long as we continued to identify with our thoughts or the people and objects around us.

Happiness: The frequency of the emotion of happiness is higher than satisfaction; however, the happiness that most of us experience is dependent on the conditions of our life being to our liking, which is a challenge given that everything in the phenomenal world undergoes change. To seek out relationships for the purpose of finding happiness is like building sand castles on the ocean edge; it will remain standing only till the next wave.

Joy: Joy is a higher vibration than happiness; however, it is an unstable emotion if the source of joy is found outside of us.

Gratitude: Gratitude is a higher vibratory level than joy because gratitude is an energy that focuses on the people, animals, or objects around us. Because it has an outward focus, it is a more stable energy frequency. The problem with gratitude is that it is often expressed in response to the receiving of a gift. For this reason, it is an energy frequency that is still vulnerable to changes in external conditions.

Appreciation: Appreciation is a higher frequency than gratitude because the emotion of appreciation can be experienced independently of any external conditions. For example, we can have an appreciation for a beautiful sunset or the work of an artist.

Love: We frequently think of love as being the most powerful force in the universe, which is true, if that love is unconditional. Since the love that we experience is normally conditional, it is subject to the changes of our external conditions, such as when our partner does not meet our expectations.

Enlightenment: Enlightenment has the highest vibratory level of any energy. Unconditional love can be equated with enlightenment; however, enlightenment can be achieved without first developing unconditional love, which is extremely rare. A more practical approach to enlightenment can be achieved by practicing meditation and self-inquiry. Both of these practices can lead to the expansion of awareness where we come to the realization that who we are is beyond our mind and body. However, this awareness must be achieved through the direct experience of it; it cannot be achieved intellectually or by reading about it. In the exercise portion of this book, I have offered exercises for this.

In my discussion of the energy levels of the various emotions, you may have noticed a pattern. The lower the emotion, the lower the vibrational level or frequency. The reason why the frequency is low is due to the amount of identification with the mind and body, which leads to a sense of separateness. Because we experience separateness, we are reactive when the conditions around us change.

The higher the vibrational level of the emotion, the less identification there is to the mind and body; hence, we become less reactive toward changes in our circumstances.
Someone who is fearful or has not allowed themselves to grieve (as in the death of a partner) have a low life frequency as they deeply identify with their thoughts and emotions. A common example of this is the person who feels that they need to be in a relationship in order to feel good about themselves.

If they find a relationship with another person, that person will have the same energy level as they do, though they may express their neediness differently. They may have a need to control or take advantage of other person in their attempts to feel more powerful.

Now consider the person who focuses on understanding themselves, instead of finding a relationship. If they practice meditation, their life's energy will be at higher levels; hence, they will attract someone whose life's energy is also high. It is impossible for a person of a high frequency to attract a person of low frequency, or a low frequency person to attract a high-level one.

Attracting a healthy and fulfilling relationship requires that we focus on raising our life first, while the norm for society is to seek out a relationship in order to feel better about ourselves.

The Mirror of Relationships

The greater consciousness, whose' quality is oneness, differentiates itself into localized consciousness in order to gain information through the experience of contrast. We can think of the greater consciousness as a CEO of a major company.

For him or her to understand what is happening in the company, he relies on numerous individuals that serve beneath him. Each of these individuals has a specific task that they are responsible for. In order to accomplish their tasks, they need to interact act with others, which creates the experience of contrast.

Part 5 – Law of Attraction for Amazing Relationships

How can the CEO understand anything about the sales of the company if he or she does not have a sales report? For this information to be generated, there needs to be individuals who are conducting sales. For sales to be created, there needs to be interactions between the sales people and their clients. The conducting of sales with clients is an experience of contrast as the client needs to determine if agreeing to buy will create added value for him or her. The decisions that are made at this level inform the CEO of the sales of the company.

Another metaphor for the larger consciousness system is from physicist Tom Campell who compares the larger consciousness system to a video game. You in your manifested form are like the avatar in the video game, while the larger consciousness system is the one who is playing the video game.

The virtual environment provides a context for the avatar to interact in, while the joy stick symbolizes the intentions of the larger consciousness.

When the avatar interacts with its environment in ways that earn points, that information provides feedback to the video game player. If the avatar interacts with its environment in a manner that leads to its destruction, then that information is provided to the player. Similarly, every moment that you are interacting with your environment informs the greater consciousness. The larger consciousness continuously responds back to this feedback by creating experiences that are consistent with the feedback that it has received.

We are localized aspects of consciousness that interact with each other for the purpose of creating experiences of contrast, which in turn informs the larger consciousness system to the nature of itself. Each person that we interact with is an experience in contrast that informs the larger consciousness system. Here is an example:

Jon and his wife are having an argument over an incident; he took offense over something that she said to him.

Jon perceives his wife as the source of his upset. His upset is a natural reaction given that Jon identifies himself with his mind and body, meaning that Jon believes that he is the culmination of his thoughts, emotions, perceptions, and his sense of physicality.

This self-identification creates a sense of separation where he experiences his wife as being a separate individual that exists apart from him. Since she is the one that made the comment, and he is the one that felt offended, he believes that she is the cause of his upset.

From the perspective of higher levels of consciousness, a whole different story is unfolding. Jon's wife is serving as a mirror to Jon's vibratory level.

Just as the bell was a stimulus that activated a response in Pavlov's dog, his wife's comments acted as a stimulus to activate Jon's life condition.

The comments made by Jon's wife were not the initial cause for Jon feeling offended. Rather, the initial cause for Jon's offense took place far earlier in his life, perhaps in a different lifetime even. Regardless of when that initial cause occurred, it was the result of Jon self-identifying with his mind and body.

However, this self-identification is not a mistake of the universe, nor is it a mistake on our part; rather, it is part of the process of the evolution of consciousness.

Part 5 – Law of Attraction for Amazing Relationships

Chapter 7: Love: The Evolution of Consciousness

Remember the previous example of the CEO? How does the CEO know if the sales strategy of his company is working or not? He or she knows this by whether or not they are getting the results that they want. There is a term in science called entropy.

While there are several definitions for entropy, one definition involves the simplicity or complexity of a system. The qualities of greater consciousness are of oneness and inclusiveness, making it a low entropy system.

As entrophy increases, the system increasingly experiences disorder. High entropy systems consume a lot of energy while low entropy systems are energy efficient. Systems are constantly fluctuating between high and low entropy.

The relationships in our lives, along with other forms of experience, are a mirror for us to examine our own energy level based on how we respond to ourselves and others. In a previous section, we discussed the frequencies of different emotions. Shame has a very low frequency while appreciation is very high. Which emotion do you think consumes a great deal of energy and which one do you think is energy efficient? To answer that question, all you have to do is ask yourself how you feel during these times. Which of these emotions are more draining?

There is nothing that exists in this universe that can cause us to experience shame except our own minds. Similarly, there is nothing in this universe that can make us feel appreciation except for our own minds.

Words like "shame" and "appreciation" are just concepts that we created and of which lack any inherent meaning; it is us that give these and other concepts meaning. When we remove these labels from the emotions that we experience, all that we have left is energy. It is the meaning that we give to our experience in relationships that create the fluctuations in the frequencies of our life's energy.

Your relationships are providing you with a mirror to how you interpret your experience. No relationship can make you feel anything; it is you that projects meaning on the other person. The quality of that meaning is determined by your vibratory level.

Because we attract that which is of the same vibratory level, everything that enters our lives, including our relationships, will be affected by that vibratory level.

Part 5 – Law of Attraction for Amazing Relationships

By learning to control your vibratory level, you can raise your vibration to attract people into your life who are also of a higher vibration, and you can affect the vibratory level of those who you are in a relationship with already.

Part 5 – Law of Attraction for Amazing Relationships

Chapter 8: When the Lines of Communication is Crossed

There are people who have sincerely used the Law of Attraction to find Mr. or Miss. Right, but ended up with something less than satisfactory. As stated later, we are manifesting all the time; it is impossible for us to not manifest.

We may believe that the Law of Attraction does not work, that it is just a New Age talking point, or that we just lack some ability that others have. The only reason why we attract that which we do not want is because we are not directing your focus in a manner that supports us.

Not doing the work
If the person of your dreams is a 10 but your life condition is a 3, there is no way that you will be able to attract that person into your life and maintain a relationship with them.
If you want a partner that is a 10, you need to focus on becoming a 10 yourself. In fact, regardless of what you want in a partner, you need to be at least at their energetic level.
Remember, you attract into your life that which matches your frequency.

Attachment to outcome
Earlier in this book, I gave two personal examples that I had in trying out the Law of Attraction. The first one was a success where I encountered a magazine cover that I had visualized.
The second attempt was unsuccessful because I had become attached to my outcome. The key to manifesting anything in your life is to create the intention for it, release that intention, and then move on with your life, don't spend time thinking about it.

Conscious beliefs
Imagine this scenario: You have been studying the Law of Attraction and you want to attract that special person.

You quiet your mind, create your intention, and go on with your life. As you are waiting for that special person to enter your life, you engage in thinking like:
- "I wonder if I am doing this (Law of Attraction) right?"
- *"What happens if doesn't work?"*
- "Maybe I am fooling myself about this manifesting thing."
- *"Things never work out for me. Why should this?"*
- "What happens if the person of my dreams shows up and I am not ready for them?"

If most of this person's focus is on thoughts such as these, then that will affect the level of their frequency that they are transmitting to the greater consciousness.
If you want to effectively use the Law of Attraction, you need to take charge of your beliefs and replace them with more empowering ones. We will discuss how to do this in Chapter 13.

Part 5 – Law of Attraction for Amazing Relationships

Subconscious beliefs

One of the most important principles for learning how to use the Law of Attraction is the understanding of how subconscious beliefs impact our ability to attract that which we desire. Even if you understand the importance of focusing on what you want, even if you create your intentions and become detached from them, you will not attract what you want if you have not explored your subconscious beliefs.

I want to start off this discussion by first saying that there is no such thing as a "subconscious" or "conscious" belief. Terms like "subconscious," "conscious" or "greater consciousness" are just concepts that we have created. As manifested beings, we use concepts to communicate our experiences to each other.

However, concepts are a creation of the mind, which is also a concept. There is no way that we can communicate without the use of concepts.

The problem is not the use of concepts, which are necessary to get along in this world. Problems arise when we identify with our concepts when we accept them as being true. Just as shadows were to the allegory of the cave, concepts are to our daily lives; they are experienced but they are not truth.

The following is a simple exercise that will allow you to briefly experience life free of concepts:
1. Sit down and view your surroundings, taking your time to take everything in.
2. When you are ready, close your eyes and allow yourself to relax.
3. Imagine that you are an alien from a distant planet who has arrived on Earth to study it. You have no information about this planet, nor do you have any past experience to draw from. Because of this, you are unable to define, identify, analyze, or judge anything that you experience. In other words, you are a blank slate.
4. No open your eyes and look at your surroundings again. Take your time.
5. How did your experience observing compare with your first observation?

If you did not notice any difference between the two observations, practice this exercise until you do.

The higher you raise your vibratory level, the less you will identify with your concepts. The less you identify with your concepts, the greater will be your experience of reality. As your experience of reality becomes greater, you will become aware of all of the universe.

Now that we have laid some ground work let us discuss how subconscious beliefs affect our ability to attract that which we desire. We will do so using the following scenario.

Janet was born to parents who were authoritarian and critical of her and her siblings. Like all children, Janet wanted their approval but nothing was ever good enough for her. By nature, Janet was very friendly and loved to explore new things. However, these natural qualities of her gradually diminished as Janet became more self-critical of herself. She had taken what was given to her by her parents and had directed it toward herself.

Janet cultivated this critical aspect of herself until it became her dominant personality. Because she is self-critical, she is also critical of others. The natural qualities of being friendly and loving to explore were suppressed in her subconscious; she lacks any awareness of them.

Based on the Law of Attraction, you would think that Janet would attract people in her life who were also self-critical; however, this is not necessarily the case.

Janet's qualities of being friendly and loving to explore, while being repressed, still give off their energetic vibration. Because she is unaware of these qualities, they will actually have a stronger impact in what manifests in her life!

This is why we sometimes see a couple who seem so different from each other that we find it puzzling how they ever got to together. This is also the reason why sometimes we have an instant dislike or attraction toward someone one who we do not even know.

All of these are examples of how our suppressed beliefs trump our conscious beliefs or intention as to what we want to attract in our lives. In Chapter 13, you have an opportunity to do an exercise to uncover your subconscious beliefs.

Part 5 – Law of Attraction for Amazing Relationships

Chapter 9: The Face of God

You are the face of God. This statement that I just made may seem provocative and may offend some of you.

My hope is that, by the time that you complete this book, you will understand my reasons for making this statement, for it's at heart of not only understanding the Law of Attraction but your truest essence.

Also, when I use the word "God," I am not making reference to any specific religious belief, or preconceptions as to the nature of God, except one. That preconception is that there must be a source from which everything that exists arises from.

I want you to do the following exercise as I believe it can help you understand why I have repeatedly made the comment that you are consciousness.

It may also help facilitate your understanding to what I meant by "You are the face of God." But first, I need provide some important instructions: When conducting this exercise, do not rely on anything that you know, or that you think you know. Do not refer to memory or guessing.

Also, do not employ your imagination either. During this exercise, I want you only to refer to your immediate and direct experience.

1. Sit down, make yourself comfortable, and close your eyes.
2. Breathe normally, and follow your breath until you feel relaxed.
3. Now open your eyes and, with a relaxed gaze, look around at your surroundings.
4. Now find an object that interests you or attracts your attention.
5. As you look at the object, I want you to allow the object to come to your attention, rather than directing your attention at the object. In other words, look at the object with a relaxed gaze.
6. As you look at the objects, determine for yourself as to whether the act of seeing ends at the point where the object begins or does the act of seeing and the object merge into each other.
7. My hope is that you will agree that the act of seeing and the object seen merge into each other.
8. Now determine for yourself whether the act of seeing occurs from within you, or does it originate from outside of you. My hope is that you agree that the act of seeing originates from within you.
9. So far, I hope that you have come to the conclusion that seeing and the object being seen cannot be separated from each other; they are one. Also, that seeing occurs from within you.

10. You are aware of the object. Now determine for yourself if there is an awareness of seeing. My hope is that you will agree that there is an awareness of seeing.
11. Now determine for yourself if awareness of seeing and the act of seeing are separate from each other or if they are one. My hope you will agree that the awareness of seeing and the act of seeing are one.
12. How is that you were able to answer these questions? You were able to answer these questions by way of thought, thoughts like "seeing and the object seen merge into each other."
13. You are aware of thought. Determine for yourself whether the awareness of thought and thought itself are separate or are they one. My hope is that you will agree that these two things are one.
14. Now, are you aware of you? How do you know that you exist? You know that you exist, there is no disputing this. How do you know that you exist? You know that you exist because there is an awareness of you. Can you separate the awareness of you from you? My hope is that you agree that the awareness of you and that which you experience as being you, are one.
15. Now for the ultimate question, the question that surpasses all other questions: "Who or what is aware of you?" To be aware of something there must be the object that is being perceived and the perceiver of the object.
16. If you are aware of you, then that which you refer to as "You" must be the object of awareness; but, you cannot be both the perceiver and the perceived.
17. My first guidance to you was to determine if seeing and the object being seen are separate or do they merge together. This is the question that you must ask yourself now. Is the awareness of that which you refer to as "you" and that which you refer to as "you" separate or do they merge together?

My hope is that you agree that they merge together. That which you refer to as "you" is the localized manifestation of the greater consciousness. That which is aware of "you" is the larger consciousness, the essence of who you are.

This essence of who you are cannot be perceived by the mind or the five senses.
It can only be known intuitively. It is this aspect of you that is aware of all existence.
It is aware of the objects around you. It is aware of the act of seeing. It is aware of the awareness of seeing. It is aware of that which is within you and around you, and it is aware of that which you refer to as "you," which is just another object floating in the unlimited field of consciousness.

Consciousness is aware of all of existence while at the same time being intimately connected to all of existence.

Nothing can exist unless there is an awareness of it. This is why I made the statement that you are the "face of god." Everything that you experience, be it a rock, a fly, or another person, is the face of god, a god that expresses itself in innumerable forms.

Part 5 – Law of Attraction for Amazing Relationships

Chapter 10: The Mirror of Relationships

As the face of god, which is your manifested form, it is the purpose of your life to wake-up from the dream that is created by the mind that leads us to believe that we are just a physical body with a mind.

It is your purpose to wake-up from the dream that you are separate from the rest of life and return to wholeness and oneness of being, which is the greater consciousness.

The return to wholeness and oneness does not require us to dismiss the physicality of our bodies or the physical realm that we find ourselves in. It does not require that we die and merge with some spiritual realm.

It does not mean we have to abandon our current lifestyle and become monks or adopt spiritual practices. The return to wholeness and oneness is an inner journey where we gain the courage to challenge the deep seated beliefs that we have of ourselves and learn to let go of them.

The greater consciousness, or god, is the ultimate manifester because it lacks any sense of identity or beliefs about itself; it is simply pure awareness.

At this level, just an intention manifests into existence instantly. As manifested beings of the greater consciousness, we too can manifest; however, our manifestations do not occur instantly as there is lag time involved.

This lag time is due to the restrictions imposed by the physical realm and because of the ego. Our beliefs that we have about ourselves and others creates resistance, which creates lag time for our manifestations to appear.

The more that we overcome our inner resistance, the more effective we will become in manifesting. Fortunately, the universe has offered us the ultimate mirror for recognizing resistance, that mirror is our relationships.

As indicated earlier, the people who enter our lives did so because there was a vibrational match to ours.

Part 5 – Law of Attraction for Amazing Relationships

Since the vibrational match may come from subconscious beliefs, identifying that vibrational frequency is not impossible unless we explore our subconscious beliefs. Regardless if the beliefs are conscious or subconscious, we project those beliefs on others, which then becomes our image of them. In truth, we can never know another person. From the perspective of our "normal" level of consciousness, we never have a relationship with another person; rather, we have a relationship with our interpretation of them.

It is because of our projections that we make on others that the people in our lives serve as a mirror to our inner realm. When we realize this, we can understand why relationships are complicated and why misunderstandings occur.

We project our inner lives on the people around us, which then becomes our image of them. When they do not meet our expectations, we become hurt or frustrated; we hold them responsible for our unhappiness.

Because the collective consciousness of the world has only recently (evolutionary speaking) begin to rise toward higher levels, ours is a history that viewed relationships not as mirrors but as objects for experiencing fulfillment and wholeness.

From fairy tales to Hollywood, from romance novels to the traditions that we uphold, we have looked to find Mr. or Miss Right to deliver us from our sense of separation from the world and to make us feel loved, desired and whole. Such a recipe for finding happiness is doomed to failure. No person or object outside of you can ever give you want you are looking for.

To do so is no different than asking your mirror at home to provide you with love and fulfillment. Everything that you will ever experience is a projection of yourself that becomes superimposed on the object of our experience.

Ultimately, everything that you experience is an aspect of yourself. Ultimately, you are the source of all experience as well as being found in all of experience. It is like a person who sprays their garden with a hose.

Everything in the garden is covered with water and water become an aspect of every plant. Consciousness is to water as the garden is to experience. Everything that you could ever desire already exists within the realm of consciousness because consciousness is the source of all that exists.

The Law of Attraction is just a conceptual model for how consciousness operates. The only thing that prevents us from being intentional creators is the limiting concepts that we identify with due to our attachment to our manifested form.

Ultimately freedom lies in transcending all beliefs, including spiritual beliefs, and opening up to all of experience with complete acceptance and abandon.

Finding your true love or the relationship of your dream requires that you stop searching for it and investigate the timeless and boundless realm that exists within you and is you. To experience that realm, the most effective tool is meditation.

Part 5 – Law of Attraction for Amazing Relationships

Chapter 11: Using the Law of Attraction in Relationships

We have covered a lot of information so far. It is time make this information practical and apply it to your current and potential relationships. There are three simple steps to applying the Law of Attraction:
1. Identify what you want your outcome to be.
2. Identify what has prevented you from achieving your relationship outcome in the past.
3. Raise your vibration

You can think of your relationship outcome as your intention. When you identify the limiting beliefs that have prevented you from achieving your relationship outcome in the past, you can then raise your vibration.

When we change our limiting beliefs and adopt empowering ones, we raise our vibration. By raising your vibration, you increase the probability that you will manifest your intentions.

Here is an example of how this process works. My relationship outcome is to improve the quality of my relationship with my spouse.

I would ask myself "What has prevented me from improving my relationship with my wife/husband in the past? In the next chapter, I have provided you with a number of exercises that you can use to identify your underlying beliefs.

Upon identifying your belief, I would next raise my vibration. All of the exercises in Chapter 13 can be used to raise your vibration. In fact, all of the exercises in this chapter can be used to raise your vibration. It is important to note that these steps do not always have followed in this order. Sometimes raising your vibration can lead you to identify your beliefs.

By raising your vibration, and maintaining it, along with releasing your intention, you will be intentionally manifesting your relationship outcome. Here are some examples of how you can apply **the Law of Attraction in Relationships**:
- Attracting a compatible partner: Think of the qualities that you want in a partner; you can be specific as possible. Consider all the attributes you would desire in a partner, including physically, emotionally, mentally, spiritually, and financially. When you have identified these qualities, make them the focus of your intention.
- Improving the quality of an existing relationship: To improve an existing relationship, you must first start off by asking yourself some questions about you! Ask questions like:
    - Would I want to be in a relationship with someone who was just like me?
    - *How have I contributed to the challenges that we are currently experiencing in our relationship?*
    - What beliefs do I hold about myself and the other person that are creating challenges for the relationship?

- *How have I contributed to the unhappiness of my partner?*
- How have my own beliefs contributed to my own unhappiness?

After acknowledging your role in creating relationship challenges, you can create the intentions that will bring happiness for both you and your partner.

It is important in relationship challenges that your intentions be pure and unconditional, meaning that your intentions for your partner's happiness are independent of your own needs. In fact, when releasing your intentions, do not even consider the relationship; consider the happiness of the individual.

To make your intentions even more powerful, let your intentions be how you can contribute to the happiness of the other person. Likewise, you can create intentions for your own happiness, using the same methods just described but with you as the focus.

It is important; however that I make the following qualifier. If you are in an abusive relationship, emotionally or physically, do not employ the Law of Attraction in an attempt to save the relationship.

As I stated before, everything starts with us. We attract into our life that which is a match for our vibration. Before you can change anything, you must change yourself first, and to change yourself means to change your vibration.

You cannot do this if you are in an unsafe situation. Take care of yourself first, and the universe will accommodate the changes that you make.

Part 5 – Law of Attraction for Amazing Relationships

Chapter 12: Conscious Relationships

Many spiritual teachings that are available; however, which teaching is best? Why do some spiritual teachings contradict each other? Why do some spiritual teachings resonate with us, while others leave us uninterested?

The answers to all of these questions can be known by considering the following: Spiritual teachings are just another form of thought, and we attract those teachings into our lives that best fit us at the given moment of our conscious awareness.

The best spiritual teaching is the one that resonates with you. Spiritual teachings contradict each other because everyone is at a different place in their evolution of consciousness.

What one person is ready to hear will be unsuitable for another person. Everything that we attract into our lives, be they relationships or spiritual teachings, has entered because it was a vibrational match to our frequency. What most people who practice the Law of Attraction fail to realize is that they are focusing on the small and limited scale instead of focusing on the ultimate prize, which is becoming firmly established in your true essence.

You can attract money; you can attract relationships or anything else you could want. But as long as we are focusing on attracting what we want, we are missing the opportunity to attract the realization of who we truly are!

When we realize this, we will not even think of the Law of Attraction or relationships. Instead, we will be focusing on how we can serve and elevate others for a more compassionate, more loving, and more highly evolved society where we support each other in our own growth, which is how a conscious relationship functions.

Conscious relationships are drastically different from the traditional relationships that most of us are involved in. In traditional relationships, we look to our partner to fulfill our needs and expectations.

In conscious relationships, we do not look to our partner to fulfill our needs and expectations; we realize that no one can fulfill our needs or expectations except ourselves. In traditional relations, we may feel threatened if our partner wants to pursue their desires when we do not share those same desires. In conscious relationships, we encourage our partner to pursue their desires, even if it could potentially cause them to leave us.

The foundational characteristic of a conscious relationship is that the partners support each other in discovering their own truth.

Conscious relationships are the ultimate mirror because there is a common understanding that relationships are not about depending on the other person to make us feel fulfilled; rather, it is about providing our support to the other person so that they can discover the fulfillment that lies within themselves.

The Power of Meditation

Unfortunately, the practice of meditation has been widely misunderstood, both culturally and spiritually. Meditation originated with the indigenous people of India, before the creation of its major religions like Hinduism and Buddhism.

In its original form, meditation was used as a vehicle to connect with the original source of all that is. Meditation was not used to reduce stress and relax but to transcend the mind and experience our inherent connection to all of existence.

In the Western world, the practice of meditation and yoga have been popularized as way to achieve a certain outcome such as improved mental, emotional, or physical well being. However, this approach has just reinforced the misunderstanding what we are just physical beings that inhabit a physical world.

Compare this perspective to the perspective that we are multidimensional beings, that we are consciousness that has manifested as localized consciousness and having physical form. It is our conceptual thinking and the beliefs that we have of ourselves that prevent most of us from experiencing both aspects of ourselves.

From perspective of pure consciousness, you do not do meditation; rather, you are the one that is observing the meditator. As pure consciousness, you become whatever your intentions are. As previously stated, you are an aspect in all that you experience.

In combination with relationships, meditation becomes another mirror in your arsenal of self-realization tools. Meditation, in its purest form, is discovering who you are at deepest level and your relationship to all of existence, which is more substantial and fulfilling than a method for reducing stress!

When practicing the kind of meditation that I have been describing, the idea is to transcend all concepts and thinking. The exercises in Chapter 13, if followed in the sequence that they are ordered, offer you the opportunity to transcend how you experience yourself and the world around you.

If what I have written so far seems too abstract or deep, don't let that bother you. Words are just concepts.

As stated earlier, the best guide to experiencing realignment with your higher power is to learn to develop greater awareness to your feelings and to learn to trust them.

When we learn to become in tune with our feelings and trust them, we have taken a major step toward attaining enlightenment, also known as loving yourself. The next chapter offers meditative exercises for raising your vibration and lowering your resistance.

Chapter 13: Law of Attraction Exercises for Relationships

We have covered a lot of information in this book, and it is time to put that information into practice. The following are exercises that will benefit you by identifying your limiting beliefs, changing your limiting beliefs, lowering your resistance, developing greater awareness of the nature of your mental phenomena, becoming aware of your projections, and enhancing your ability to experience love and compassion for yourself and others.

There is no specific way to approach these exercises. You can pick the ones that resonate with you, or you can do all of them.

For best results, I recommend that you do all of the exercises and that you do them in the order that they are sequenced. I have staggered these exercises from simplest to the most difficult, especially for meditation exercises.

Exercises for Beliefs

Uncovering deep seated beliefs

Previously in this book, we discussed subconscious beliefs and how they impact the manifestation process. The following are two exercises for uncovering your subconscious beliefs:

Exercise 1

To show you how this exercise works, I will provide you with an example.
1. The first step is to think of an ongoing challenge that you are experiencing in your life. My example will be:
   I am afraid of being rejected by others.
2. My next step is to start a line of inquiry using the phrase "What would be so bad if..." So my first question would be "What would be so bad about being rejected?"
3. My answer to that question would be "I would feel that people saw me as being less, that I am not good enough.
4. I would then use my response and rephrase the question: "What would be so bad if people saw me as being less or not good enough?"
5. My response to that would be "It would make feel like I am worthless."
6. I would continue to repeat this question by asking: "What would be so bad if I felt like I am worthless?"
7. My answer to that would be "I would feel like I am unlovable."
8. Keep going through this line of questioning until you are unable to any further. When you have reached this point, you will have identified your subconscious belief. At the conscious level, I am aware of the fear of being rejected; however, the core belief behind this belief is "I feel like I am unlovable."

Part 5 – Law of Attraction for Amazing Relationships

Exercise 2:

This next exercise can be used to find the subconscious beliefs for the things that we want. For this exercise, I will use the example: "I want to get married."

1. What would getting married give me?
2. It would give me someone to spend my life with.
3. What would having someone to spend my life with give me?
4. It would give me a sense of security.
5. What would a sense of security give me?
6. It would give me a sense of peace.
7. My subconscious belief is that I want a sense of peace, but my conscious belief is that I want to get married.

Habitual Patterns

1. Start becoming more aware of your daily thinking and actions.
2. When you catch yourself thinking a habitual thought or behaving habitually, ask yourself the following questions:
    a. Do I have a choice of thinking or behaving differently?
    b. Is there a payoff for me thinking or behaving in this habitual way?
    c. How would I like to think as opposed to my current habitual thinking?
    d. How would I like to behave as opposed to my current habitual behavior?
    e. Would these new ways of thinking or behaving retain the payoff that my current thinking or behaving offers?
    f. Would these new ways of thinking or behaving bring me greater happiness?
3. If you said yes to the last two questions, start incorporating your new way of thinking or behaving in your daily life.
4. Whenever you catch yourself repeating your old thinking or behaving, remind yourself that you are now dedicated to your new ways of being.

Changing a Belief

When you have identified a belief that is limiting you (subconscious or conscious), you can use the following procedure to weaken your old belief and replace it with a more empowering belief:

11. Get two sheets of paper. Select paper sizes of 8" x 11" or larger.
12. Take the first sheet of paper and fold it in half lengthwise.
13. On the top of the paper, write down your belief.
14. Make a list on the left-hand side of the paper of all the ways this belief has cost you in your life. When doing this part of the exercise, think of how this belief has affected you in all your life areas. Ask yourself how this belief has affected you in the way that you see yourself, how it has affected your emotional health, your relationships, your physical health, your work, your finances, and so on.
15. When writing, keep in mind the following:
    - When writing this list, write down the first thing that comes to your mind, even if it seems irrelevant.

- Write as fast as you can and feel the emotions that arise. This is a heartfelt exercise, not a thinking one.
- Keep writing until you run out of things to write.
16. By each item that you write down, assign an arbitrary point value as to how much impact this item has had on you. When selecting the point value, choose the first number that comes to mind.
17. When you have completed assigning the point values, find the total of all the point values and place it at the bottom of the page.
18. For the right side of the page, repeat Steps 6-7, except this time, you will write down all the ways that this belief has benefited you.

When you have completed Step 8, think of a new alternative belief that empowers you. For example, if the original belief was "No one will ever love me," my new belief maybe "The only love that I can depend on is the love that I give to myself."

On the second paper, repeat steps 1-8, using your new belief, with the following exceptions: Reverse Steps 6 and 8 by writing down all the ways that you believe that you would benefit from this new belief for Step 6. When doing Step 8, write down all the ways you believe it will cost you.

When you have completed the two sheets, do the following:

3. Immediately review your lists, allowing yourself to fully experience any emotions that arise.
4. Review yours lists every day, once in the morning and once before you go to bed until you become fully associated with the emotions that you experience.

When you become fully associated with the costs for holding on to your old belief with the benefits of adopting your new belief, your mind will become re-programmed with your new belief.

The following is an alternative to the last exercise for changing your beliefs and involves meditation:

1. On the piece of paper, write down a belief that you have which limits you or is causing you unhappiness.
2. When you have written down the belief, sit down in a comfortable position and close your eyes.
3. Allow yourself to follow your breath during inhalation and exhalation. Place your attention on your breath. Feel it as it courses through your body. Relax.
4. I want you to think of the belief that you wrote down. Feel the heaviness and the weight, which this belief has had on your life.
5. What has been the cost to your happiness for holding on to this belief? Can you think of specific instances? Did this belief cost you a relationship? If so, who is no longer in your life because of this belief?
6. Has this belief cost you money? Did this belief lead you to engage in risky behavior with your money or health? What about your sense of self?
7. How has this belief affected your self-confidence or self-esteem? Take the time to feel the pain that this belief has created for your life.
8. Allow yourself to experience it fully, allow yourself to experience the emotions and feelings that come with living with this belief.

Part 5 – Law of Attraction for Amazing Relationships

9. How will this belief affect your future? If you continue to hold on to this belief, what will your life be like a year from now, five years from now, 15 years from now? See your life in the future. What consequences will you experience if you continue to maintain this belief?
10. As mentioned before, thoughts and beliefs do not have any power other than the power we give them. Unto themselves, our thoughts and beliefs lack any power. Our beliefs are not true or untrue, they just exist. It is us who grant them power over our lives.
11. Now open your eyes and get your writing instrument. This negative belief you just meditated on existed because you perceived in your mind that there was a benefit to having this belief.
12. Write down how all the ways this belief benefited you, even if how it benefited does not sound rationale. For example, if you have a belief that you cannot depend on or trust other people, the benefit of this belief may be that it protected you from getting hurt.
13. Now think of a belief that will offer the same benefit but will not create limitations for you. Using the previous example, a new belief could be "I can trust others because I am learning to trust myself." Write down your new belief.
14. When you have written down the belief, sit down in a comfortable position and close your eyes.
15. Allow yourself to follow your breath during inhalation and exhalation. Place your attention on your breath. Feel it as it courses through your body. Relax.
16. I want you to think of the new belief that you wrote down. Think about what your life would be like if you operated from this new belief from this moment on.
17. How would living with this new belief make you feel about yourself? How would it impact those that you care about? What would your life be like? Think about what your life would be like one year from now if you started to live by this new belief today. What do you think it would be like five years from now?
18. As you think about what your life would be like, allow yourself to experience the emotions and feelings that you experience. Allow yourself to sink into these emotions and feelings. You may want to visualize yourself acting from this new belief.
19. Practice this meditation every day for three weeks, which is how long it normally takes to create a habit. The mind cannot tell the difference between visualization and actual doing. Meditating regularly will reprogram your subconscious, leading you to take the appropriate action.
20. Start becoming more aware of your daily thinking and actions.
21. When you catch yourself thinking a habitual thought or behaving habitually, ask yourself the following questions:
    a. Do I have a choice of thinking or behaving differently?
    b. Is there a payoff for me thinking or behaving in this habitual way?
    c. How would I like to think as opposed to my current habitual thinking?
    d. How would I like to behave as opposed to my current habitual behavior?
    e. Would these new ways of thinking or behaving retain the payoff that my current thinking or behaving offers?
    f. Would these new ways of thinking or behaving bring me greater happiness?

22. If you said yes to the last two questions, start incorporating your new way of thinking or behaving in your daily life.
23. Whenever you catch yourself repeating your old thinking or behaving, remind yourself that you are now dedicated to your new ways of being.

Exercises for Emotions

Diving Deep into Emotions

We discussed earlier that emotions are a mirror to our thoughts. We also discussed how our subconscious beliefs can override our intentions to manifest. The purpose of this exercise is to guide you in transforming your emotions at their deepest level; thus, changing them at the subconscious level.

1. Identify a concern that you are experiencing. Since this book is about relationships, I will use the following concern as an example: I am frustrated with my child being irresponsible.
2. Now that I have identified my concern, the next thing would be to identify how I feel about the situation, which I have done already.
3. Upon identifying how I feel about the situation, the next thing to do is to get into a relaxed state. Using the basic meditation that was presented earlier in this book is ideal for this.
4. When you are relaxed, ask yourself "What does being frustrated feel like?" Notice: You want to describe what the emotion feels like, not what you think about it. To avoid falling into this trap, phrase your response as "It feels like_____?
5. Here are some examples:
6. "It feels hard and edgy."
7. "I feel like I want to cry."
8. "It feels heavy."
9. My response to this question would be that feeling frustrated feels heavy, like I am being pulled down."
10. I would then follow-up by asking "What does heavy or being pulled down feel like?"
11. I would then respond with "It feels like I am stuck."
12. I would continue my questioning by asking "What does being stuck feel like?"
13. My response: "Feeling stuck makes me feel like I want to go to sleep or escape."
14. I would follow-up by asking "What does going to sleep or escaping feel like?"
15. My response would be "It feels like I am freeing myself."
16. My last response, "It feels like I am freeing myself" has a whole different feeling than my initial feeling, which was feeling frustrated. When your line of questioning leads you to feeling a neutral or positive emotion, you have transformed your original emotion at its deepest level.
17. When doing this exercise, it is important to mention that there is no way that you can do it wrong or come up with the wrong answer. As long as you are responding at the feeling level, your response will be valid for this exercise.

Part 5 – Law of Attraction for Amazing Relationships

Exercises for Resistance

Allowing of the body

The following exercise is good for learning to be mindful of your body. To do this exercise, do the following:

1. Sit in a chair or on a pillow and allow yourself to be comfortable.
2. Close your eyes and relax.
3. Allow your awareness to roam freely; do not try to focus on anything particular.
4. Now place your awareness on the body. Allow your body to move any way it wants. Do not try in any way to control your posture or the way you are sitting. Whatever your body is telling you, allow your body to assume that movement or positioning.
5. Enjoy the allowing of your body. Maintain this allowing for as long as you desire.

A Day without Resistance

It is the resistance that we create within ourselves that prevent us from experiencing our full potential for manifesting. All of us, at one point or another, have engaged in actions that went against how we felt.

The purpose of this exercise is to start honoring your feelings by only engaging in those actions that are consistent with how you feel.

To live your life in accordance to how you feel is to be in alignment, which eliminates resistance. It is important to note that this exercise is about feelings, not emotions. If we lived according to our emotions, the results could be troublesome.

Unlike your emotions, your feelings are those messages that are guiding you to either move toward a situation or to move away from it. You can think of feelings as "approaching for avoiding. I want you to commit to one day where you will only engage in those activities that are consistent with how you feel. If you do not feel like doing something, then do not do it. If you are feeling like doing something, do it! If you find yourself having trouble doing this exercise for a whole day, then do it for a shorter period of time, even if it is for just 20 minutes then extend that time until you can do it for a whole day.

Obviously, there are things that we need to do which we rather not do. To not do them would not be irresponsible. In cases such as these, use the following guidelines:
-Change your perspective of the task that is creating resistance in you by focusing on all the benefits that you would gain by completing it.
-Find ways to change the way that you approach doing the task by making it more enjoyable for you. Example: Listen to your favorite music while doing yard work or invite a friend over to do your taxes together.
-If none of the previous techniques work, do not take on the task until you have come to accept the fact that you need to do this task and that it will not be enjoyable. Regarding this technique, I want

you to focus on the word "accept." It means you do the task with complete acceptance for what it is; you have lost any sense putting up a fight against it.
-These guidelines lead to an important point. This exercise has nothing to do with the activities that we do; rather, it is about recognizing the resistance that we experience and honoring it.

Exercises for Relationships

Projections

From the perspective of higher levels of consciousness, there is no distinction between your inner world and the world around you.

All relationship problems occur when we experience others as being separate from ourselves and mistakenly believe that which we project on them originates from them. The following is a meditation for reclaiming your projections.

Exercise 1: Projections
1. Sit down in a comfortable position, close your eyes, and relax.
2. Follow your breath during inhalation and exhalation.
3. When you are feeling calm, I want you to think of someone whom you believe has treated you unfairly. When you have identified this person, I want you to recreate in your mind the specific situation where this person mistreated you.
4. Where did the situation take place?
5. Imagine the surroundings of this location.
6. Where was this person when the situation happened? What were they doing at the time? See it in your mind; visualize it with as much detail as possible.
7. What did they say or do to you that caused you to be angry or hurt?
8. How did you feel when the situation happened? What did it feel like? What did you tell yourself?
9. Now I want you to recreate this same situation in your mind with one difference. I want you to relieve the situation without any form of judgment or analysis.
10. As you run through the situation a second time in your mind, focus on the other person that you believe hurt you. Can you say that you are absolutely sure that this person intended to hurt you? Is it possible that you were projecting your own beliefs on this person's intent?
11. If while reliving the situation you experiencing hurt or anger, from where do these feelings arise? Did this person impose these feelings on you, or are these feelings generated from within you?
12. The hurt that you believe that this person caused you, whether they intended to so or not, are you not committing the same offense against yourself at this moment? How long will you continue to carry this hurt?

Exercise 2: Projections

1. Think of a people in your life who have qualities about them that bother you.
2. When you have identified the qualities, write them down on a piece of paper. I recommend that you use one piece of paper for each quality that you identify.
3. For each quality, write out all the reasons why this quality bothers you. For example, if the quality is that the other person is insensitive, you could write something like this:
4. By being insensitive, you make the world colder. It can lead to others feeling hurt, and it prevents you from experiencing the emotions and feelings of others. Being insensitive is like living in a barren desert.
5. Remember that how you experience the outer world around is a reflection of your inner world. That which bothers you in others is also found to some degree within you as well. If you are disturbed the insensitivity of others, it is because you have insensitivity within you, and you associated emotional pain to being insensitive.
6. Now reflect on the benefits of having that quality that you find bothersome in the other person, if not to a smaller degree.
7. Using the previous example, a benefit of having a degree of insensitivity in you may be that you would not be bothered by what other people think of you. You might not be less reactive emotionally, or you may feel a greater degree freedom in doing what you want to do without worrying about what other people might say.
8. By acknowledging the nobility of your subconscious aspects, that which you are keeping suppressed, you relinquish your resistance to it. In doing this, it will lose its potency as a counterforce when you are using your conscious mind to attract what which you desire.

Compassion

What of the most fundamental qualities that are needed for a healthy relationship is compassion? You may think of love as the most important quality for a relationship; however, love is often experienced as being conditional. In other words, we have a thought that goes like this: "I will love you as long as you_____." You can fill-in the blank. Compassion is unconditional; you feel compassion for another because you can connect to their suffering. The following is an exercise for expanding your compassion. This exercise is a series of sub exercises, with each one creating the foundation for the following exercise.

Step 1:

I want you to think of a person or animal that you love. When you have identified the subject of this reflection, I want you to think of all the ways that you appreciate them. Experience the feelings and emotions that you have for your subject and fully experience them. I want you to think of all the hardships and challenges that they have experienced. Think of the sufferings that they have experienced and make their suffering your own. When you have connected with their sufferings, express your love to them and wish them happiness.

Step 2:
In this next exercise, you are going to repeat what you did in the first exercise; however, this time you are going to choose a subject that you have neutral feelings for. For example, your subject could be the clerk at the register where you do your shopping or the mailperson. Even though you may not know anything about this person, I want you to imagine the sufferings that they may have experienced in their life. Use your intuition or your imagination but make their suffering as real for you can. Allow yourself to experience their sufferings as your own. When you have connected with their sufferings, express your love to them and wish them happiness.

Step 3:
In this third exercise, you are going to repeat what you did in the last two exercises; however, using another subject. In this exercise, your subject is going to be someone who you dislike, avoid, or you do not get along with. I want you to think of the sufferings that they have experienced in their life. As in the previous exercise, you can use your intuition or imagination if you do not know this person's background. Allow yourself to experience their sufferings as your own. When you have connected with their sufferings, express your love to them and wish them happiness.

Step 4:
This exercise differs from the previous three exercises because you will not be identifying your subject ahead of time. Instead, you perform this compassion exercise as you go about your day. I want you to notice the people around you as you conduct your daily business. Take time to imagine the potential sufferings of the people that you see. Allow yourself to experience their sufferings as your own. When you have connected with their sufferings, express your love to them and wish them happiness.

Step 5:
This is the final exercise, and for many people, the most difficult one. In this exercise, you will be the subject of your reflection. I want you to reflect on the sufferings that you have experienced in your life. Allow yourself to experience your sufferings fully; do not minimize anything. Get in touch with pains that you have experienced. When you have connected with your own sufferings, express love to yourself and wish yourself happiness.

The exercise that you just completed was an exercise in experiencing compassion, and the subject of your compassion began with the ones that are the easiest for us to experience compassion for, those whom we love. Each succeeding exercise became more difficult because the subject of your compassion became further removed from you emotionally. Most people have trouble loving or showing compassion for themselves, which is why you were the subject of the final meditation.

Part 5 – Law of Attraction for Amazing Relationships

The power of your compassion for others is dependent on your ability to have compassion for yourself. When we lack compassion for others it is because we lack compassion for ourselves; we project our lack of compassion for ourselves on those who are around us.

Conversely, when you develop compassion for yourself, you can truly have compassion for others. The power of compassion is also vital if you are to become an intentional manifester because compassion increases your vibration to a high level.

Meditation Exercises

One of the most effective ways to raise your vibrational level is through meditation. Mediation allows us to expand your awareness of your mental phenomena such as thoughts, perceptions, and sensations. By developing greater awareness of your mental phenomena, you will weaken your sense of identification with them. By losing your identification of them, you will lower your resistance toward them. By lowering your resistance, you raise your vibrational level. We will start off with a basic meditation.

Basic Meditation
1. Sit down either on the floor or in a chair and make yourself comfortable.
2. Allow yourself to relax and close your eyes as you breathe normally.
3. Place your awareness on the sensations that you experience as your breath flows into your body during inhalation and flows out of your body during exhalation.
4. As you focus on your breath, do not judge or analyze anything that you experience. Fully accept everything that you experience just as it is.
5. Whenever you get distracted by a thought, gently return your attention back to your breath, regardless of how many times you lose your concentration. With continued practice, your mind will become calmer as the amount of attention that you give your thoughts will become less and less.

Meditation on Thought
The purpose of this exercise is to expand your awareness to the nature of thought.
1. Make yourself comfortable, close your eyes, and relax.
2. Place your attention on your breath as you breathe normally.
3. As thoughts enter your awareness, observe them by maintaining your awareness of them. When observing your thoughts, do so without any sense of judgment or resistance. What happens to your thought when you observe them in this manner?
4. As you maintain the awareness of your thoughts, notice their qualities. Do your thoughts undergo changes or are they fixed and unchanging?
5. Where to do your thoughts appear from? Can you locate this place?
6. Where do your thoughts go when as they fade away from your awareness? Can you locate this place?

7. What do you experience when one thought fades away and your next thought has yet to appear?
8. This is the end of this exercise; continue meditating as long as you want.

Exercise 1: Emotions

The purpose of this meditation is to expand your awareness of your emotions.
1. Make yourself comfortable, close your eyes, and relax.
2. Place your attention on your breath as you breathe normally.
3. As you experience emotions, observe them by maintaining your awareness of them. When observing your emotions, do so without any sense of judgment or resistance. What happens to your emotions when you observe them in this manner? What do you notice?
4. As you maintain the awareness of your emotions, notice their qualities. Do your emotions undergo changes or are they fixed and unchanging?
5. Where to do your emotions appear from? Can you locate this place?
6. Where do your emotions go when as they fade away from your awareness? Can you locate this place?
7. What do you experience when one emotion fades away and your next emotion has yet to appear?
8. This is the end of this exercise; continue meditating as long as you want.

Exercise 2: Emotions

1. Sit down and make yourself comfortable.
2. Close your eyes and allow yourself to relax.
3. Place your attention on your breath as it enters and exits your body, focusing on the sensations you experience as you inhale and exhale.
4. Identify any negative emotions that you may be experiencing. If you are not experiencing a negative emotion, think of a problem or negative experience. When you experience a negative emotion, offer it total acceptance. Do not try to avoid it, deny it, or change it; allow the emotion to fully express itself.
5. Place your full awareness on the emotion, allow yourself to observe it with your attention but do not engage it. Allow yourself to experience the sensations that accompany the emotion. Pretend that you are diving into the emotion; allow yourself to become fully immersed in it. Remember, your emotions have no power as long as you do not try to resist them to or try to interpret them. As long as you involvement with them is restricted to observing them and experiencing them, you will be in charge.
6. What happens to the potency of your emotions when you just observe them and allow them to fully express themselves?

Part 5 – Law of Attraction for Amazing Relationships

Feelings

Exercise 1: Feelings

The purpose of this exercise is to expand your awareness of your feelings.

1. Make yourself comfortable, close your eyes, and relax.
2. Place your attention on your breath as you breathe normally.
3. As you experience feelings in your body, observe them by maintaining your awareness of them. When observing your feelings, do so without any sense of judgment or resistance. What happens to your feelings when you observe them in this manner? What do you notice?
4. As you maintain the awareness of your feelings, notice their qualities. Do your feelings undergo changes or are they fixed and unchanging?
5. Where to do your feelings appear from? Can you locate this place?
6. Where do your feelings go when as they fade away from your awareness? Can you locate this place?
7. What do you experience when one feeling fades away and your next feeling has yet to appear?
8. This is the end of this exercise; continue meditating as long as you want.

Exercise 2: Feelings

We previously discussed how our feelings are like a GPS in that they indicate how aligned we are with the larger consciousness. The following meditation can be used to expand your awareness of your feelings.

1. Sit down, make yourself comfortable, and relax.
2. Breathe normally as you focus on your breath, just as you did in the basic meditation exercise.
3. As you become more relaxed, be aware of any feelings that you are experiencing.
4. Allow yourself to experience your feelings without any judgment. Do not try control or change any feeling that you experience. Do not classify any of your feelings as being good or bad, pleasant or unpleasant for these are value judgments that exist solely in the mind. I want you to just place your attention on the feelings that you experience.
5. Are the feelings that you experience stable? Are they always the same or do they change? Are they always there or do they come and go?
6. Just stay in the awareness of your feelings, allow yourself to experience them for as long as you desire.
7. This is the end of this meditation. Feel free to allow yourself to continue to meditate on the body for as long as you wish.

Part 5 – Law of Attraction for Amazing Relationships

Beyond the Image of You

This final meditation is the ultimate meditation as it involves self-inquiry into the nature of your own existence. To understand the nature of your own existence is to challenge every belief that you have ever had about yourself and the world around you. As in all meditations, do not judge, criticize, or analyze any aspect of your experience. Greet every experience will complete acceptance. Do not turn to your knowledge, experience, imagination, or ideas during this meditation. Approach this exercise purely through your direct experience.

1. Make yourself comfortable and relax.
2. Close your eyes and place your attention on your breath.
3. Observe the perceptions, thoughts, sensations, feelings, and emotions that arise from within you. Notice how they come and go on their own, that they appear and fade away on their own accord.
4. Notice how these mental phenomena appear and fade away, but you, the observer of them, always remains.
5. Notice that perception, the ability to hear sound, and the ability to feel occur without any effort by you. These sensory functions occur without any of your involvement; you are the witness to these things.
6. The functions of your mind and body all carry on without any effort on your part. Who or what is aware of all of this?
7. If you tell yourself "I am the one who is aware of this," there must be an awareness of this answer. Who or what is aware of the response that you give? How can you be "I" when there is an awareness of this "I"? Where is this "I" located?
8. Who you are is the one that is aware of thought, sensations, perception, sound, and smell. Who you are is aware of every response that you give when conducting this inquiry. Who is this one? Regardless of how you respond to this question, there is awareness of it as well.
9. The word "phenomenal" means something that can be seen, thought, touched, heard, or detected somehow. The truth of who you are cannot be phenomenal. How can you be both the perceived and the perceiver? Who you are is non-phenomenal, for you are consciousness itself!

Part 6- Book 6

Law of Attraction for Abundance

How to Change Your Relationship with Money to Manifest the Wealth You Truly Desire

Introduction

I remember watching a cartoon as a child where a man was making his way across the desert. He struggled as he walked under the merciless sun. All that he could think about was having water to drink. He felt like each step that he took would be his last when suddenly he saw an oasis in the distance. Excited, he ran toward the oasis. As he got closer to the oasis, it began to fade until it disappeared. Instead of life-giving water, there was just more desert sand.

Midas was well-known for his greediness. He wanted to be the wealthiest man in the world. In Greek mythology, there is the story of Midas, the king of Phrygia.

One day, Midas performed an act that pleased the god Dionysus. In return for his thoughtful gesture, Dionysus offered to grant Midas the wish of his choice. Midas told Dionysus that he wanted to be able to turn anything he touched into gold. Dionysus warned Midas of the dangers of such a wish; however, Midas persisted with his request. Unable to refuse Midas, Dionysus hesitantly granted Midas his wish.

Midas was thrilled with his new powers. Everything that he touched turned into gold. He had the "Midas touch." He now could become the wealthiest man in the world. However, the thrill of his new gift was short-lived. Midas realized that he was unable to eat or drink, for they also turned to gold.

Both the man traveling through the desert and the story of King Midas are metaphors for two different mindsets toward money. Like the man traveling across the desert, many of us struggle financially and are searching for the opportunity to quench our thirst for financial stability or wealth. Unfortunately, it never appears. There are others who are like King Midas who pursue money with a laser-like focus and end up being cursed.

Regardless of our intentions for wanting more money, most of us pursue the traditional approach, which is to expend a great deal of energy at the expense of others or ourselves.

This book was written to provide a radically different perspective on success. And not just financial success, but success in all areas of our lives. The perspective this book takes is through the Law of Attraction. There are plenty of books on the market about the Law of Attraction. However, this book is different.

Because it's written from a higher perspective, this book provides insights that most other books on the Law of Attraction fail to address.

They fail to address these insights because they are written from a dualistic perspective. This book begins with a discussion on higher levels of consciousness and works downward to the nuts and bolts of attracting anything that you could desire, especially money.

By adopting the principles in this book and consistently applying them, you will be able to transform your life. All that's required for this transformation is to have an open mind, an open heart, and the determination to challenge some of your most deep-seated beliefs.

Part 6 – Law of Attraction for Abundance

Chapter 1: The Secret Behind the Secret

The 2006 bestseller, *The Secret,* introduced a mass audience to the Law of Attraction. *The Secret* was well-received because the timing was right. The timing was right because universal consciousness is continually evolving, and it reached a point where *The Secret* resonated with us.

However, *The Secret,* and many other books on the Law of Attraction, only examined the Law of Attraction from a surface level. Because of this, a lot of crucial information was not communicated; information that you need to know to more effectively use the Law of Attraction.

That this information was not contained in *The Secret* was not due to ignorance on the part of the author. Rather, it was written to conform to our dualistic understanding of the world. The purpose of this book is to pick up where *The Secret* left off and provide you with that vital information so that you can use the Law of Attraction to more effectively attract wealth into your life.

To do so, we will first explore the non-dualistic view of life so that we can understand the Law of Attraction, and ourselves, from a broader context. Using this understanding, we will explore practical steps you can take to develop a mindset that is more open to attracting and receiving money with less frustration and mental energy. We will start by exploring our relationship with consciousness itself.

Chapter 2: From Nothing to Something

What is the source of existence? Where did we come from? What is the true nature of reality? These are the big questions that philosophers, scholars, poets, and scientists have pondered through the ages.

Though it may seem that the answers to these questions are out of reach, I believe that we are much closer than we think.

In many religious faiths, the answer to these questions would be God. In Buddhism, which does not believe in an external deity, it would be Ku. Ku is the essential aspect of existence. It is formless, timeless, and non-changing. In other words, it cannot be perceived by our senses and is beyond our ability to comprehend.

From it arises everything that we experience, including us. In quantum physics, there is the quantum field, which has the qualities of Ku and is made of energy. From religion to quantum physics, it appears that everything that is known arises from the formless. In this book, I will refer to this source of everything as consciousness. Consciousness is the awareness that creates all of existence.

Everything that we experience arises from consciousness. The water cycle is a helpful metaphor for understanding how consciousness manifests into form. Water in its gaseous state cannot be perceived by us. The air contains water in its gaseous state. When the moisture in the air cools, it condenses and forms clouds. When the moisture in the clouds becomes saturated, it becomes rain. When rain is exposed to cool enough temperatures, it becomes ice. In this manner, water in its formless state manifests into the form that we know as rain or ice. Regardless of its form, water's essential nature remains the same, which is two hydrogen atoms and one oxygen atom.

Consciousness is a form of intelligence and information and has the infinite potential to express itself, which it does to expand. To expand, consciousness needs to experience itself.
What we refer to as manifestation is consciousness expanding, and the expansion process begins with desire. Desire is the genesis of physical manifestation. Consciousness manifests desire from the information that it receives from our sense of experience. Desire manifests as thought, which we experience as the mind. Thought manifests as emotion, which motivates us. Emotion manifests as action, and action creates the effects that we experience. The effects that we experience create new desires in us, which completes the manifestation cycle and the expansion of consciousness.

Like gas, consciousness is formless, or non-phenomenal, and expresses itself as the phenomenal. The term "phenomenal" refers to that which we can perceive through our mind and senses, while non-phenomenal refers to that which we cannot perceive. Desires, thoughts, emotions, and action are phenomenal.

Because we identify with these phenomena, we experience ourselves as the mind and body. Because we experience ourselves as a mind and body, we experience ourselves as being separate from our surroundings. Because we experience ourselves as being separate from our surroundings, we experience contrast. Because we experience contrast, we can have experiences. Here is an example of what I mean:

I am a physical expression of consciousness, which is my essential nature. Because I experience myself as being a separate being, I experience the world as "me and other." I am "me," and everything else that I experience is "other." I am not my home, my family, my dog, or my car; all of these things are perceived to be something outside of myself. Because I see myself as being separate from these things, I experience contrast. I can see how my home is different from me. I can see how my family is different from me, and so on. That contrast creates experience. My experience appears to me in the form of thought. It is my thoughts that inform consciousness of my experience.

My thoughts, which result from experience, inform consciousness, which allows it to experience itself. By experiencing itself, it creates new potentials that are consistent with the information that it receives. Here is another example:

I, who sees myself as a separate being, sees my car parked next to a fancy sports car. Seeing my old Toyota next to this shiny new sports car creates contrast. I can see the major differences between the two vehicles. This contrast leads to an experience, which may appear as thoughts such as:

- I need to wash my car.
- *I am going to save my money to buy a car like that.*
- I will never be able to afford a car like that.

These thoughts inform consciousness which then manifests as phenomena that are consistent with my thoughts. If my previous thought was, "I need to wash my car," then all the conditions that are needed for me to wash my car will appear.

If my thoughts are, "I am going to save my money to buy a car like that," consciousness will manifest conditions that make this possible. It is this attracting of conditions that match our thoughts that is known as the Law of Attraction. As our essential selves, the Law of Attraction does not exist because the nature of consciousness is "oneness."

It is only in our phenomenal form, which is characterized by a sense of separateness that the Law of Attraction exists.

Part 6 – Law of Attraction for Abundance

The level of our ability to use the Law of Attraction is dependent on how effectively we can align our phenomenal self with our essential self.

Part 6 – Law of Attraction for Abundance

Chapter 3: The Illusion of Separation

As you read this book, you most likely experience yourself as being separate from the book. You also probably experience yourself as separate from that which you are sitting on. You also most likely experience yourself as different from your environment.

Except for light and sound, everything that you experience, including yourself, is made of molecules. Molecules are made of atoms. In fact, the carbon atom is the basic atom of all living and non-living beings.

Once thought to be the fundamental unit of matter, we now know that the atom is not solid. Rather, the atom is made of subatomic particles that are separated by vast distances of space. Additionally, the subatomic particles are not solid. Atoms are fluctuations of energy.

What this means is that, at the most fundamental level, there is no difference between you, this book, your electronic device, and your environment. Further, you and this book are no more solid than the air around you. At the atomic level, you and the money that you desire are one in the same. At the most fundamental level, everything is energy.

The cause of our experience of separation is our identification with the mind and body's functions. We experience ourselves having thoughts, perceptions, emotions, and feelings. We also experience ourselves as having a body that appears to be solid.

Because of how we experience the mind and body, we believe that we *are* the mind and body. Everything else that we experience is perceived to be something separate from ourselves, including the money that we desire.

Here are some exercises to challenge your perceptions of being separate from the world:

Exercise 1
Note: It is recommended that you first review this and other meditations in this book before performing them as they contain a lot of information. Another alternative is to read them out loud while recording them and then play them back when you are ready to meditate.

In this meditation, you will have the opportunity to challenge the nature of experience itself. When conducting this exercise, do not involve your knowledge or thinking. Rely solely on your immediate and direct experience.

6. Sit down and view your surroundings, taking your time to take everything in.
7. When you are ready, close your eyes and allow yourself to relax.

8. Imagine that you are an alien from a distant planet who has arrived on Earth to study it. You have no information about this planet, nor do you have any experience to draw from. Because of this, you are unable to define, identify, analyze, or judge anything that you experience. In other words, you are a blank slate.
9. Now, open your eyes and look at your surroundings again. Take your time.
10. How did your experience observing compare with your first observation?

If you did not notice any difference between the two observations, practice this exercise until you do. When we impose our thoughts on that which we are experiencing, what we are experiencing becomes a reflection of our thoughts.

Thought reconfigures everything that we experience. It is for this reason that Buddhism teaches us that our environment is a mirror of our inner world. Being able to observe without utilizing conceptual thinking is being mindful and present.

Exercise 2
Note: When conducting this exercise, do not involve your knowledge or thinking. Rely solely on your immediate and direct experience.

1. Sit down and make yourself comfortable. Allow yourself to relax. If you would like, you may close your eyes for now.

2. Allow yourself to relax as you focus on your breathing. Place your attention on your breath as it enters your body, travels through your body, and then leaves it as you exhale.

3. Breathe normally without exerting any effort. Relax.

4. When you are ready, open your eyes.

5. Now, look at an object in your surroundings.

6. As you look at the object, ask yourself, "Does seeing occur outside of me or from within me?" I hope you agree that seeing occurs from within you.

7. Does seeing require any thought or effort?

    For most of us, the answer to both of these questions would be "no." Even a blind person can "see" mental images.

8. Now, look at the object again. Ask yourself the following question: Does seeing stop at the point where the object begins, or does the object being seen and the act of seeing flow into each other?

I hope you will agree that seeing and the object being seen flow into each other.

9. How do you know that seeing is taking place? You know that seeing is taking place because you are aware of it.

10. Now, ask yourself whether you can separate the awareness of seeing from the act of seeing. I hope you agree that the awareness of seeing and the act of seeing are inseparable.

By practicing this exercise, I hope that you realize that seeing an object, the act of seeing, and the awareness that seeing is taking place are inseparable. They are one in the same.

That the act of seeing seems to originate from within us, and the object being seen appears to be outside of us, is an illusion created by the mind. From higher levels of perspective, there is no "inside" or "outside." You and what you experience are inseparable from each other.

You can repeat this exercise by replacing "seeing" with "hearing" or "touching. With enough practice, you will inevitably realize that who you are cannot be separate from the world around you.

Thought leads us to believe that we are separate from life. When we base our understanding on our direct experience, we find that we can never be separate from life, including the money that we desire to attract.

Exercise 3

The following exercise is similar to the preceding one, but it involves the senses of touch and hearing. As with the previous exercise, it is intended to challenge how you perceive the world around you. When conducting this exercise, do not involve your knowledge or thinking. Rely solely on your immediate and direct experience.

1. Sit down and close your eyes.
2. Now, touch your leg. As you touch your leg, ask yourself, "Am I experiencing my leg, or am I experiencing the sensation of touching my leg?"
3. I hope that you agree that you are experiencing the sensation of touching your leg.
4. Now ask yourself, is sensation experienced outside of me or within me?
5. I hope you agree that sensation is experienced within you, just as in seeing.
6. How do you know sensation is being experienced? You know of sensation because there is an awareness of it.
7. Now, listen to a sound in your environment. When you hear a specific sound, do not attach a label to it. In other words, if you hear a bird singing, do not think, "A bird is singing." Instead, just listen to the sound that it makes without thinking about it.

8. As you listen to the sound, touch your leg again. As with listening, do not attach any labels or think about it. You only want to experience the sensation. Are the sound that you hear and the sensation that you feel separate from each other?

Practice this exercise (with your eyes closed) until you reach the realization that both sensation and sound are aspects of experience that appears in your awareness. Sensation and sound appear in awareness and are indivisible from each other.

When we do not conceptualize our experience, meaning that we do not label or think about it, we realize that all we can ever know is experience and our awareness of it. Further, awareness is indivisible from experience itself. Your direct experience of this will give you a major advantage in manifesting. The reason why is this: Everything that you could want already exists in your life.

All challenges in manifesting through the Law of Attraction are the result of us putting our attention on our sense of separateness. If there is anything that you desire that is not currently evident in your life, it is because you have not made yourself open enough to receive it. The reason why we are not open to receiving is that we see ourselves as being separate from it.

At the level of our ordinary awareness, we believe that we can use the Law of Attraction to attract money into our lives, or that we have to do it the old fashion way, which is to work at it. From the perspective of higher levels of awareness, having the desire for money is enough to manifest it in our lives if we do not prevent ourselves from receiving it. To become effective manifesters, we need to adopt a mindset that is consistent with consciousness.

The degree that we can manifest is dependent on our alignment with consciousness, which we will be exploring in the upcoming chapters. But before we do, let us explore the most essential tool for understanding the manifestation process. That tool is meditation.

Chapter 4: Meditation

Meditation is an essential tool for increasing awareness of the nature of the mind and overcoming the illusions of reality that it creates. Most of us have lost our inward focus and concentrate on the outer realm that surrounds us, which is what we refer to as the world. Meditation makes it possible for us to see beyond this illusion of separation and realize that the outer realm is reflecting our inner realm.

We will use meditation techniques throughout this book to expand our awareness of the nature of the mind. For now, here is a simple meditation to practice that will build the foundation for the upcoming meditative exercises.

Basic Meditation

6. Find a quiet place to sit that is comfortable. You may sit either on the floor or in a chair.
7. Close your eyes and allow yourself to relax by placing your attention on the flow of your breath. Keep your awareness on your breath as you inhale by focusing on the sensations. Do the same thing during exhalation by placing your attention on the sensations that are experienced as your breath travels out of your body. Breathe naturally; it is vital that you make no effort at any time during this meditation. An alternative to following your breath is to focus on the rising and falling of your abdomen.
8. Keep your focus on your breathing. If at any time you catch your mind wandering, just return your attention to the sensations of your breath. Do this as often as necessary without any form of judgment of yourself.

By continuing to practice this meditation, you will increase your awareness to the coming and fading of thought. By focusing on your breathing, you deprive your thoughts of the attention that you have been giving them; thus, slowing down your mental activity.

Part 6 – Law of Attraction for Abundance

Chapter 5: The Vibrational Universe

You and I are multidimensional beings in that we are simultaneously non-phenomenal and phenomenal. Our essential self is consciousness while our experience of being a person is the manifestation of consciousness.

Your manifested self is the aspect of you that can have an experience. Your essential self, which is consciousness, creates new manifestations based on the information that it gains from your experiences. The information that is gained from experience takes on the form of thought.

The quality of our thoughts determines the quality of manifestations that are expressed by our essential self. More specifically, the quality of the thoughts that we focus on determines the quality of the manifestations that are expressed by consciousness.

In the following chapters, we will discuss the role of thoughts in the manifestation process as well as the roles of emotions and feelings. However, before we discuss these mental functions, we need to understand the vibrational nature of reality.

While consciousness is the essence of existence, everything that is expressed by consciousness is a vibrational expression of it. To better understand this, we can go back to the water cycle as a metaphor. Water can take on the form of a gas, liquid, or solid. What determines the form that water takes is the behavior of its molecules.

In the gaseous state, water molecules are further apart than in any other state. The reason why water is invisible as a gas is because of the great distances between its molecules. Not only are the molecules far apart from each other, but they are also very active and vibrate at a high frequency.

When water becomes a liquid, the molecules are closer together but still have a lot of distance between them. It is for this reason that water, as a liquid, can flow and take on the shape of the container that it is in. As a liquid, the molecules are active and vibrate at a high frequency, though its activity and vibrational frequency are lower than that of gas.

When water becomes solid, the molecules are close together. It is the close proximity of the molecules that give ice its solid form. Because of their proximity, the molecules are far less active than liquid water and have a low vibrational rate.

Just as with water, the different manifestations of consciousness also have a vibrational quality to them. Thoughts, feelings, emotions, and the physical body are different vibrational qualities of the consciousness.

Only consciousness is conscious. The mind, thoughts, feelings, emotions, and physical body are not conscious. Our phenomenal selves are experienced by us within the field of consciousness, so we believe that our phenomenal self is conscious. Thoughts, emotions, and feelings are the vibrational qualities of conscious energy that we experience in our phenomenal form. In this manner, the only difference between a thought and a pile of money is the vibrational level.

Thoughts

Imagine that you go to the Grand Canyon and see the mighty Colorado River. The river is vast with torrential waters that travel through the canyon at high speeds. Now imagine that you take an eye dropper and place it in the river to collect a sample of its water. We would never confuse the water sample with the river. However, most of us confuse thought with reality.

The Colorado River is a metaphor for consciousness. Consciousness is infinite, without boundaries or limits. All information that has ever existed, or will exist, is found within consciousness. In our manifested form, we can tap into consciousness for information. Just as with dipping an eyedropper into the Colorado River, the information that we receive from consciousness is just a minute sample of reality.

Not only is it a tiny sample, but it is also subjectively influenced by our past conditioning. For example, the thoughts that we have for a piece of art is distorted by our past experiences. One person may see a piece of artwork as being brilliant while another may find it to be nonsense.

Thoughts lack any power that is inherently their own. Rather, they become energized by us giving attention to them. When we give thoughts our attention, they become our reality. The popular adage that we create our reality cannot be understated.

Our reality consists of the thoughts that we identify with.

When we have a sense of certainty about our thoughts, we refer to them as beliefs. Our beliefs define our experience of reality. Because we have such a sense of certainty about our beliefs, we are unable to perceive anything that lies outside of them. If I believe that I will never experience a million dollars, I will never notice the opportunities to make a million dollars. One aspect of aligning our manifested self with our essential self is transforming our limiting beliefs.

Exercises for Beliefs

Identifying limiting beliefs

The following are exercises that can be used to identify or change your limiting beliefs:

Exercise 4

To show you how this exercise works, I will provide you with an example.

9. Think of an ongoing challenge that you are experiencing in your life. For my example, I will use: "I can never get ahead financially."
10. My next step is to start a line of inquiry using the phrase, "What would be so bad if…" So my first question would be, "What would be so bad about not getting ahead financially?"
11. My answer to that question would be, "I will continue to struggle."
12. I would then use my response and rephrase the question: "What would be so bad if I continue to struggle financially?"
13. My response to that would be, "I will never feel financially secure."
14. I would continue to repeat this question by asking: "What would be so bad if I do not feel finically secure?"
15. My answer to that would be, "I would feel inadequate or like a failure."
16. Keep going through this line of questioning until you are unable to go any further. When you have reached this point, you will have identified your subconscious belief. At the conscious level, my challenge was that I cannot get ahead financially. At a deeper level, my challenge is that I feel inadequate and that I am a failure. For me to attract wealth, I need to transform my belief that I am inadequate and a failure. My difficulty in getting ahead financially is just a symptom of this.

Exercise 5:

This next exercise can be used to find the subconscious beliefs about the things that we want. For this exercise, I will use the example: "I want to be rich."

8. What would getting rich give me?
9. It would give me a sense of financial security.
10. What would having a sense of financial security give me?
11. It would make me feel more relaxed.
12. What would feeling more relaxed give me?
13. It would give me a sense of peace.
14. My subconscious belief is that I want a sense of peace, but my conscious belief is that I want to be rich.

Changing a Belief

Exercise 6:

When you have identified a belief that is limiting you, you can use the following procedure to weaken your old belief and replace it with a more empowering one:
1. Get two sheets of paper. Select paper sizes 8" x 11" or larger.
2. Take the first sheet of paper and fold it in half lengthwise.
3. At the top, write down your belief.
4. Make a list on the left-hand side of all the ways this belief has cost you in your life. When doing this part of the exercise, think of how this belief has affected you in all of your life areas. Ask yourself how living by this belief has affected the way that you see yourself, how it has affected your emotional health, relationships, physical health, work, finances, and so on.
5. When writing, keep in mind:
    a. Write down the first thing that comes to your mind, even if it seems irrelevant.
    b. Write as fast as you can and feel the emotions that arise. This is a heartfelt exercise, not a thinking one.
    c. Keep writing until you run out of things to write.
6. Next to each item that you write down, assign an arbitrary point value as to how much impact this item has had on you. When selecting a point value, choose the first number that comes to mind.
7. When you have completed assigning the point values, find the total of all the point values and place it at the bottom of the page.
8. For the right side of the page, repeat Steps 4-7, except this time, you will write down all of the ways that this belief has benefited you.

When you have completed Step 8, think of a new alternative belief that empowers you. For example, if the original belief was, "I will never enjoy financial success," my new belief may be, "Financial success is just an expression of who I am that I have not yet tapped into."

On the second paper, repeat steps 1-8 using your new belief with the following exceptions: Reverse Steps 4 and 8 by writing down all the ways that you believe that you would benefit from this new belief for Step 4. When doing Step 8, write down all the ways you think that it will cost you. When you have completed the two sheets, do the following:
5. Immediately review your lists, allowing yourself to experience any emotions that arise.
6. Review your lists every day, once in the morning and once before you go to bed until you become fully associated with the emotions that you experience.

When you become associated with the costs of holding on to your old belief with the benefits of adopting your new belief, your mind will become re-programmed with your new belief.

Emotions

I previously offered the metaphor of the water cycle with its different phases of water's manifestation as a gas, liquid, or solid.

If thought is like water's gas phase, emotions are like the liquid form. What we call "emotions" are the next level of manifestation from thought. Emotions are the tangible expression of our thoughts. They are the universe's way of making our thoughts more evident to us.

Though we have many thoughts, our thoughts are just indicators of whether or not we have a pleasurable or painful experience. The thought, "I will never be rich," can be a painful thought, which alerts my nervous system to this understanding. Conversely, the thought, "I can attract wealth if I have the proper mindset," is pleasurable and will register in my nervous system in that way.

The crucial thing to understand is that neither thought is inherently true. They are just interpretations that our minds make out of the information that it receives from consciousness.

Because we are not always able to identify the thoughts that we are experiencing, especially our subconscious thoughts, our emotions provide a palpable message to the quality of our thoughts. If I am experiencing happiness, it is because I am having thoughts of the same quality. If I am experiencing anger, it is because I am having thoughts of that nature.

We experience a range of emotions with each having its own vibrational frequency.

At the low end of the spectrum are feelings such as shame, humiliation, or guilt. Further up the spectrum are things like disappointment, anxiousness, or fear. While low in their vibrational frequency, they are higher than the first category of emotions because they are more likely to lead us to take action.

Next up the spectrum are emotions like anger, determination, and pride. These emotions have a vibrational frequency that is higher than the last category, and they are more likely to cause us to take action to change our situation.

Going further up the spectrum are the emotions of happiness, allowing, and acceptance. These have a higher frequency than the ones below them because they are further away from the vibration of fear.

The feelings of gratitude and appreciation are even higher than the previous category because they cause us to have a more outward focus than the previous categories.

The last categories centered on how we feel about our situation; they inform us as to whether our situation is pleasurable or if we need to avoid it.

Gratitude and appreciation cause us to focus less on our situation and more on the object of our gratitude and appreciation. I can have gratitude because I see that I live a higher standard of living than most people in other parts of the world. Appreciation has a higher vibration than gratitude because gratitude implies that we are grateful for something that we received. Appreciation can be experienced without having received something in return. In other words, it can be unconditional. I can have an appreciation for a beautiful flower or the work of artists.

Exercises for the Mindfulness of Emotions

The following meditative exercises will allow you to develop a greater awareness of your emotions and how to transform them.

Exercise 7
The purpose of this meditation is to develop a greater awareness of your emotions.
1. Find a quiet place where you will not be disturbed and make yourself comfortable.
2. When relaxed, close your eyes and place your attention on your breath. For approximately one minute, use your attention to follow the path of your breath as it enters your body during inhalation and leaves it during exhalation. Do not put any effort into this. Simply observe your breath flowing through you. If you wish to extend this step for more than one minute, feel free to do so.
3. Adopt the attitude that you will allow anything that you experience to exist without any involvement by you. Do not resist or try to change anything. Let everything that appears do so without judging it.
4. If you experience an unpleasant thought or emotion, allow yourself to observe it like a birdwatcher observes a rare bird from a distance. Do not try to interfere in any way with the unpleasant emotion. Do not give any thought or concern to it. Simply observe it calmly without getting involved.
5. As you observe the thought or emotion, what happens to it? Does it get weaker and fainter? The change in potency happens because you are no longer engaging with these mental functions. Like thoughts, emotions depended on you for their power.

Exercise 8
The purpose of this meditation is to become more deeply aware of the nature of your emotions:

1. Sit down and make yourself comfortable.
2. Close your eyes and allow yourself to relax.
3. Place your attention on your breath as it enters and exits your body, focusing on the sensations you experience as you inhale and exhale.
4. Identify any negative emotions that you might be experiencing. If you are not experiencing a negative emotion, think of a problem or negative experience. When you experience a negative emotion, offer it total acceptance. Do not try to avoid it, deny it, or change it. Allow the emotion to fully express itself.

5. Place your full awareness on the emotion. Allow yourself to observe it with your attention, but do not engage it. Allow yourself to experience the sensations that accompany the emotion. Pretend that you are diving into the emotion and allow yourself to become fully immersed in it. Remember, your emotions have no power as long as you do not try to resist them to or try to interpret them. As long as your involvement with them is restricted to observing and experiencing them, you will be in charge.
6. What happens to the potency of your emotions when you just observe them and allow them to express themselves?

Exercise 9
1. Sit in a comfortable position and close your eyes.
2. Allow yourself to follow your breath during inhalation and exhalation. Place your attention on your breath. Feel it as it courses through your body.
3. Take on an attitude of complete allowing. Whatever arises in this meditation, you will have complete acceptance of it.
4. Observe the perceptions, thoughts, sensations, feelings, and emotions that arise within you. Allow them to come and go on their own. All you need to do is be the observer of them.
5. Now, pay attention to any emotion that arises. Become an observer of it. What happens when your focus is placed on your emotion?
6. Do not place any meaning on the emotion you experience. Do not think of it as being positive or negative. Words such as "positive," "negative," "pleasant," or "unpleasant" are products of the mind
7. There is no intrinsic meaning to anything in life. All meaning is derived from our minds. Emotions and feelings have no power of their own. They derive their power from the attention we give them.
8. When observing emotions, do so with complete allowing. Do not try to change anything about it.
9. As you observe your emotions, do you notice a change in how you experience them? Do they change in intensity? Do they become stronger or milder? Can you locate where the emotions came from? Can you observe where they go?
10. As you observe emotions, ask yourself, "Am I my emotions, or am I the one that is aware of them?" If a feeling or emotion is experienced as being unpleasant, does awareness feel unpleasant? If an emotion is experienced as being pleasant, does awareness feel pleasant?
11. Awareness does not experience anything; it can only know of experience. Awareness is like a beam of light shining on a snow-covered field. The light does not feel the cold of the snow, it only illuminates it. As you observe emotions, become the beam of light.
12. This is the end of this meditation. Feel free to remain in meditation for as long as you wish.

Exercise 10

The purpose of this exercise is to transform your emotions once you have become comfortable with the previous exercises. It will involve you playing a more active role than in the previous exercises, and it is a powerful tool if you have a strong negative emotion that has been lingering in you. Do the following:

1. Sit down and make yourself comfortable.
2. Place your attention on your breath as it enters and exits your body, focusing on the sensations you experience as you inhale and exhale.
3. If you are not already experiencing a negative emotion, relive a memory that will activate one. Think of a negative experience from the past or one that you are currently experiencing.
4. When the negative emotion appears, identify what the emotion feels like. Remember, you want to describe what the emotion feels like, not what you think about it. To avoid falling into this trap, phrase your response, "It feels like_____."

Here are some examples:
- "It feels like there is a weight on me."
- "I feel like I want to hide."
- "It leaves me feeling defeated."
- "It feels like I am being crushed."

After you identify what the emotion feels like, use the following process to transform your emotion using your response from Step 4. Here is an example:

1. If the emotion that I am feeling is anger, my response to what anger feels like would be, "It feels like my I am going to explode."
2. I would then repeat the process by asking, "What does exploding feel like?"
3. My response to that would be, "It feels like tension is filling my body."
4. I would follow up with, "What does tension feel like?"
5. With every response that I give, I would repeat the same line of questioning until the emotion transforms into a positive emotion.

The key to this exercise is to become fully associated with the emotions that you experience. Also, when trying to identify the feeling of the emotion, go by the first answer that comes to you.

Do not worry about getting it wrong; you can't. As long as you describe the feeling of the emotion without getting intellectual about it, you will be on the right track.

Every time you describe an emotion, you allow it to transform itself. By continuously describing it every time that it transforms, the emotion will eventually transform into a positive emotion. Using this process allows the emotion to go full circle and heal itself.

When you learn to transform your emotions, you will automatically transform your thoughts. By transforming your thoughts in a way that feels empowering to you, you will improve your alignment with consciousness, which is your essential self.

Feelings and Sensations

Our thoughts and emotions are forms of conscious energy that become altered by our past conditioning. For example, I may feel angry, but I would never harm another person or animal. However, some people would. Why do I act differently under anger than some other people? It is because of my past conditioning, which is based on how I was raised, the norms of the society that I grew up in, and my experiences. All of these things created my conditioning.

There is a conscious energy that is pure and unaltered by my personal experience, and that conscious energy is my feelings. Our feelings are our direct connection to consciousness. For this reason, our feelings are like our GPS for determining our alignment with our essential selves.

Anytime we experience feelings of well-being, we are in alignment with our essential selves. Anytime that we are not experiencing the feelings of well-being, it means that we are out of alignment. Many of us have lost touch with the feelings of the body because we are preoccupied with our thoughts, or we are trying to avoid our feelings because we find them threatening to our emotional being. The following exercises will help you increase your awareness to the feelings and sensations that you experience in your body.

Exercise 11
8. Close your eyes and allow yourself to follow your breath during inhalation and exhalation. Place your attention on your breath. Feel it as it courses through your body.
9. Now, place your attention on the sensations of your body. Place your attention on any sensation that appears in your awareness.
10. Do you feel a tingling in your hands or feet? Do you feel tensions in your back, shoulders, or face? Do you feel the weight of your body or the pressure on your buttocks from the chair or ground that you are sitting on?
11. Allow yourself to experience the sensations of the body without any judgment, even ones that may feel unpleasant. There are no good or bad sensations. Good and bad, pleasant and unpleasant, these are value judgments that exist solely in mind. The same thing is true with perceptions, sounds, and thoughts. They just exist.
12. Are the sensations that you experience stable? Are they always the same, or do they change? Are they always there, or do they come and go?
13. Just stay in the awareness of your body's sensations. Allow yourself to experience them for as long as you desire.

14. This is the end of this meditation. Please feel free to allow yourself to continue to meditate on the body for as long as you wish.

For many of us, there is a lack of awareness of our inner world. This is because we spent most of our waking hours focusing on the world outside of ourselves. For the same reasons, we often lack an awareness of our bodies. We may be unaware of subtle sensations and feelings. The body is the interface that allows consciousness to experience the physical world. In fact, the physical body plays a vital role in allowing us to develop greater levels of consciousness.

Exercise 12

Most instructions for meditation advise you to sit in a comfortable position while sitting in an upright position. One of keys to meditation is learning to be allowing of all experiences and to not control anything, including your body. In this meditation, you will listen to the body and allow it to move or position itself in complete freedom.

1. Sit down and make yourself comfortable. Allow yourself to relax. Close your eyes and focus on your breath. Allow yourself to become relaxed.
2. Forget about what you learned from your mother about sitting straight. If your body feels like slumping over, let it. Allow your body to do whatever it wants.
3. Place your awareness on your body and its sensations. Let your awareness be soft and do not get caught up in your thinking.
4. Observe the sensations of the body and any messages that you are getting.
5. Honor the messages from the body by allowing it to express itself freely.
6. This is the end of this meditation. Feel free to allow yourself to listen to your body for as long as you desire.

Exercise 13

In this meditation, you will experience the power of awareness on the body.

1. Sit down and make yourself comfortable, if you like, you can close your eyes.
2. Place your attention on your breath as it travels in and out of your body. Allow your awareness to wash over your body and experience the sensations.
3. Now, scan your body with your awareness for a relaxed, calm, or pleasant sensation. When you find such a sensation, allow yourself to focus on it.
4. As you observe this sensation, I want you to ask yourself the following question. "What color is this sensation?" Accept the first response that comes to mind.
5. Now ask, "What size is this sensation?" Again, go with the first answer that comes to mind.
6. Now ask yourself, "Does this sensation have a texture to it? Is it smooth, rough, soft, or hard?"
7. Now, search the body for a sensation that is not relaxed, calm, or pleasant. Perhaps it has tension, pressure, heaviness, or hardness to it.
8. Now, just as with the pleasant sensation, inquire about the color, size, and texture of this sensation.

9. Using your awareness, allow yourself to imagine that the qualities of the unpleasant sensation taking on the qualities of the pleasant sensation. If the pleasant sensation had a green color, imagine the color of the unpleasant sensation turning green. If the texture of the pleasant sensation was soft, imagine the unpleasant sensation growing soft, and so on.
10. Take your time and transfer the qualities of the pleasant sensation to the unpleasant sensation.
11. Place your attention on the unpleasant sensation. Has it changed? Does it seem more pleasant as a result of transferring the positive qualities? If not, continue to practice this meditation.

Exercise 14

Our feelings inform us whether we are moving toward or away from our integrity as a human being. When we do not trust our feelings, we are unable to trust ourselves. This next meditation demonstrates how our feelings change with changes in our perceptions.

1. Sit down, close your eyes, and relax.
2. Allow yourself to become silent and observe the thoughts, feelings, emotions, and sensations that arise. Allow all of these phenomena to present themselves to your awareness.
3. Relax.
4. I want you to think of a situation that is currently causing you feelings of uneasiness, concern, or hurt. When you identify such a situation, allow yourself to focus on it. Relive the experience in your mind.
5. As you focus on the situation, become aware of the feelings that arise. Allow them to arise naturally.
6. Remember, your feelings are like a compass in that they have a message for you. They are telling you to move toward or away from that which you are focusing on.
7. When we are making decisions, taking actions, or focusing on things that bring about pleasant feelings, we know that we are on the right track and that we are consistent with our sense of integrity.
8. Conversely, when we have feelings that are unpleasant, it is a message that we are focusing on things that are inconsistent with our sense of integrity.
9. Ask yourself, "What can I do, believe, or focus on that will make me feel better about this situation?" Is there a decision that you need to make? Do you need let go of something? Do you need to question your thinking? Do you need to take time for yourself? Do you need to risk disappointing others?
10. Keep inquiring with yourself until you have identified a way to address the situation that leaves you with feelings of ease, relief, calm, or peace.
11. Whatever you come up with to address the situation, if it leads you to experience positive feelings, trust that it is the correct decision for you.
12. Your feelings are completely accurate and reliable at this moment in time. If your feelings regarding your solution or the situation change, honor them as well.

Part 6 – Law of Attraction for Abundance

   Be sure not to confuse your feelings with your thoughts or beliefs. Your feelings are reliable, but your thoughts and beliefs are not.
13. If you are unable to find a way to make yourself feel better, that is okay, too. Allow yourself to remain with the feelings. Honor them by fully accepting them.
14. Accepting our feelings and being at peace with them is an act of self-love and an indication of integrity.
15. This is the end of the meditation. Please remain in your stillness for as long as you like.

Part 6 – Law of Attraction for Abundance

Chapter 6: Meditation on the Self

In this book, you engaged in exercises for increasing your awareness of the nature of experience, thoughts, emotions, and feelings.

The purpose of these activities was to move you toward the realization that the phenomena of the mind and body are in constant flux and that who you are is the observer of these phenomena. Through this observation, we can arrive at the realization that the nature of who we are is beyond the phenomenal.

The more we lift the veils of illusions that are created by the mind, the closer we come to understanding our true nature. It is this understanding that will liberate you from the limiting thinking that impedes your ability to attract the wealth that you desire.

The following meditative exercises are the most profound of all, for they involve inquiring about the nature of who you are. By continually practicing these meditative exercises, you have an opportunity to make the most profound discovery a human can ever make. However, making this discovery requires that you be willing to let go of all of your beliefs about yourself.

Self-Inquiry
Exercise 15

Anytime we ask ourselves a question, we are engaging in inquiry. You will now engage in self-inquiry or the inquiry into the nature of your existence.

1. Sit down in a comfortable position and close your eyes.
2. Place your attention on your breath as you breathe. Feel it as it courses through your body.
3. Take on an attitude of complete allowing, that whatever arises in this meditation you will have complete acceptance of it.
4. Observe the perceptions, thoughts, sensations, feelings, and emotions that arise from you. Allow them to come and go on their own accord. All you need to do is to be aware of them.
5. You are the observer of thought, sensation, perception, emotions, and feeling. You are the one that is aware of experience. But who are you? You refer to yourself as "I." Who is this "I?"
6. Can you find where this "I" is located? Is it in your body? Is it in your heart?
7. The word "phenomenal" means something that can be seen, thought, touched, heard, or detected. Any response that you give to these questions is also phenomenal.
8. Anything that you experience and everything you know is phenomenal.
9. Even if you experience space, a sense of emptiness, or bliss, you are none of these. Space, emptiness, and bliss can be detected by you.
10. Your experiences come in and out of awareness. Who is observing experience coming in and out of awareness? Are you coming in and out of awareness?

Part 6 – *Law of Attraction for Abundance*

11. Your emotions and feelings are constantly changing. Is your sense of being, the sense that you exist, constantly changing?
12. Any responses that you give to these questions is also observed, and there is a knowing of it. What is aware of this? What is observing this?
13. When answering this question, do not rely on your thinking. You will not get an answer.
14. Do not use your imagination or mind. Neither of these will answer this question.
15. Do not put any effort into answering this question. Just observe and be allowing. Continue asking yourself this question. Continue to inquire within.
16. The question of who you are is more important than the answer. Pursuing this question will lead to you experiencing the answer. You cannot know the answer; you can only experience it.
17. Whatever you are aware of cannot be you, for you are the awareness itself.
18. Who you are does not arise or fade. Who you are has no sense of identity or personality.
19. Who you are has no color, shape, or texture. Who you are never changes; it is eternally present.
20. Who you are cannot be experienced. Who you are is awareness itself. Just as a ray of light cannot shine on itself, the awareness that is you cannot observe itself. But you have a knowing that you exist.
21. Though you cannot perceive yourself, you can perceive that which you are not.
22. You are not your experience of life, nor are you your experience of yourself.
23. The more you discover that which you are not, the closer you will come to realizing who you are.
24. This is the end of this meditation. Allow yourself to remain in silence for as long as you desire.

Exercise 16

1. Sit in a comfortable position and close your eyes.
2. Allow yourself to follow your breath during inhalation and exhalation. Place your attention on your breath. Feel it as it courses through your body.
3. Take on an attitude of complete allowing, that whatever arises in this meditation that you have complete acceptance of it.
4. Observe the perceptions, thoughts, sensations, feelings, and emotions that arise from you. Allow them to come and go on their accord. All you need to do is be aware of them
5. Allow yourself to release all desires for effort, discovery, or any expectations of what you should be experiencing.
6. Allow your life to flow through you unhindered. Whatever arises within you, let it be. No action by you is required.
7. Allow yourself to sink into the depths of your being. Feel the sense of lightness and spaciousness within you.
8. You may experience a pleasant, warm sensation. Enjoy them and allow yourself to sink into these sensations.

9. Thought, emotions, and sensations will continue to arise. Allow them to be. Stay in the stillness of your being.
10. Anything that you experience is merely a projection of who you are. You are not your projections. You are the awareness of your projections.
11. Who you are cannot be observed or felt. Who you are has no shape, size, color, or sensation.
12. Who you are cannot be perceived or imagined. You can only know that which you are not.
13. You are like a movie screen, and your experiences are like the movie projected on it.
14. When we watch a movie, the movie and the screen seem to be one. There is no thought of the screen. We are only interested in the movie.
15. The movie is not the screen, and you are not your experience. Who you are is the invisible and undetectable screen that is behind all of experience.
16. Allow the movie of your experience to play before you. You are the awareness of them.
17. Who you are cannot be experienced, but you, the awareness, knows of experience.
18. All of experience in all of its diversity and form depends on your awareness for it to exist.
19. Experience arises from awareness and consciousness.
20. You are not your experience, but you can be found in all of experience.
21. At the level of consciousness, we are not separate from anything.
22. At the level of consciousness, our being merges into oneness.
23. At the level of the mind, we experience separateness.
24. All of this is happening without our involvement. This is ultimate reality, the union of non-duality and duality.
25. The mind or ego resists ultimate reality. It wants to dictate how life should be. But, the mind arises from consciousness as well. It makes it possible for your sense of self to experience the world.
26. Simply allow life and experience to happen. There is nothing to control or change.
27. Everything that is happening was meant to happen.
28. Let go of all intentions, outcomes, strategies, and plans.
29. Let go of your memories, dreams, or thoughts on the future.
30. All mental and physical activity is experienced through consciousness
31. You are not your mental and physical activity.
32. You are the observer of mental and physical activity.
33. You are not the one who is meditating or doing self-inquiry. You are the observer of the one who is meditating and doing self-inquiry.
34. This is how consciousness experiences itself. It learns about itself through experiencing itself as a physical body and mind, a physical body and mind that has experienced.
35. You are informing consciousness through your experience and consciousness is providing you with the experience.
36. Do not resist any of this. Embrace it and surrender to it. This is true freedom, joy, and happiness.
37. This is the end of this meditation. Allow yourself to remain in silence for as long as you desire.

Chapter 7: The Law of Attraction and Money

The previous chapters focused on the nature of consciousness and experience, and a variety of exercises were provided for you to experience what would otherwise be theoretical. There is a reason why we spent most of this book on these topics.

The only reason why we experience difficulty in attracting money into our lives is that we are personalizing our experience of the mind and body. In other words, we are still under the illusion that somehow we are separate from what we want. It is these beliefs that are preventing us from experiencing the object of our intentions.

Of all the areas of our lives, few affect us as profoundly as money. Whether it is an abundance or a lack of it, money can have a powerful emotional impact on us.

Whether rich or poor, money plays a dominant role in the consciousness of most people. Because of this, we have developed strong beliefs and attitudes about money. Here are just a few examples of the more common ones:

- Money is the root of all evil.
- Money does not grow on trees.
- The desire for money is not spiritual.
- Most rich people got that way by taking advantage of others.
- It is selfish to ask for things that we cannot afford.
- I cannot become financially successful because I have too many things stacked against me.
- It takes money to make money.
- I do not deserve to be wealthy.

All of these beliefs were developed in response to a misunderstanding of money. They point to the mistaken belief that money has inherent power or value, or that money causes us to behave in a certain way.

Money is just a means to measure the exchange of value. If I pay a merchant $50 for a product, then both the vendor and I have agreed that the product is worth $50.

The value of money is purely subjective and established by the government. Its value is subject to change during periods of inflation. The mistake that many people make is that they focus on making money, which has no inherent value, instead of focusing on the value that they have to offer, which creates money.

Money is made when we find a way to create value for others and they are willing to compensate us for it.

There are people who have accumulated millions of dollars only to lose it all. Many of these individuals were able to rebuild their fortunes. On the other hand, there are people who live out their lives in financial scarcity despite their desire for money.

The only difference between these two groups of people are the beliefs that they hold. While it is true that some people have the resources and opportunities that others may lack, that alone is not the cause for the discrepancy between these two groups. There are plenty of people who started off with nothing but built fortunes.

Whether we are aware of it or not, our financial situation is the result of the Law of Attraction. The rich person who lost their money rebuilt their fortune because of their sense of certainty that they could do so. They had that sense of certainty because they experienced wealth before. It is that sense of certainty that allowed them to attract the opportunities to generate wealth into their lives.

For the person who lives out their life in scarcity, wealth is an abstract idea while scarcity is their daily experience. By focusing on their daily experience, they create an opposing force that works against their intentions for money. Thus, they continue to attract scarcity into their lives.

Interestingly, even the wealthy have a sense of scarcity, which is why some people accumulate millions and then lose it. As stated before, they were able to accumulate their fortune because of the beliefs that they held.

However, it is also their beliefs that cause them to lose their wealth. Like a thermostat, their limiting beliefs kicks in when they reach a certain income level, causing them to self-destruct financially.

They recover their losses because their empowering beliefs become activated. If they do not become aware of their limited beliefs, they will continue this cycle of wealth and loss.

When our dominant belief is that we can create wealth, regardless of our current situation, we can attract wealth into our lives provided that we apply ourselves and find a way to create value for others.

Conversely, if our dominant belief is that we will never move beyond financial struggle, that belief will attract the conditions that support it.
The difference between wealth and poverty has less to do with money and opportunity than it has to do with mindset. Henry Ford, Steve Jobs, Oprah Winfrey, J.K. Rowling, and Chris Gardner are just a few examples of people who came from very modest beginnings or even homelessness only to generate fortunes as adults.

Regardless of your story, your life conditions do not determine your ability to become financially successful. Rather, your life condition is a reflection of where you are placing your attention.

Part 6 – Law of Attraction for Abundance

What is receiving the greater amount of your attention, your beliefs about your current situation or your sense of certainty that you can create wealth? The following sequence of exercises will guide you to guiding your focus toward attracting money. The steps include:

- Examine your beliefs about money
- Knowing yourself
- Identifying your qualifications
- Identifying needs
- Coming up with a winning idea and the Law of Attraction
- Attracting money using the Law of Attraction

Examine your Beliefs about Money

Exercise 17
Write out a list of all of your beliefs about money. If needed, refer to the examples in the earlier part of this chapter. When you write your list, do not make it an intellectual exercise. Instead, write whatever comes to mind.

When you have completed list, review each belief. If the belief does not make you feel empowered, draw a line through it and create a new belief that both resonates with and empowers you.

Note: Refer to the Exercise 6 in Chapter 6 for instructions on how to install your new belief.
Example:
Old belief: Money does not grow on trees.
New belief: Money grows from the ideas that I foster and pursue.

Knowing yourself

Exercise 18:

Money manifests when we create value for others by fulfilling an unmet need. When the value that you provide also aligns with your passion and joy, you have a winning formula.

Take time to reflect on what you enjoy doing. Think about what makes you happy or passionate. If there is something that you enjoy doing, then odds are you are also good at it. Make a list of all the things that you enjoy doing. It could be as simple as talking to being as complex as repairing computers.

Identify your qualifications

Exercise 19

Once you have made a list of the things that you enjoy doing, your next step is to make a list of all of your skills, talents, and knowledge base.

Skills are considered those abilities that you had to learn. For example:
- Accounting
- Repairing cars
- Scuba diving

Talents are those abilities that come naturally to you. They did not require any learning. Examples:
- Being compassionate
- Having a sense of humor
- Being persuasive
- Being athletic

Knowledge bases include the knowledge that you gained from formal education, training, or from being self-taught.

Identifying needs

Exercise 20:

This exercise involves identifying an unmet need. This need can be local, national, or global. Think of needs as problems, which can vary in magnitude.

Problems can be as minor as forgetting where you left your keys or glasses to being as relevant as water or energy shortages. Make a list of all the unmet needs that are meaningful to you.

Part 6 – Law of Attraction for Abundance

Coming up with a winning idea and the Law of Attraction

Exercise 21:
Take time to reflect on the information that you gleaned from previous exercises. Can you come up with an idea that fuses all of those components together? Coming up with a winning idea can take time and research. If you find yourself unable to come up with an idea, you can use the Law of Attraction.

The Law of Attraction will attract the ideas, people, and circumstances for manifesting a money-making enterprise. It is critical that you do the first three exercises before turning to the Law of Attraction.

The information that you gain from these exercises will clarify your intentions. To attract a winning idea, do the following:

1. Review your work from the previous exercises in this chapter.
2. After reviewing the list, create an intention. For example:
   a. I will find an idea that addresses a need and creates happiness for all involved.
   b. I will find a way to align my joys and strengths with service to others.
   c. I will attract the people and circumstances that will allow me to successfully serve others.
3. Enter your meditation. When you reach a calm state, release your intention. Upon releasing your intention, give up all attachment to it. Simply continue to live your life.
4. Repeat this meditation until your request is manifested.

Attracting money using the Law of Attraction
Exercise 22
The following is a supplementary meditation that can be used to enhance the effects of the previous one. It was previously stated that we do not want money.

Rather, we want what money will give us. When you know what you want from money, do the following:

1. Sit down in a comfortable position, close your eyes, and breathe normally.
2. Place your attention on your breath by focusing on the sensations of it traveling in and out of your body.
3. As your focus on your breath, you will experience the appearance of thoughts. When they appear, simply ignore them and return your attention back to your breath.
4. If you keep your focus on your breath, there will come the point when you can maintain your awareness of it without any effort. When you reach this stage, think about how you

would feel emotionally if you had the money that you desired. Experience these emotions as entirely as possible.
5. Imagine what you would see if you had the money that you desired.
6. Imagine what you would touch if you had the money that you desired.
7. Imagine what you would hear if you had the money that you desired.
8. Make these experiences as real as possible, making them more intense whenever possible, and then let them go.
9. When you are ready, awake from your meditation.

Part 6 – Law of Attraction for Abundance

Chapter 8: Law of Attraction Mindset

As previously stated, everything in this universe has a vibrational quality. The dominant vibration in our life attracts manifestations of like kind into our life. If we give attention to our beliefs of limitation, difficulty, scarcity, or lack, then the vibrations of these beliefs inform consciousness that we want more of it.

It is no more difficult for consciousness to manifest $10,000 than it is to manifest a quarter. What hampers our ability to manifest is our resistance. We express resistance when we experience doubt about our ability to manifest.

To attract money, we need to raise our vibration so that our lives are conducive to receiving money.

The mistake that many people make is that they try to raise their vibration through techniques that are designed to be "one size fits all," or they do not sincerely believe what they are telling themselves as they try to raise their vibration.

I could meditate and repeat affirmations all day of how I want $10,000. However, if any part of me harbors doubt, I most likely will not manifest that $10,000. Now, if I meditated and repeated affirmation of how I want a quarter, I most likely would manifest a quarter. Why the difference? I am a lot more confident that I can manifest a quarter than I am manifesting $10,000.

However, there is another component that makes a difference, which is detachment. A quarter is not too meaningful to me, so I will not give much thought about it after I express my intentions for its manifestation. The same is not true of the $10,000.

I want that $10,000, and you better believe that I will be thinking about it long after I express my intentions for its manifestation. So, how can we overcome these obstacles and communicate our intentions for money effectively? The answer to this question is incredibly simple, as you will find in the next chapter.

Chapter 9: How to Remove Resistance

As previously stated, our feelings are our direct connection to consciousness, or our essential selves. When we are not experiencing happiness or peace, we are out of alignment with our essential self. When we experience these feelings, then we are in alignment. One of the challenges that many of us have is that we often avoid experiencing our feelings.

We have become experts in distracting ourselves to avoid experiencing them. We avoid experiencing our feelings because we fear or do not trust them. When we distance ourselves from our feelings, we distance ourselves from the rest of the universe.

The best thing that we can do to increase our ability to manifest is to start becoming more aware of our feelings and honoring them. When we learn to accept our feelings, both negative and positive, we are not only honoring them but honoring ourselves.

When we go against our feelings, we go against our Internal Guidance System. When we learn to trust our feelings, we regain our alignment with consciousness and rebuild trust in ourselves. The Law of Attraction is a function of our focus. When we resist anything in life, we are giving it our focus. It is for this reason that we often attract that which we do not want. By removing our resistance, we can focus on what we want while maintaining our alignment with our essential self. The way we remove our resistance is through acceptance.

The principle of acceptance is often misunderstood, especially among the spiritual community. The practice of acceptance does not mean that we try to convince ourselves that things are okay or that they do not matter. To do so would dishonor our feelings. Rather, the spirit of acceptance is that we accept the existence of everything that we are experiencing in our lives. It means not to deny or resist those things that we find unpleasant.

When we can accept the existence of everything that enters our life, we create the space to give our focus to what we want. By doing so, the consciousness does not receive the mixed messages that resistance provides.

Letting Go and Allowing

I hope that by now that you realize that nothing about your experience is permanent. Your thoughts, feelings, and sensations are in constant flux. There is nothing in your experience that does not arise from within you. So what are you holding on to? What are you trying to control? This next meditation is about allowing.

Exercise 23

1. Sit down, make yourself comfortable, and relax. If you would like, you may close your eyes for now.
2. Allow yourself to relax as you focus on your breath. Place your attention on your breath as it enters your body, travels through your body, and then leaves it as you exhale.
3. Breathe normally, without exerting any effort. Relax.
4. Allow yourself to develop a sense of total acceptance. Be totaling allowing of whatever appears in your awareness.
5. Do not judge, evaluate, or analyze anything that you experience.
6. Do not hold any expectations for what you should be experiencing.
7. Do not search for, imagine, or create anything. Simply observe.
8. If unpleasant or uncomfortable thoughts, feelings, or sensation arise, let them be. Allow them to come to your awareness. Do not try to change them or replace them with something that is more pleasant or positive.
9. If you feel numbness or a sense of dullness, allow this.
10. You cannot do anything wrong. Whatever you are experiencing, this is the right experience for you.
11. Allow experience to flow through your awareness without any interference.
12. There is nothing for you to do, change, or believe in. Simply be aware of all that presents itself.
13. This is the end of this meditation. Allow yourself to remain in silence for as long as you desire.

A Day without Resistance

We all have done things that went against how we felt, and we have been doing so since we were small children. We learned early on the consequences of not meeting the expectations of our parents. As we grew older, we increasingly faced situations that demanded our allegiance. Out of social pressure, we often gave in to those demands at the expense of how we felt. The people in our lives, jobs, and societal expectations have all conspired to perpetuate the dishonoring of our feelings. The following exercises are intended to guide you back to honoring your feelings.

Exercise 24

In this exercise, you will commit to engaging only in those activities that are consistent with how you feel. If you do not feel like doing something, then do not do it. If you feel like doing something, do it! If you find yourself having trouble doing this exercise for a whole day, then do it for a shorter time, even if it is for just 20 minutes, and then extend that time until you can do it for a whole day.

Obviously, there are things that we all need to do which we would rather not. Not doing them would be irresponsible. In cases such as these, use the following guidelines:

- Change your perspective of the task that is creating resistance in you by focusing on all the benefits that you would gain by completing it.
- Find ways to change the way that you approach doing the task by making it more enjoyable for you. For example: Listen to your favorite music while doing yard work or invite a friend over to do your taxes together.
- If none of the previous techniques work to lower your resistance, do not take on the task until you have come to accept the fact that it needs to be done and that you are willing to do it.

It is important to note that the previous exercise has nothing to do with the task itself. Instead, it is about our resistance to the task. Nothing in life has inherent meaning to it. It is us who projects meaning onto life.

Part 6 – Law of Attraction for Abundance

Chapter 10: The Pathway to Reconnection

Earlier, I offered the example of manifesting $10,000 versus a quarter. I indicated that it is easier to attract a quarter than it is to attract $10,000 because of our resistance and attachment toward manifesting the $10,000. In the previous chapter, we discussed ways to reduce your resistance. In this chapter, you will learn a technique to increase your vibration by moving up the vibrational scale. What is amazing is how simple this step is.

To enter the space where intentional manifesting occurs, we need to not only reduce our resistance but raise our vibration. The process for doing this involves focusing on the things in your life that bring you enjoyment or a sense of well-being and becoming fully associated with the feeling and emotions that accompany it. I will outline the steps to this process by using myself an example. If I wanted to attract $10,000, I would reflect on what is it that I enjoy or what makes me feel good. My thoughts may be:

- "I enjoyed the time that I took just to relax and not do anything."
- "I enjoyed getting up early this morning and seeing the sunrise and experiencing the quiet calm of desert."
- "I love seeing my wife's smile and hearing her laugh."
- "I am enjoying the sense of peace that I experience when I practice accepting everything that enters my life."
- "I feel revitalized when I think about how I can use the manifesting process to improve my family's life."
- "I love the sense of peace that comes from knowing that I am supported and loved by the universe."

By identifying those aspects of my life that sincerely bring me happiness or comfort, I am raising my vibration. By making this a continuous practice in my life, I am not only raising my vibration, but I am maintaining it.

When I maintain a high vibration, then all that is left for me to do is to express my intention for the $10,000. After I express my intention, I return my focus back to those things that bring me happiness. My intentions will be registered with my essential self because I am in alignment with my essential self.

It is important to take note that my focus was not on the $10,000. Rather, it was on those things that I already enjoy. My intention for the $10,000 was like a seed that was planted in the fertile ground of my sense of appreciation and happiness.

Powering up your intentions
This following exercise will take the power of your intentions to the next level:

Exercise 25
Sit down in a comfortable position, close your eyes, and breathe normally.
1. Place your attention on your breath by focusing on the sensations of it traveling in and out of your body.
2. As your focus on your breath, you will experience the appearance of thoughts. When they appear, simply ignore them and return your attention back to your breath.
3. If you keep your focus on your breath, there will come the point when you can maintain your awareness of it without any effort. When you reach this stage, do the following:
    a. Imagine how you would feel if you had the amount of money that you desired. Experience these emotions as fully as possible.
    b. Imagine what you would see if you had the money that you desired. How would you spend it?
    c. Imagine what you would touch if you had the money that you desired. What would it feel like?
    d. Imagine what you would hear if you had the money that you desired. If you could buy what you wanted, what would it sound like?
    e. Make these experiences as real as possible and intensify the feelings.
4. When you are ready, awake from your meditation.

What you accomplished through this meditation was utilizing all of your senses to experience what you would get from the money you desired as though it was already yours. By making your desired experience real for you today, you are informing consciousness of what you want to be manifested in your life. By focusing on the feelings of what you desire, you are becoming a vibrational match for it to come into your life.

Perform this meditation daily until you can effortlessly experience that which you desire. This can be accomplished by taking time during your day to rehearse this meditation in your mind by focusing on what you desire and fully experiencing the feelings.

By doing this continuously, you will eventually condition yourself to experience these feelings anytime you think of what you desire from the money.

Chapter 11: What Do You Really Want?

Though this book has been focusing on how to use the Law of Attraction to attract money, it is time to move toward higher levels of awareness and discover the truth of what you want! I am confident in saying that I know something about you that you may not. What I know about you is that you do not want money. You want what you believe money will give you. Money is just paper. What you want is the emotions and feelings that you believe you experience by having money. Here is an exercise for discovering what you truly want:

Exercise 26
1. Ask yourself the question "If I had the amount of money that I desire, what would it mean to me?

Examples of responses could be:
- A sense of security
- A better life
- Not having to work
- Being able to buy whatever I want

2. For example, my reply may be that having the amount of money that I desire would mean that I would have enough money to save for the future.
3. For the next step, I would repeat the first question but incorporate my response into the question:
4. What would having enough money to save mean to me?
5. Having enough money to save would make me feel more secure. I would know that the money is there if I need it.
6. What would having a sense of security mean to me?
7. Having a sense of security would give me peace of mind.

Based on this example, my desire for money is not my root desire. My real desire is the peace of mind that I believe money would give me. However, even this root desire is just an illusion. There are people with fortunes who lack peace of mind.

In fact, there are people with more money than they will ever need who are full of anxiety and fear. Conversely, there are people in third world countries who live with a sense of peace and acceptance.

Ultimately, at the essential level, anything that you could desire already exists in your life. To realize this requires looking inward and exploring your inner world. It is through exploring your inner world that you move in the direction of self- discovery and the discovery of your essential self. From higher a perspective, the Law of Attraction is a tool that the universe uses to demonstrate to you that who you are is more than your sense of being a person.

Chapter 12: Intentions and Life Purpose

We have covered a lot of information on manifesting. We discussed the obstacles that many people encounter when attempting to manifest, including overly identifying with the mind and body functions, our limiting beliefs, not being aware of our feelings, and resistance. But even if someone was to steer clear of these obstacles, they still may not get what they want if they lack clarity in their intentions and purpose.

In the previous chapter, we discussed the question, "What you truly want?" This chapter builds on that. We could do everything right, but if our intentions are not clear, we will not manifest what we want. I previously stated that no one wants money. Rather, we want what we believe money will give us. Your answer to the question "What money would give me?" will clarify your intentions and provide a valuable clue to second part of this chapter, which is your life purpose.

Intentions

Your intentions broadcast to consciousness that which you desire and want to experience in your life. There are certain guidelines to follow when creating your intentions:

- Get clarity on your intentions before you allow them to become part of your focus. As stated before, our intentions should not be for money. Rather, our intentions should be for what we believe money would give us. Refer to Exercise 5 in Chapter 6 to determine this.

- Make your intentions impersonal. To be effective, do not personalize your intentions. When we personalize our intentions, they may be driven by our egos and be fear-based. When our intentions are for the benefit of others, we liberate ourselves from the ego. Further, we come from a place that is not fear based. For example, instead of having the intentions, "I will get the job that I desire," make your intention, "I will get the job where I can create the greatest value for all those involved." This kind of intention focuses on our strengths and what we can give as opposed to what we want, which comes from a place of need.

- Avoid making your intentions too specific. Your intentions should be focused on the final result of what you want to experience in your life, not when or how it will happen. The intention, "I want to attract the conditions that will allow me to support my family," will be more effective than, "I want $30,000 by the end of the year." Again, it is not money that you want; it is what money would give you. The intent to attract those conditions that will support my family does not limit consciousness in how it can express itself to meet that need. Asking for $30,000 by the end of the year narrows the possibilities for consciousness to express itself.

Purpose in Life

Few people are born knowing their life's purpose. For most of us, our life's purpose involves a journey through life. However, this journey is not a journey of distance and time. Finding one's purpose in life involves a journey of going within.

Though the situations and circumstances of our lives may be what grab our attention, the true magic of discovering who we are is revealed from the depth of our lives. As author Parker J. Palmer stated: "'Before I can tell my life what I want to do with it, I need to listen to my life to tell me who I am." Ultimately, your life purpose is about what you are here to give.

Many people struggle in life because they do not have a sense of purpose. Conversely, there are just as many people who are actively seeking their purpose in life but are unable to find it. From higher perspectives of awareness, having a purpose in life is moot point. Our essential self, or consciousness, does not need a purpose in life.

At the level of your essential self, you are beyond any conceptual thought. It is only in our manifested form that the need for a purpose in life may appear. If you can live happily without knowing your purpose in life, do not worry about finding it. On the other hand, if you find a need to know your life's purpose, it is best that you do not get too serious about it and approach its discovery in a light-hearted way. I say this to you because your need to find your life's purpose does not come from your essential self. It comes from your mind. To say your life's purpose comes from the mind does not negate your sense of need for it. Instead, I'm making this statement to point out that you can be happy without it. The mind creates a need for finding our life's purpose out of its own dissatisfaction.

The mind is only happy when it can keep us on our toes. The mind is always looking for a job to do. Fear, excitement, guilt, worry, pride, arrogance, superiority, and inferiority are all job titles that the mind accepts. When we identify with our minds, we become the mind's co-worker and share in its responsibilities.

When you understand how our minds work, meaning that you are no longer obedient to it, your sense of purpose, if needed, will become self-evident. It will become self-evident because you will awaken to your unbounded potentiality. The unbounded potentiality that I speak of is your essential self and is expressed in your manifested being as your passions, talents, and strengths, which we will discover in the next section.

Finding your Life's Purpose

The steps for identifying your purpose in life are very similar to the steps for attracting money. Saying that finding your purpose in life and attracting money should share similar steps is not surprising because the manifestation process is the same for everything that we want to experience. The following are steps to find your purpose:

- Focusing inward
- Getting out there
- Focusing outward
- Realization
- Problem-solving

Focusing inward
Focusing inward is the first step in finding your life purpose because everything that we experience begins there. I know the world around me through my five senses. However, the information that I get from my five senses is synthesized and assembled from within me. It is from this conceptual place that I understand the world. Further, we already discussed that our feelings are our GPS to our alignment with our essential self.

Your life purpose does not have to be sought out because it has always existed within you. Rather than searching for your life's purpose, you want to take the time to experience it. We experience our life's purpose when we pay attention to our feelings.

The reason why we spent so much time on meditative exercises is that it is one of the best ways to gain awareness of our thoughts and feelings. By becoming aware of our thoughts and losing our identification with them, we can shift our focus to our feelings and listen to the message that they are sending us. Here is your first exercise to finding your life's purpose:
Get a sheet of paper and a writing instrument.

Get into a meditative state. You can use any of the previous exercises, or you can use your own technique (Note: You may be able to do this exercise without going into meditation. If you find it difficult to recall past events, going into meditation can help).
When you are in a relaxed state, think of the times when you were the happiest. When you think of a specific time, try to remember:
- What were you were doing at the time?
- *Who was around you at the time?*
- What was it about this time that made it so enjoyable for you?
- *When you receive this information, write it down.*
- When you are finished recording, go back into meditation and think of another time when you were at your happiest.
- *Repeat this process until you can no longer recall memories of your happy times.*

When you have completed your list, I want you to think about your passions, strengths, skills, and knowledge base.

Passions
Think about what creates a sense of passion in you. Make a list of all the things that give you a sense of passion.

Strengths
For your strengths, think about the strong points of your character. What is it that you are known for? Think of your strong points as those aspects of you that come naturally to you. They are effortless. Examples could be:
- Your sense of humor
- Your patience
- Your sensitivity
- Your ability to persuade others
- Your athletic ability
- Your compassion

Skills
Unlike your strengths, your skills are those things that you do well as a result of previous training or education that you had. Make a list of your skills. Examples of skills may be:
- Computer skills
- Debate skills
- Sales skills
- Supervisory skills
- Writing skills
- Administrative skills

Note: There may be some overlap between your strengths and skills. If you encounter this overlap, place that item in the category that you believe it fits best.

Knowledge Base
Your knowledge base is the information that you have gained through past formal education or training. Your knowledge base differs from the previous category in that your knowledge may not always be evident since it may not express itself in your actions. For this exercise, think of your knowledge base as being the intellectual part of you. Make a list of your knowledge areas. Examples are:

- Being philosophical
- Legal expertise
- Knowledge of design principles
- Theoretical knowledge

When you have completed your lists, review them. You will use them later. For now, you are ready to go on to the next step.

Getting Out There
Remember that you are the physical manifestation of your essential self, which is consciousness. You appeared in your manifested form for the purpose of experiencing. Like anything else in life, we discover our life's purpose through experiencing contrast in this world. This step of the process is called *Getting Out There* because that is the only way you can discover your life's purpose.

Your instruction for this step of the process is to expose yourself to as many different experiences as you can. It means challenging yourself by stepping out of your comfort zone. Try something that you have never done before out of fear. Try something that you have never done before out of the belief that it was of no interest to you. Try something that you have never done before out of your concern over what others might think. You came to this Earth to experience and expand consciousness. It is only by doing so that you will be able to tap into the discovery of what you are here to give.

For the first half of my life, I was of a strictly scientific mindset. I had no interest whatsoever in spiritual matters. For me, if I could not examine it, measure it, or observe it, I could not give credibility to it. If someone had spoken to me about the Law of Attraction, I would have been polite about it. I would pretend to listen while my thoughts would be elsewhere.

Today, I am writing about it based on personal experience. How did I make the jump from being a devotee of science to an explorer of consciousness? I started to expose myself to experiences that I avoided before. I started to read books about the subject, I listened to experts in the field of consciousness, and I started meditating.

When you start exposing yourself to new experiences, you want to enter them the same way that you were instructed in the various exercises in this book. You want to be open-minded, be accepting of whatever you experience, and not have any expectations. Just as in meditation, allow yourself to be immersed in the experience.

Focusing Outward
In the first step of this process, you went inward and did a personal assessment of yourself. In the previous step, you exposed yourself to different experiences. In this step, *Focusing Outward*, you are going to do another assessment. Unlike your personal assessment, your assessment in this step of the exercise is going to be focused on the world around you. You are going to assess the unmet needs of those around you. The need could be a need within your family, or in your neighborhood, community, state, country, or in another part of the world.

Those who create wealth do so by providing an answer to a problem, or they find a better answer to a problem. Examples of problems could be as simple as finding a way to prevent people from losing their eyeglasses to finding a way to address water shortages on a mass scale. For this exercise, stay alert to the opportunities for making a difference in the lives of others.

Realization
In the previous steps, you assessed your passions, strengths, and other abilities. You then exposed yourself to new experiences. In the previous step, you assessed the unmet needs of others. Now it is time for realization. This is the step when you try to connect the dots. You do this by selecting an unmet need, and you think of ways you can utilize your passion and strengths to make a difference for those who are experiencing that need.

I know of a veterinarian who recognized a need in her community. Many people who have pets are unable to afford traditional veterinary care. This situation poses numerous problems. There are pet owners who love their pets and have to see them suffer. Because their pets are not getting spayed or neutered, there is a problem with unwanted births. Obviously, this veterinarian had the knowledge base and skills to meet this need. More importantly, she has the passion for helping others.

This veterinarian started a mobile service where she travels around the county to provide pet owners with veterinary care at a fraction of the cost of traditional care. The result is that she has loyal customers throughout the county, her overhead is minimal compared to other veterinarians, and she is doing what she loves.

Your exercise for this section is to determine how you can apply your passions and strengths to the unmet need that you selected.

Problem Solving
Problem-solving is the step where you take the results of the previous exercise and start developing a plan on how you would put it into action. You want to ask yourself questions like:

- Is there someone already doing what I have thought of? If so, what could I learn from them? More importantly, how can I improve on what they are already doing?
- Who do I need to talk to?
- What resources will I need?
- Where can I get help to write a business plan?
- What are the risks involved in this venture?
- How can I mitigate these risks?
- What legal or regulatory requirements do I need to be aware of?
- How can I recruit the support of others to make my vision real?

It is important to note that this five-step process is a guideline and does not need to be followed in this order. You will most likely find yourself experiencing situations that do not follow a neat order as I have outlined, which is perfectly okay, but you want to incorporate all of the steps at some point in the process. Additionally, many of these steps may present themselves to you simultaneously.

The main thing to understand is that once you start this process, your intentions will attract the people, resources, and situations that will help you move forward. In fact, this process is providing a structure for you to focus on. It is your focus that informs your essential self to what you will need in any given situation. When you give to others that which you want, you will experience what you are looking for in your life.

It deserves repeating the importance of drilling down into your desires and discovering what lies beneath. I may want more money because I believe that it will give me a sense of security. As long as I base my sense of security on the amount of money that I earn, then my sense of security is dependent upon something outside of myself.

Since everything that is outside of myself is subject to change, my sense of security will change as well. Let us say that you find a new job which triples your income. At first, you will be excited and happy with your new situation. You may increase your spending, raise your standard of living, and start building your savings. However, that increase in money can lead to a new sense of insecurity. You may become insecure about your ability to maintain your new lifestyle. You may feel insecure about losing your money and want to protect it. All of the potential concerns that arise from your increased income exist due to the illusion that money will give you what you are looking for.

Now let us look at a different scenario. Let us say you took the time to explore your beliefs. You identified your limiting beliefs and changed them into empowering ones. You also increased your awareness to the nature of your thoughts, emotions, and feelings. You realize that your essential nature is greater than these mental functions. You also reduced your resistance toward life. Doing all of these things would lead to increasing your sense of security regardless of how much money you had. Further, this sense of security would exist independently of what was happening around you.

Because your experience of life has changed, you feel the desire to help others feel more secure in their lives. This desire to share becomes your life purpose. Because you are in alignment with your essential self, your sense of security grows exponentially. It is fueled by your focus on others. Focusing on your intentions will lead to the unfolding of your life's purpose.

Part 6 – Law of Attraction for Abundance

Chapter 13: Your Ultimate Desire

At the surface level, this book appears to be about money and the Law of Attraction. However, the true intent of this book is far more profound. The intent of this book is to act as a pointer to a source of wealth that is beyond anything that you can grasp intellectually. As repeatedly stated in this book, you do not want money. You want what money can give you.

However, even this statement can be easily misunderstood. You may say that you want money because it will give you a greater sense of security, that it will allow you to take care of your family, or that it will allow you to make a difference in this world.

Previously, you were asked to drill into your thinking to find the root cause for your desire for money. However, even this exercise will fall short of reaching your ultimate desire. Regardless of our reasons for wanting more money, the root cause for wanting money is the emotional state that we experience. In fact, our emotional state is a cause for us desiring anything. However, even our emotional state is not the ultimate cause for our desire.

Our emotional desire is not for the attaining of anything. At the deepest level, our emotional desire is to return home.

Throughout this book, it was stated that we are multidimensional beings in that we are the manifestation of consciousness. We are simultaneously a physical and non-physical being. The essence of who we are is non-physical; our experience of ourselves is our physical aspect. We took on our manifested form so that we could experience the world and expand consciousness, which we do through experience.

For us to experience, we need to experience a sense of separateness. Ultimately, anything that you could ever want is rooted in your desire to leave your sense of separateness behind and return home. You want to return to your essential self where there is a sense of oneness, wholeness, and eternal peace.

Every challenge that we have as human being, be it at the individual or collective level, is due to our confusing the world of objects to be the answer to our ultimate desire. Chasing objects, however, never works. If we are honest with ourselves, lasting happiness or fulfillment does not exist in the realm of form.

You may want to use the Law of Attraction to become a millionaire. Even if you become a millionaire, you will not achieve lasting happiness or fulfillment. Having a million dollars only creates new challenges, insecurities, and desires. The reason for this is that your ultimate desire can only be quenched when you return home.

The only way to return home is to develop the qualities that your essential self inherently possesses. What are the qualities of your essential self? If you practice the exercises and guidance in this book, you will eventually experience them for yourself. In fact, there is no way you cannot experience them if you are sincere in your desire to pursue your truth. However, here are some clues regarding the qualities that I speak of:

- Appreciation
- Kindness to all, especially yourself
- Compassion to all, especially for yourself
- Non-judgment
- Acceptance of yourself and others
- And most of all, love

It may sound trite, but love is your essential self. When I speak of love, I am not referring to romantic love or even the love that we have for family. The kind of love that I speak of is unconditional. Unconditional love is the acceptance and embracement for all of life.

To reach the state of awareness that I have just described may seem to be a daunting task or an unrealistic goal. Should this thought occur to you, I have good news for you. Ignore that thought! Everything that has been discussed in this book about higher perspectives of awareness, and your essential self, already exists within you. In fact, there is no way for you to not possess them.

The only reason why we do not experience our deepest essence is that we have been conditioned from the time that we were born to focus on the world around us, not our inner world. We have spent our lives chasing shiny objects in that hopes that we will experience our ultimate desire.

It is because we have forgotten about our essential nature that this book offered so many meditative exercises. It is only when we take time to become still and silent that we can start to remember our deeper truths.

My guess is that you purchased this book because you believe having more money in your life will satisfy that which you are searching for. The good news is that you can find what you have been searching for, and have money, if you redirect your attention toward your inner realm. It is only in your inner realm that you will find the answers you have been looking for. In the next chapter, we will discuss what to do next!

Part 6 – *Law of Attraction for Abundance*

Chapter 14: Making Sense of it All

You have been presented with a wealth of information and exercises in this book. This chapter is about your next step. To read this book and not look at it again would defeat its purpose. This book is intended to be a guide for you for as long as you seek out your ultimate fortune, which is the sense of peace that comes from aligning your life with your essential self. The following are some suggestions for getting the most out of your manifesting experience:

- Do not judge anything that you experience.
- Do not hold expectations of what should happen or of what should not happen.
- Allow everything that you experience to happen, and do not resist anything. Every thought, sensation, perception, or outwardly experience has its place. Everything that exists is intended to exist.
- No thought, feeling, or sensation can harm you. It is you that they owe their existence to.

Having said this, here are some suggestions regarding the content of this book:

- Make sure that you read the entire book and do each exercise at least once.
- When you have completed the book, take note of the exercises that resonated with you or felt right to you. You do not have to do every exercise in this book to achieve your desires. However, you will not know if these exercises are right for you unless you do them.
- Once you have selected the exercises that resonate with you, practice at least one of them each day. When I say to practice them each day, I do not mean to practice them in the traditional sense. Normally, practice is viewed as repeatedly doing something to improve. When it comes to meditation, there is nothing to improve! Meditation is about being still and quiet. Its purpose is to increase our awareness of the nature of the mind. Meditation should not require any effort other than getting yourself to do it. Each time you do a meditative exercise, treat is as though it is your first time doing it.

Once you become comfortable meditating, the following guidelines can be used to attract your desires:

- Develop a clear intention of what you want to attract.
- Make sure your intentions are aligned so that everyone who will be affected by them will benefit.
- Increase your vibration using meditations in this book, especially from Chapter 10, until you have reached a state of well-being.
- When you have reached a state of well-being, express your intention to the universe. When expressing your intention, express it through your emotional state as opposed to thinking about it intellectually. In other words, if you want to manifest $1,000, experience how you

would feel if you already had $1,000. If you experience any sense of doubt during this process, refer to the exercises in Chapters 6 & 10.
- Take action that will move you toward the manifestation of your desire. If you desire is to manifest $1,000, what action can you take that will create the opportunities to receive it? Remember, you do not want $1,000. You want what it will give you. A great way to take action is to do the exercises in Chapter 11.
- It is crucial to understand that everything that you read in this book is just a pointer, a pointer that is pointing to your essential self and inviting you to follow.
- Do not get caught up with anything that you read in this book. Do not take anything written in this book as truth. There is no ultimate truth in the universe. What we believe to be truth is a product of the mind. Instead of seeking truth, seek that which resonates with you, that which brings you happiness.
- Use the information in this book to launch yourself into your inner journey. Let this book be a guide, not the pilot. It is up to you to determine what feels right for you and to honor it.
- Have the courage to trust your essential self, that part of you which is beyond your thoughts and sensations, and that part of you which you can only know intuitively.

Conclusion

We started this book with two metaphors, the man in the desert and King Midas, and so that is how we will end. In Greek mythology, there is Plato's Allegory of the Cave. There is a group of people who are imprisoned in a cave where they are chained. Against the wall of the cave, they see moving shadows.

The people of the cave believe that these shadows are living beings that also inhabit the cave. What they are not aware of is that there is a large fire at the entrance of the cave. Any time somebody walked by, between the fire and entrance of the cave, their shadow was projected onto the cave wall.

One of the people inside the cave is able to free himself from his chains and wanders outside of the cave. It is then that he realizes the truth of what he had been witnessing in the past. The shadows of the cave were illusionary. They were just representations of something greater.

Another metaphor is that of the clouds and sky. Of the two, the sky is greater due to its vastness. Additionally, the sky is non-changing, unlike the clouds, which are constantly taking on different shapes. Whatever the clouds do, the sky remains untouched.

I leave you with this final thought about your true nature and that of the phenomenal world, which includes money. As long as our sense of self is shaped or defined by the amount of money that we have, we are no better than the prisoner in the cave who believes the shadows are the real thing.

This is not only true about money, but also for anything else that is phenomenal. To define ourselves by anything that we experience, be it a thought, sensation, relationship, our jobs, or our possessions, is to identify with a shadow.

True success is achieved when we become like the sky. Like the sky, you are free. As the sky is unaffected by the clouds that travel through it. We should strive to discover that aspect of ourselves that is also unaffected by the clouds of thought, sensation, perception, and objects that float through our awareness.

What is required for this kind of liberation is to lose the personalizing of our experiences, including that of the Law of Attraction and money. Instead of viewing the Law of Attraction as a way to manifest our desires, I invite you to view it as a natural process of the universe, of which you bear witness to. To believe that we attract things into our lives is to reinforce our sense of separation.

Part 6 – Law of Attraction for Abundance

The only way that you can attract something is if that which you want to attract is separate from yourself. Who you are at the non-phenomenal level is not separate from the universe. Rather, your essential self is the universe! You will experience greater expansion if you stay as an observer to all that enters and leaves your life. Every thought, sensation, and perception is just a visitor that passes through your awareness. You are the witness to their movement. They exist only because you exist!

What we refer to as the Law of Attraction is that of the world of existence continuously parading through our awareness. The world of existence is like a current moving through the expanse of the ocean, and you are the ocean. Learn to enjoy and appreciate every experience that enters your life.

The clouds of pleasure, happiness, peace, sadness, fear, and grief, are the clouds that transverse your skies. Learn to view money, not as a measure of your success but a tool, a unit of exchange, in your encounters with other manifested beings. When you can live your life in this spirit, you will be wealthy regardless of your net worth!

Personal Message from Elena

Thank You so much for reading this book to the very end! I hope you found it inspiring and discovered at least one helpful idea to help you grow on your Law of Attraction journey.

If you have a few minutes, I'd really appreciate it if you could leave me a short review on Amazon. Let other LOA readers in our community know who this book can help and why.
Thank You Thank You Thank You,
I hope we "meet" again,
Much love,

Elena

For more information and resources about LOA, please visit my website:

www.LOAforSuccess.com

If you'd like to say hi, please email me at elena@LOAforSuccess.com

Free LOA Newsletter + Bonus Gift

To help you AMPLIFY what you've learned in this book, I'd like to offer you a free copy of my **LOA Workbook – *a powerful, FREE 5-day program (eBook & audio)*** designed to help you raise your vibration while eliminating resistance and negativity.

To sign up for free, visit the link below now:

www.loaforsuccess.com/newsletter

You'll also get free access to my highly acclaimed, uplifting **LOA Newsletter.**

Through this email newsletter, I regularly share all you need to know about the manifestation mindset and energy.

My newsletter alone helped hundreds of my readers manifest their own desires.

Plus, whenever I release a new book, you can get it at a deeply discounted price or even for free.

You can also start receiving my new audiobooks published on Audible at no cost!

To sign up for free, visit the link below now:

www.loaforsuccess.com/newsletter

I'd love to connect with you and stay in touch with you while helping you on your LOA journey!

If you happen to have any technical issues with your sign up, please email us at:

support@LOAforSuccess.com

More Books by Elena G. Rivers

Money Mindset: Stop Manifesting What You Don't Want and Shift Your Subconscious Mind into Money & Abundance

How Not to Manifest: Manifestation Mistakes to Avoid and How to Finally Make LOA Work for You

Visualization Demystified: The Untold Secrets to Re-Program Your Subconscious Mind and Manifest Your Dream Reality in 5 Simple Steps

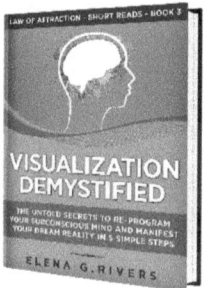

Law of Attr-Action for Entrepreneurs: Advanced Identity Shifting Secrets to Manifest the Income & Impact You Deserve

www.ingramcontent.com/pod-product-compliance
Lightning Source LLC
Chambersburg PA
CBHW080632170426
43209CB00008B/1551